AGAINST EXOTICISM

AGAINST EXOTICISM
Toward the Transcendence of Relativism
and Universalism in Anthropology

Edited by

Bruce Kapferer and Dimitrios Theodossopoulos

berghahn
NEW YORK • OXFORD
www.berghahnbooks.com

First published in 2016 by

Berghahn Books

www.berghahnbooks.com

© 2016 Berghahn Books

Cover: Emberá child, counter-exoticizing. Parara Puru, River Chagres, Panama.
Photograph © Dimitrios Theodossopoulos

Library of Congress Cataloging-in-Publication Data

Names: Kapferer, Bruce, editor. | Theodossopoulos, Dimitrios, editor.
Title: Against exoticism : toward the transcendence of relativism and
    universalism in anthropology / edited by Bruce Kapferer and Dimitrios
    Theodossopoulos.
Description: New York : Berghahn Books, 2016. | Includes index.
Identifiers: LCCN 2016044417 (print) | LCCN 2016047698 (ebook) |
    ISBN 9781785333705 (pbk. : alk. paper) | ISBN 9781785333712 (ebook)
Subjects: LCSH: Cultural relativism—Case studies. | Ethnology—Case studies.
Classification: LCC GN345.5 .A43 2016 (print) | LCC GN345.5 (ebook) |
    DDC 305.8–dc23
LC record available at https://lccn.loc.gov/2016044417

British Library Cataloguing in Publication Data

A catalogue record for this book is available from the British Library.

ISBN 978-1-78533-370-5 (paperback)
ISBN 978-1-78533-371-2 (ebook)

CONTENTS

INTRODUCTION
Against Exoticism

Bruce Kapferer and Dimitrios Theodossopoulos

The exotic, in its countless connotations, stirs our imagination. Marvelous and mysterious, dangerous, deceptive, or corrupt, the exotic is an inherently relational term that presupposes an awareness of Otherness. Etymologically, it is rooted in externality, derived from the Greek adverb *éxo* (outside) and adjective *exotikós* (from the outside).[1] Seen as what comes from the outside—the strange, the outlandish, the unexpected—the exotic predicates evaluations, metaphors, and categories of knowledge (Fernandez 1986; Lévi-Strauss 1962).

For many, anthropology as an idea and as an academic discipline begins in the encounter with the exotic. The exotic here is conceived as what lies outside ordinary experience, a meaning rooted in the etymology of the term, which projects a view of exteriority. This association of exteriority provides the term with broad meaning and guides much of our discussion here. There are some additional, value-laden connotations linked with the exotic. Barbarism, for example, indicating forms of life at the edge of civilization (as defined by the ancient Greeks and the historian Herodotus, who is sometimes described as an early anthropologist), or the 'savage slot', a term introduced by Michel-Rolph Trouillot's (2003) critique of the anthropological domain in the context of colonialism and the neo-imperialism of globalization. Such negative associations darken the anthropological encounter with the exotic. They reproduce a pervasive dualism between the Self and the Other, in which ethnocentric values provide the measure for evaluating difference. Much of the negativity that forms around the idea and imagination of the exotic in anthropology is contained in the charge of its Orientalism.

Notes for this section begin on page 20.

The overall critique of Orientalism is tied to anthropology's beginnings as a discipline that focused on the subject peoples brought within the net of imperial expansion. The exotic Other was defined and described in relation to the non-exotic ideal of the Western metropolitan Self. In this, early anthropology was thoroughly participant in a colonizing, civilizing discourse whereby an interest in the expansion of knowledge concerning the exotic Other was linked to interests of political control. In this respect, Enlightenment reason was a legitimating ideology in excess of any justification in science. This involved an unscientific version of evolutionism based on an ethnocentric conception of 'progress' and a hierarchization of cultural knowledge and practice. Max Weber's all-embracing global comparative scheme that opposed Western Protestant-influenced rationality to that of China is one major example. The exacerbation of this orientation in anthropology, as Clifford Geertz (1984) points out, often enhanced its value in an intellectual merchandizing of the exotic, threatening to elaborate preexisting stereotypes of a racist nature. Anthropology, of course, was far from alone in such orientalizing, simply one of the more egregious examples of a self-admiring Eurocentrism that underpinned much, if not all, academic disciplines at the time of their establishment. This is not to excuse the discipline but to suggest that the matter of orientalizing exoticism is more profound than the charge of Orientalism and associated critiques allow.

By and large, late-twentieth-century anthropology attempted to turn away from the exotic. It aspired to expunge its scandal by following one or more redemptive approaches—for example, by (a) renouncing earlier interests to do with the non-modern (understood as the chief domain of what might be termed the anthropological exotic), (b) modernizing the discipline by focusing on more contemporary issues (see MacClancy 2002), or (c) insisting on universalizing theories shorn of problematic evolutionist and racist assumptions. Such reaction is frequently more cosmetic than anything else—as, for example, the excision of the concept of tribe from the anthropological lexicon. Thus, more deep-seated problems connected with the Eurocentricity—not just of anthropological thought but also of the modes of thinking and theoretical reflection in the humanities and sciences as a whole—can contribute to the risk and persistence of exoticism or Orientalism, despite an intention otherwise.

The dualism of much Euro-centered thought, and sometimes a restricted view of rationality and the nature of reason, is a factor in the creation of an exoticism of understanding, for want of a better expression. We cannot find a more pervasive example than the social-evolutionist, linear view that conceives human reason as progressive, evolving from unreason to reason with Western thought at the higher end. Such issues have long been at the center of methodological debate in anthropology and are tied to an aim to overcome exoticism and in fact to de-exoticize understandings of difference. In this objective anthropologists have anticipated the critique of Orientalism and, furthermore, have—in their own methodological angst—revealed the dangers of exoticism even in perspectives that would expressly eschew it. We address aspects of this in the following discussion, in which we will sustain the importance of the concept of the exotic in anthropology, although definitely not exoticism.

Our notion of the exotic expands on the idea of the exotic as the outside in the more abstract, as well as the more concrete, sense of practices and/or ideas or values that demand the reconsideration of prevailing conceptual and theoretical understanding. Additionally, we are concerned to deterritorialize (also detemporalize) the concept so that the exotic in our usage is a potential of any practice or value in any space or time whatever. From this broader point of view, all is potentially exotic to everything else. It is through the exotic, or the potentiality of it, that anthropologists can reveal continuities and similarities underpinning apparent as well as critical differences that may open toward a more general understanding of the fundamental unity of human beings despite and perhaps because of their very diversity.

Starting from this deterritorialized and detemporalized perspective, we set out to explore the exotic in two broad senses. Our first and main concern is to examine the exotic and the problem of exoticism as an issue of particular methodological import for anthropology—a discipline that is concerned with understanding the human being in its cultural and social diversity, through its differences and similarities. Comparison is central in anthropological practice, and the concept of the exotic is vital to the anthropological project and to what we will discuss as its methodological openness: in particular, the idea that certain practices and ideas may express perturbations and potentialities that are irreducible to prevailing general or universalizing understandings. The awareness of the exotic in anthropology, the value that is placed on the exotic, even in our specific usage, always risks exoticism: that is, a misrecognition of difference through the inappropriate application of descriptive/analytical categories, or else the constraint of interpretation to unsubstantiated highly localized and, in effect, relativist modes of comprehension. These matters are at the heart of anthropological methodological discussion and what we will by and large concentrate on in this introduction.

Our second concern relates to the exotic/exoticism as a sociocultural practice or as a dimension of the way the exotic—as difference, the strange, the unusual—enters into everyday processes of sociopolitical construction (e.g., nationalism) or into the imaginary in the routine formation of social relations or into memory. Here our interest is in the exotic as a value in social discourse and some of the varieties of its effects. In this focus there is some overlap with our methodological examination of the role of the exotic in anthropological understanding, and we attend to certain aspects of this. An example concerns the exotic as a method of anthropological distancing or of accentuating the strangeness of a phenomenon in order to highlight an analytical problematic. In such an instance, the very familiarity of practices to the analyst can obscure understanding, which clothing them in the language of the exotic may overcome. This is what Horace Miner (1956) famously attempted in his well-known study of the Nacirema. In effect he employed exoticism in an anti-exoticizing intention. Our broad aim in the second part of this introduction is to engage the exotic as an ethnographic phenomenon.

Anthropology and the Aporia of the Exotic

Much methodological debate in anthropology centers upon the issue of how social and cultural (or value) differences, sometimes of an irreducible and radical kind, can be grasped in a way that recognizes their integrity while simultaneously showing how they contribute to a general understanding of human being as a whole. In this regard, anthropology is generally concerned to give authority to those who are involved in the creation or construction of the realities in which they live. This, to some degree, has a distinct emphasis according to whether the orientation is relativist or universalist. Relativists tend to give general priority to the values integral to the constructions and practices of the anthropological subjects. For universalists this tends to be a first-order strategy in analysis that will eventually become subordinate to a logic of conceptual and theoretical understanding that transcends the phenomenon as it has been constituted by its practitioners.

The distinction between relativism and universalism in anthropology has further significance in the context of our discussion of the exotic and exoticism. In relativism, the exotic—with which the concept of culture was virtually synonymous—was overvalued. In universalist perspectives, the exotic was undervalued as something to be explained ultimately through universal modes of understanding that achieved their veracity in their apparent deconstruction or de-exoticization of cultural difference. This opposition still persists, as some of the chapters in this volume illustrate. As we have indicated, the culture relativist/universalist contradiction or opposition is endemic and virtually the aporia of a discipline that asserts the unity of human kind but is also alert to its radical, often irreducible, differences. Methodological discourse in the subject is broadly directed to the resolution of this contradiction, which contributes, we consider, to the particular dynamic of the discipline. In this, relativism and universalism are better conceived as complementary and dialectically interwoven rather than simple opposites.

Anthropology in our opinion is not as theoretically driven, or at least not in the same way, as many of the other social sciences—e.g., economics, psychology, sociology—with which it is cognate. Theory is more a point of arrival than a starting place or, more accurately, a continually shifting horizon of open potential. This is certainly the orientation of relativists, such as Geertz (1984), whose relativism, as we read him, does not necessarily rule out the establishment of universal theoretical and conceptual understanding. What he stresses, in effect, is that global cultural and social diversity is such as to limit, at the present moment, a universally or generally valid conceptual and theoretical scheme. This is so especially for universalist theory that is initiated within Western perspectives and grounded in their value assumptions, which is one of the points of Geertz's celebrated essay on the Balinese cockfight.

There is a strong sense in Geertz that the only possible universalism, if paradoxically so, is relativism itself—that is, given the global view of anthropology, difference is all there is. The best that can be hoped for, through specific ethnographic investigation, are some concepts (and perhaps theoretical schemes) that have some application beyond the particular ethnographic instance from which they may be derived. An example might be Geertz's concept of the 'theatre state' that he develops from his Bali research. But this is already founded in a universalizing vision (one that threatens a Eurocentrism based as it is in Goffman-esque drama-conceptual metaphors of 'performance'). This is true also of his concepts of 'status bloodbath' and his employment of Gregory Bateson's notion of 'deep play' in the cockfight essay. For all his relativism, Geertz's work is founded, from the very start, in universalist perspectives that are premised on certain a priori assumptions and frequently of a strongly Western kind.

If in Geertz the falsity of a relativism/universalism opposition can be easily detected, this is so in general. Moreover, as Geertz does not escape universalist perspectives in his relativism, the same is true the other way about. Universalist conceptual and theoretical orientations in anthropology can recognize relativistic difference but generally, as we have said, as a first step in analysis (a setting of the problem at hand), which is dissolved when processes are examined in their depth. Relativism, for universalists, is a surface phenomenon that obscures underlying unities. However, the unities that are postulated may nonetheless embed relativist assumptions that the generalizing theory that is propounded does little more than substantialize ethnographically in an exercise of teleological confirmation.

Both relativism and universalism risk exoticism either in the form of mistaken difference—sometimes impelled in that ideology of anthropology that celebrates its practitioners as "merchants of astonishment" (Geertz 1984: 275)—or in the search for unity that is motivated to ignore or reduce that which otherwise refuses categories of general understanding in grand acts of totalizing theoretical narrative. It is in the failure by anthropologists to recognize their relativism within the universal that they can fall into the trap of exoticism, that is, misconceive a real difference as merely a variation in the universal. Levy-Bruhl's participation perspective insisted that much magical and ritual practice could not be reduced to the universalizing pretensions of Western reason, a point that Wittgenstein also made in reaction to anthropological analyses of Azande witchcraft. Many stock concepts in anthropology, indeed those of magic, witchcraft, ritual, fetishism—to list but a few—derive their force in an exoticism impelled in a rationalist universalism deeply centered in Euro-American commonsense and theory. This is not to deny their appropriateness when directed, for example, to describe the irrational consequences of certain ideological political and economic rationalities in American and European realities with global effect in contemporary processes. Nonetheless, the conceptual labels of such irrationalism rest on a potential exoticism of the Orientalist kind resting on evolutionist assumptions concerning the lesser rationality of other cultural practices.

Broadly we consider that the exoticizing difficulties of relativism and universalism are aporetically endemic to anthropology. Anthropologists have by and large recognized this. It is nothing less than a key problematic of the discipline that it is continually oriented to overcome, and here rests its methodological contribution in the humanities and sciences for the understanding of human beings as a whole. This methodological potential, we add, is continually unfolding in a constant differentiating diversity of existential circumstances. Human being, if not a story without end, is far from over, and for this reason, we think, the idea of a final totalizing all-embracing conceptual and theoretical system is unlikely. In anthropology conceptual construction and theoretical formation is in continual process. Our reconceptualization of the idea of the exotic is intended to communicate the conceptual and theoretical openness of anthropology that at once acknowledges the problematic imbrication of relativism with universalism (that in many ways is inescapable) and attempts to transcend an opposition between them in opening to novel possibilities created in the flux of human action. The exotic is a concept that is open to potential and allows for the continual realization of novel possibilities.

We critically address three major orientations in anthropology that exemplify the idea of the exotic as open potential. In each there is a relativist/universalizing mix that is given in the primacy of ethnography in anthropology but is secondarily directed to its transcendence or a capacity to extend, through the ethnographic, a larger conceptual and theoretical understanding of human cultural and social diversity. In other words, the perspectives we address here, albeit briefly, are different attempts to arrive at a more general or universal understanding that variously attempts to avoid an exoticizing Eurocentricity.

Lévi-Strauss and a Structuralist Universalism

Lévi-Strauss' structuralism is the major initiator of an anthropology with a universalizing ambition that both gave primacy to the ethnographic and in certain ways attempted to decenter Euro-American authority (e.g., *The Savage Mind* and its particular attack on the hegemony of Sartre's existentialism). He, of course, drew from within Western Enlightenment and post-Enlightenment modernist philosophical traditions (of Kant, Hegel, Marx, and Freud). Much criticism has been directed at his Euro-centered dualism—notably his universalist assertions of a nature/culture opposition and binary mentalism (see MacCormack and Strathern 1980), and an ahistoricism: for example, that so-called cold societies (the worlds of an anthropology examining realities at the edges of imperial expansion) are outside history, which Marshall Sahlins resolved with a historical structuralism and Eric Wolf overcame in an insistent historical materialism. The latter especially but also Max Gluckman (1965, 1966), well before Wolf, stressed that those apparently outside history were still well within history and particularly the hot centers of colonializing and imperializing America and Europe.

While we recognize the point of many of the major criticisms of Lévi-Strauss, we stress that he largely refused what we discuss as exoticism—that is, the creation of peoples marginalized (and dehumanized and destroyed) in the relentless push of capital into objects for the touristic gaze, and/or to become regarded as primitive forms of the modern (as Werbner also argues in chap. 2). Rather, he represented them as exotic in a value-free and exteriorizing sense: as forms of existence independent and/or outside of the modern—of the hegemonically dominant in contemporary realities—whose practical comprehension of the nature of human realities is no less legitimate. The idea of the exotic here—as an outside, a formation of human potential in itself (see Kapferer 2013)—implicitly indicates a mutuality of the exotic: that is, the hegemonically dominant (e.g., systems organized within the terms of Western capital) are no less exotic than those they often too easily demean.

The anti-relativism of Lévi-Strauss is thoroughly concerned with establishing general understandings through the exploration of the exotic, or that which demonstrably stands outside and threatens currently prevailing understandings of the nature and potential of human being. Lévi-Strauss's paradox is that he asserts a Western cognitive and conceptual way of organizing and sensing phenomena that for many he fails to transcend. Effectively he is bound to the Kantian paradox within which he begins and does not transcend its dualism. In other words, the moderate relativism—conceived here as a social and historical standpoint—that is part and parcel of the positioning of any anthropologist is not, for many of Lévi-Strauss's critics, overcome in his universalism. In other words, an exoticism remains Lévi-Strauss's possibility. This is the matter that directs what may be regarded as major poststructuralist developments in anthropology, approaches inspired by Lévi-Strauss attempting to overcome his specific dualism. Two in particular stand out: Philippe Descola (and to a lesser extent Eduardo Viveiros de Castro and Marilyn Strathern) on the one hand and Louis Dumont on the other.

Descola, Viveiros de Castro, and the Poststructural Ontological Turn

The recent so-called ontological turn is a move toward overcoming, in effect, false generalism or universalism and is strongly influenced by philosophical directions such as that of Michel Foucault and Gilles Deleuze. There are different anthropological examples (e.g., Holbraad 2012; Holbraad and Pedersen 2016), but the best known are the perspectivist and cognitivist approaches of Viveiros de Castro (1998, 2004) and Descola (2013). Descola relativizes the Euro-centered dualism of Lévi-Strauss, specifically that of the nature/culture distinction that has been at the crux of much criticism, reconceiving it as a particular ontology of naturalism. The notion of ontology at first thought might appear to be linked to Lévi-Strauss's concept of the overarching paradigm, or paradigmatic logic, for action. But the idea of ontology engaged is far more foundationalist—ontology as the orientational ground for thought and action in which being in the world is constituted and directed. Thus, for Descola, what we have discussed as the exotic—another potentiality of being human outside prevailing conceptions—can, if established as such through ethnographic investigation, manifest an orientation to existence that is effectively ontological in import.

Descola does not necessarily eschew universalism.[2] What Descola does is develop a set of ontological possibilities or combinations from a basic set of principles that he claims underpins any ontological cognitive and relational order. He generates a total set of possibilities, not all of which have so far been discovered to exist through a search of the ethnographic and historical record. In his analysis the total set of ontological possibilities reduces, in effect, to a fourfold ontological set—naturalism, analogism, animism, and totemism. These major ontologies are then deterritorialized in Descola's development so that they are to be found potentially in a diversity of geographical locations and without any necessary historical connection (e.g., through diffusion).

Descola's major contribution is that he gives no particular ontology commanding or overarching authority, not privileging one over another. Furthermore, the various ontologies, which are actualized in historical societies—there are many logical possibilities in his schema that as far as is known have not eventuated—are then brought into play by Descola in developing a general anthropologically and ethnographically grounded understanding of human being as a whole. Through them he can understand the global differentiation and distribution of human institutional arrangements and related practices (e.g., cosmic kingship, human-animal interactions, orientations to the environment and ecology, sacrifice).

Despite his ingenuity, Descola does maintain the Kantian formalism (and nominalism) of structuralism. This is so despite an effort to engage Husserl's phenomenology, which in itself is Eurocentric (and naturalistic) and especially so in Descola's usage (see Kapferer 2014). It also continues to insist on an ahistoricity (see Kapferer 2014; see also Ramos 2012 and Nugent in chapter 3 for criticisms that apply the Marxist criticism of earlier structuralism to Descola's development). Descola may still be seen to risk an exoticism founded in the overriding value given to Euro-American philosophical and scientific assumptions even though they receive a degree of relativization. Nonetheless, it is an important attempt to overcome Lévi-Strauss's paradox while continuing in his tradition. He maintains the highly exotic categories (e.g., animism, totemism) that are subject to the Orientalist critique. However, he reconfigures their value effectively, giving them equality with other ontological possibilities, for example, the naturalist ontology of Euro-American thought and action. Descola has lifted old anthropological categories from out of their evolutionist and hierarchical meanings of earlier anthropological usage. By revaluing them, he has reinvented them as relatively distinct ontologies that stand in an exotic relation—as an outside (see also Kapferer 2013)—to Western ontologies and vice versa.

Thus, it may be fair to say that Descola has realized a positive dimension of the exotic in anthropology whereby the differences established through anthropological ethnographic analysis contribute to the genuine critical understanding of human potential. Despite some of our serious reservations in other respects—including a tendency to over-homogenize difference and a continuing essentialism still rooted in Western philosophical and scientific reason—Descola has addressed the vital paradox in the comparative vision of anthropology: a tension to exoticization whereby one ontological frame (usually Euro-American thought and practice) is given an undemonstrated authority (even a modern evolutionist superiority), both in the definition of others and in the discerning of their general import.

We single out Descola and separate him from other major poststructural and posthuman approaches in anthropology because he advances a comparative perspective that stresses the exotic as consciously attempting to escape exoticism. No one among his four ontological perspectives is necessarily privileged over any other or constitutes the standard against which others are identified as divergent, different, or exotic—which is a major factor in exoticization. Of further interest, and related to our concern with the exteriority of the exotic, is Descola's emphasis on interiority and physicality, which demarcates his fourfold ontological scheme and represents a variety of possible standpoints towards the exotic as the outside.

Strathern's poststructural orientation is another attempt with a similar objective. But in our opinion it tends to privilege a Melanesian perspective[3]—and in this risks an orientalizing exoticism, one that is inversionary of a Self/Other dualistic kind. Somewhat paradoxically, Strathern's concept of the 'dividual' (Marriott 1976) can also be conceived as extending within dominant Euro-American individualist value. Moreover, her relational and dividualist perspective bears some consistency with contemporary globalizing even corporate processes as they are often conceived. It is an approach that is as much internal to contemporary modern/postmodern dynamics as it may appear to be external to them.

The same might be said of Bruno Latour's actor-network orientation, which we also note expresses some degree of affiliation with that of Strathern. His perspective intends to break out from the philosophical metaphysics that underpinned major anthropological perspectives particularly in the tradition of Durkheim and Mauss. It is powerfully oriented in the direction of current scientific advances (a cybernetics, engineering perspective), and there is a marked effort to suspend more conventional anthropological emphases on the social/ society, as well as on value. The focus is on assembling dynamics that decenters the hitherto anthropological focus on the human and the restriction of agency to human being.

In a broad sense, Latour's approach avoids exoticism both in its suppression of value and in its stress on assembling processes. Effectively, there is no outside (exotic): all difference is conceived as a continually shifting potential of organizational principles that are not constrained within the confines or limitations of particular cultures or systems of value—although specific historical and contemporary instances may give intense expression to the effects of certain kinds of dynamic assemblage. This notion is carried to the extreme by Manuel DeLanda (see Kapferer 2011 for a critique), whose general approach is very close to that of Latour. He argues that any consideration of culture or value does not have any significant consequence for the understanding that perspective promises. Theoretically, there is no outside, no exotic in the sense that we think is crucial to the anthropological contribution. In certain aspects it joins other sociological universalisms such as Durkheimianism, and also some Marxist approaches, but in a vein that many would say is more conservative.

Latour and DeLanda would claim that they are leaving the ideological plane of previous sociologies, although paradoxically such a view likely masks the potential of a highly ideological position that many Marxists, for example, would detect. Their break with a history of Western metaphysics (this can be wondered at!) and what Latour and DeLanda dismiss as its constructionism (the stress in anthropology on social processes of value definition) may remove a vital factor in anthropological exoticism, but at the risk of reasserting universalizing values of the center (if now global rather than specifically Euro-American). They champion a neorealism (see Harman 2016 on Latour), which risks a return of a kind of positivism that was implicated in the exoticizing evolutionism and hierarchies of the anthropology of yore. Further, the loss of the anthropological exotic, the demonstrated recognition of distinct logics of practice that are not necessarily reducible to a general scheme, neutralizes or radically weakens the potential—indeed the scientific potential—of anthropology either as critique and as a testing of generalizing theory or as an expanding of the ground for the development of concepts and theory of potentially genuine general or universal value.

Another example of neostructuralist confrontation with the exotic can be detected in the popular and stimulating interventions of Viveiros de Castro (1998, 2004). Perspectivism alludes to the acknowledgment of different Amerindian perspectives, which become ethnographically apparent in the negotiation of human and nonhuman subjectivities. The perspectival approach collapses standard Western categorical distinctions between humanity and animality, nature and culture. In this respect, a committed engagement with another (exotic) point of view has provided perspectivism with a spark of originality, the recognition of a world defined by different ontological premises— although the proposition that different worlds exist as alternative realities is an issue resisted by many anthropologists, and with persuasive arguments (see Pina-Cabral 2014a, 2014b).

Much more relevant with respect to our exploration of the exotic is that Viveiros de Castro's perspectival point of view is undertaken in isolation, within an exotic ontological realm that is "only visible to the eyes of trans-specific beings such as shamans" (Viveiros de Castro 1998: 471) and the academic experts who conduct the anthropological interpretation on their behalf. They permit the thoroughgoing relativism of other systems of thought (Euro-American naturalizing reason, for instance), and they may open space for critiques such as those of contemporary ecological movements (see Descola 2013) even though they are centered within the logics of Western reason (and the romanticism that is its potential). A problem with perspectivism is that it may be little more than a situationally specific orientation (relative to hunting; e.g., see Henriksen 2008; Willerslev 2007) rather than fully ontological. This is the counterargument presented by other Amazon specialists (Ramos 2012 and especially Turner 2009), which implies that a more conventionalist Durkheimian and Marxist-influenced universalism maintains relevance.

The powerful implication of these critiques is that perspectivism continues to run the great risk of exoticism. Steve Nugent (chap. 3) puts under critical light the image of the undifferentiated, exoticized Amazonian Indian, which is so central in perspectivism and presents us with a good example of an exoticized stereotype that has achieved a certain transcendental ahistoricity. As Nugent argues, the image of the Amerindian falls comfortably within conventional Western referents of the primordial exotic: closer to a naturalized ur-condition representative of a mythologized human state before Westernization.

All this being said, Viveiros de Castro, Descola, and Strathern give renewed life to that anthropology that is concerned with opening up the importance of different formations of human existence—past or present—for the general understanding of human being, an understanding that decenters dominant or dominating perspectives, including those of some of their critics. As such, their approaches represent important junctures in anthropology's attempt to reposition itself with respect to the exteriorizing and/or orientalizing connotations of the exotic.

The Comparativism of Louis Dumont

Louis Dumont presents another orientation that maintains the importance of the exotic in the anthropological comparative project. It is, in effect, a postructuralism directly intended to overcome the Eurocentric dualism of Lévi-Strauss' structuralism. Moreover, Dumont grounds his approach in the recognition that anthropology is first and foremost a comparative discipline. Unlike Descola, who affirms the authority of Eurocentric scientific and philosophical reason, Dumont is concerned to more thoroughly decenter Eurocentric authority, despite acknowledging that it is impossible to fully escape. Dumont confronts the methodological aporia at the heart of anthropology, giving the discipline, perhaps, a unique position in the social sciences. His approach works strongly in the space of the exotic as one of open potentiality whereby a relatively universally applicable methodology can be built and tested.

Dumont has been singled out as the figure of anthropological Orientalism par excellence, particularly regarding his India research on caste, which comprises the basis for his comparative methodology. However, Dumont's objective is thoroughly antagonistic to Orientalism and anthropological exoticism in general, which he most explicitly locates in Eurocentrism and also in certain modernist universalisms of a well-tried Marxian and Weberian sort. Dumont identifies himself as oriented to a Marxist position and thoroughly in accord with its liberating ideas. But he is wary of the way his political ideology may interfere with an anthropology that, in the interests of being scientific and rigorous in its investigations, must at first be prepared to suspend judgment (a kind of Husserlian epoche).

Caste is conventionally conceived as the extreme instance of inequality largely of a general economic kind. For perhaps most social scientists, caste is the worst instance of class oppression legitimated in religious ideology: an oriental system that could be overcome in a Western modernizing advance. In contesting this still ruling opinion—and without avoiding the undoubted dehumanizing possibilities of caste—Dumont showed how this misconception carried into practice (indeed through an orientalizing imperialism) in effect contributed to new human destructions of caste (and of ethnicity) associated with the 1947 Partition of India. Developing a new set of concepts—for example, a non-stratificationist notion of hierarchy and the idea of encompassment—Dumont analyzed how caste was part of a specific overarching ideational logic of practice, ingrained in diverse social relations from kinship, through politics to the economic, that could not be reduced to conventional Western-derived sociological understanding.

While Dumont's orientation starts by contrasting India (the Orient) and the Occident, the ultimate aim is not to oppose them—and certainly not as homogeneous totalities (see his Appendices in Dumont 1980)—but to indicate them as historical divergences from out of common ground. Thus, their apparent difference disguises an underlying unity: the societies of Western Europe and North America being a suppression of forces to which India in its diversity gives varieties of open expression. There is no Self/Other dynamic in the comparison that hitherto defined the Euro- and America-centric orientation of much anthropological comparative work. This is how Dumont's arguments have been systematically presented (e.g., Rio and Smedal 2010), and we question such orientation. Dumont's objective is to overcome such dualism: what is treated as distinctly opposed is reframed as emergent in a dynamic of historical differentiation.

From this historical orientation Dumont develops a distinctive comparative method that strives to create concepts derived from underlying unities (demonstrated ethnographically), rather than on the basis of difference, or upon surface and untested assumptions of similarity and difference. Thus, in Dumont's view the concepts of comparative and universalizing Euro-American dominant sociologies assert the validity of concepts (and their theoretical articulation) that are inherently contradictory and oppositional. They are based in assumptions that defy their generalizing purpose, compounded by the fact that they spring from ideologies and values peculiar to a particular and relatively recent Euro-American historical experience.

Dumont's point has some similarity with the otherwise distinct ontological perspective of Descola, although Dumont prefers the term 'ideology' for a similar usage, but, we think, is less closed and homogeneously totalizing. Ideology for Dumont is not a surface phenomenon but deeply layered (like Descola's ontology) in the dynamics of relations constituting, as revealed through analytical abstraction, the overall impetus and organization of social processes in particular contexts. We should say here that Dumont's (unlike Descola's) is not a finished project. Descola's approach is highly formal—logically formulated in all its possibility—establishing a priori categories to be substantiated by ethnographic work. It is a typological frame for comparison as it is a method for identifying exotic difference without asserting Euro-American conceptual hegemony. Thus, it may avoid the Orientalizing type of exoticization and invite the possibility of developing counter-exoticizing interpretations.

Dumont also avoids exoticism by attempting to develop concepts that are both phenomenologically sensitive to the nature of practices in specific contexts and open to refinement in the interests of comparison. The analytical concepts that Dumont tries to develop for comparison are in many respects dislocated.

That is, they are in their pure abstraction independent or outside any extant context while having a potential and particular organicity to specific practices. The concepts (and their logic) to be applied, in Dumont's orientation, needs continual ethnographic demonstration as to their specific relevance, which also involves defining the limits of certain concepts as they are articulated in analysis. In our opinion, Dumont's comparative strategy is more ethnographically grounded than that of Descola. It takes the form of anthropology as an ongoing experiment, a continuing archaeology of the exotic in the constantly differentiating realities of human realities anywhere and everywhere, with an emphasis on the structures of limitation within practices that might restrict their applicability to other contexts. Thus, Dumont is able to show why the logic of caste hierarchy in India might not be expected to operate in Indonesia, where, for example, the relation of power to ritual is markedly distinct. That is, power is identical with ritual potency and not subordinate to it (see Geertz 1980).

We have seen so far how different theoretical interventions in anthropology have attempted to address exoticism in anthropology and especially to overcome the ever-present risk of Orientalism. Our concern also has been to break out of the relativism/universalism oppositional dialectic in anthropology in which the discipline has become needlessly bogged down.

The Ethnographic Exotic: A Counter-Exoticizing Opportunity

It is time to shift our attention from theory to ethnography, focusing on the burdens, but also the advantages, of studying the exotic—this time, adopting a perspective from the grassroots. Once more, the connotations of exteriority, inherent in the etymology of exoticism, guide much of the discussion that follows and encourage us to focus on two emerging challenges.

The first challenge relates to the nostalgic identification of the ethnographer with the ethnographic object. Ethnography always addresses a time other than that of writing. In its attempt to capture social life as enacted somewhere else (or sometime before), ethnographic practice bears the mark of nostalgia. Is this an indelible mark, unredeemable, the ultimate sign of orientalizing exoticism? A deluded desire to salvage what is unsalvageable? Or, as we would like to argue here, ethnographic nostalgia presents an opportunity to reposition oneself with respect to exteriority: to deterritorialize and detemporalize ethnographic practice? And in that process, discover new meaning and unexpected, alternative perspectives?

The second challenge of the exotic for ethnographic writing emerges from its reemployment by the ethnographic subjects themselves: the appropriation and reuse of previous exoticized referents to articulate new identity narratives, which provide (often peripheralized) local actors with new opportunities to renegotiate their cultural representation. We refer to this process as counter-exoticization, and we recognize in it an opportunity for rewriting history from the bottom up, but without departing completely from preexisting exoticizing (mostly colonial) registers. In this respect, and as we are about to show, counter-exoticizing narratives may reproduce ambivalence and the very source of Orientalism they attempt to deny. This is why we approach self-exoticization, and the exoticization introduced by (more powerful) Others, as mutually constitutive and interrelated processes.

De-exoticizing Ethnographic Nostalgia: Salvaging Anthropology No More

As a wistful longing for how things used to be—themselves more frequently fantasy than not—the nostalgic view can distort the ethnographic project in discreet, not always directly detectable, but often mildly exoticizing ways. To expose the consequence of such distortions, anthropologists have identified a number of distinctive, ideal types of nostalgia (Angé and Berliner 2015).[4] One among them, 'imperialist nostalgia', introduced by Renato Rosaldo (1989), encapsulates a longing for disappearing worlds affected by modernizing change.[5] Nostalgic predilections of this variety can be detected in the exoticizing preferences of Western travelers and writers who contemplate exotic worlds, but also in the salvaging motif of some anthropological accounts. Ethnography's disappearing object is lost and textually reclaimed, rescued at the very moment of its transformation, or presented as resisting the inevitable advance of Westernization (see Clifford 1986; Marcus 1986; Marcus and Fischer 1986).

Such a deconstructive approach may entice us to approach ethnographic writing as a redemptive Western allegory (see Clifford 1986: 99) and nostalgia itself as a mechanism for rescuing cultural difference: Western anthropology salvaging what Western colonialism has already damaged. Pnina Werbner (chap. 2) places under critical examination these stimulating criticisms. She argues that behind the apparently romanticist, pastoral, or exoticizing outlook of much mid-twentieth-century anthropology, we can detect a committed antiracist and anticolonialist stance. To elucidate her point of view, Werbner focuses on *Tristes Tropiques*, a paradigmatically nostalgic—but for Werbner also historical—book that confronts the question of cultural survival at the face of extinction (see also Kapferer 2013). For Werbner, Lévi-Strauss's lament for what is fractured and lost emerges from his condemnation of the Western colonial project and its destructive effect on vulnerable colonized societies. His pessimistic tone, Werbner argues, has much to do with the traumatic World War II experience—the Holocaust, the extermination of millions—that informs a view of irrevocable transformation, the uprootedness of cultures.

The critics of late twentieth-century anthropology—Werbner refers to George E. Marcus and Michael M. J. Fischer (1986), Marcus (1986), and Geertz (1988)—have, in her opinion, overlooked the anticolonial protest intended by *Tristes Tropiques*; in this respect, their criticism "lacks attention to the very historicity they advocate" (Werbner, chap. 2; see also Fardon 1990). Such thoughts lead Werbner to argue that it is time to reconsider, ideally with a more sympathetic eye, the nostalgia that emerges from traditional anthropological accounts, such as those of the salvaging cultural diversity variety. Ethnography's disappearing object, she argues, is not a mere rhetorical construct, as James Clifford (1986: 112) has argued—for example, a made-up justification of an ethnographic pastoral. In some cases, certain societies—or more often, particular cultural practices—are irreversibly affected by Westernization, state policies, consumerist trends, and noticeably postcolonial inequalities.

The anthropological commitment to engage critically with such processes brings anthropologists face-to-face with disappearing, fractured cultural practices, and invites attention to the following dilemma: is it appropriate to consider our engagement with what is irrevocably transformed as salvaging preoccupation? A starting point for resolving this dilemma, we believe, is to draw a firm distinction between, on the one hand, the anthropological commitment to study vulnerable, peripheral societies—a decision that, as Werbner points out, does not in itself engender nostalgia—and on the other, the exoticizing collapse of time and space that emanates from some ethnographic accounts, which may lead to the imprisonment of the ethnographic object in a depoliticized time capsule, an alochrony of a sort (see Fabian 1983).

A certain degree of exoticizing nostalgia, argues Theodossopoulos (chap. 1), is predicated on our fieldwork memories and on our reading of the work of previous authors—for example, the literature that constitutes a particular ethnographic record. Field notes and previous ethnographies provide a well-articulated (thematically organized) view of the society under study that, very often, compares unfavorably with the disorderly dynamism of the everyday social reality. From this incongruity emerges 'ethnographic nostalgia', claims Theodossopoulos, the inclination to pursue nostalgic connections between a present social reality and the ethnographic record, which often provides the fleeting impression that the past is repeated in the present, as if it has emerged from the pages of a book.

The nostalgic, exoticizing biases outlined so far represent a never-ending challenge for ethnographers: the more distortions we uncover, the more we are bound to discover. As with ethnocentrism, the temptation of the exotic resurfaces in almost every new confrontation with alterity. But are such enticements unsurpassable? We believe that the ethnographic project engenders the very conditions that may lead to the demise of exoticism—or, ethnocentrism, for that matter. The more closely we experience the complexity of everyday social life, the more likely it is that we realize how our nostalgic predilections do not always represent the concerns of the people we study.[6] An engagement with what we (or others) may erroneously deem exotic entails the potential that, in time, familiarity with the Other's point of view will bring about a de-exoticizing perspective: the detemporalization of exteriority in culturally meaningful and socially embedded terms.

It is in this fundamental respect that our treatment of nostalgia communicates a more positive message than that of Clifford (1986) and Rosaldo (1989). Our insistence to continue engaging ethnographically with social reality may—and often does—provoke a multitude of exotic recognitions that pose de-exoticizing challenges to our understanding (see Kapferer 2013). Thus, although exoticism, in the Orientalist sense, cannot be redeemed, the confrontation with alterity—conceived as what comes from outside—invites the consideration of new perspectives: the exotic as a gained opportunity, enabled by ethnography itself.

Self-Exoticization as Counter-Exoticization

Just as native or indigenous anthropologists look inward, making the familiar exotic (Sax 1998; see also MacClancy 2002: 8), so too the everyday protagonists of social life, especially those in the periphery of economic power, look at their own culture from some temporal distance to reflect upon cultural practices of the past and valorize them in terms relevant to the present. In this process they may embark in the exoticization of their own culture. Self-exoticization involves a certain degree of self-distantiation: the repackaging of cultural products and practices—"a curious mix of the intimate and the remote" (Comaroff and Comaroff 2009: 3)—that invites foreign consumers of the exotic. In this respect, self-exoticization, as a more encompassing process, may also inspire the re-articulation of local histories—often as representative and prototypical, ideal for repetition in performance, or worthy to serve as symbols that accentuate cultural distinctiveness.

Emerging identity narratives of that type can be broadly contrasted to institutionalized identity constructions, for example, nationalist practices such as those Eric Hobsbawm (1983) described as 'invention of tradition'. The term 'invention' in this use carries its own semantic baggage—a particular association with inauthenticity (Theodossopoulos 2013)—that fails to capture the innovativeness, creativity, and improvisation of local discourse (Bruner 1993; Hallam and Ingold 2007), including cases of self-conscious depictions of the Self as exotic. Instead of invention, Sahlins (1999) recommends the term 'inventiveness' as a more appropriate alternative, which better conveys the idealization, irony, and self-caricaturing involved in the bottom-up revaluation of particular representations. The latter may be the product of political or economic contingencies—or marked inequalities—that inspire local actors to take their representation into their own hands and modify previous exoticizing images or narratives to fit new purposes.

From this point of view, we can see self-exoticization as dependent upon, or as a reaction against, notions of the exotic that are externally imposed—for example, previous, already established imaginaries such as tourism imaginaries (see Salazar and Graburn 2014). It is undeniable, however, that self-exoticization subverts top-down exoticization to reconstitute the exoticized subject in new, locally meaningful terms. In this respect, self-exoticization may instigate local, vernacular forms of counter-exoticization, such as the cases examined by Maurice Said in chapter 4, Theodora Lefkaditou in chapter 5, and Urmi Bhattacharyya in chapter 6. Such local vernacular types of counter-exoticization invite attention to a significant feature of the self-exoticizing process: its close interrelationship with the exoticizing narratives and images that it attempts to replace, which lead us to argue that exoticization and self-exoticization are mutually constitutive processes. They closely communicate with one another and borrow each other's referents. It is more appropriate, thus, that they are analyzed in terms of their dialectic relationship.

We can detect this dialectic between exoticization and self-exoticization in the imaginary about capoeira teachers in Bahia, a topic explored ethnographically by Theodora Lefkaditou in chapter 5. There is a particular sensualized reputation, she argues, about male capoeira teachers in Bahia. The latter are stereotyped by other members of their society as 'hunters of foreign women'. The racialized stereotype of the attractive, black male capoeira teacher who pursues relationships with foreign female tourists (or capoeira students) rests upon a much wider exoticized imagery about this Brazilian martial art and its practitioners. This wider imagery contributes to the appeal of capoeira and Bahia as a tourist destination. Young Brazilian men, interested to pursue short-term erotic relationships (and establish connections that may help them travel abroad) take advantage of a preexisting sensualized reputation to present themselves in a manner that perpetuates an exoticized myth.

This mutually reinforcing process of exoticization and self-exoticization provides opportunities for local actors to reflect upon and redefine their identifications with Bahia, capoeira, and the wider world. The male capoeira teachers who pursue erotic relationships with foreign women understand that their exotic reputation offers an escape route out of marginalization. Other local actors, however, such as Brazilian women in Salvador and older, more established capoeira teachers, comment disparagingly about the young Brazilian men who engage with capoeira in a performative, flirtatious, or more superficial manner. In everyday conversation, argues Lefkaditou, the Bahians discuss the flirtatious practices of male capoeira teachers with ambivalence: admiration is mixed with contempt—including a growing concern about how Brazilian male sexuality, and the reputation of Bahia more generally, is appropriated by outsiders. The interface of exoticization and self-exoticization in this case poses identity dilemmas for many Bahians who remain so far unresolved.

Maurice Said (chap. 4) explores some similar dilemmas in Sri Lanka. Focusing on the period following the catastrophic tsunami of 2004, Said identifies two exoticizing tropes articulated in local contexts. The first of these involves the stereotyping of the undifferentiated generic Sri Lankan by foreigners (e.g., expatriates or aid workers) who present the local population in either patronizing (e.g., passive victims in need of humanitarian aid) or denigrating terms (e.g., 'unreliable', 'uneducated', 'uncivilized'). Local Sri Lankans respond to these exoticizing views with counter-exoticizing narratives of their own, portraying the generic foreigner as businesslike and calculative but also gullible and exploitable. Both of these exoticizing tropes are predicated on contradictions; they inform complicated expectations that oscillate between idealization and disappointment (in the case of the foreigners) or dependency and exploitation (in the case of the Sri Lankans).

The dialectic of exoticization and counter-exoticization engenders identities formed in mutual opposition and reminds us, as does Said, that exoticization is never unidirectional. On a wider scale, the exotic imagery of Sri Lanka as a tropical paradise stimulates economic development. Those locations that are more heavily (or successfully) exoticized have received increased levels of humanitarian aid and foreign investment. In addition, European expatriates have taken advantage of local fears of another tsunami to buy and develop beachside properties. They have attempted to promote Sri Lanka as an untouched paradise, a refuge from the banality of life in Western societies. Unable to sanitize the local landscape and its inhabitants of Westernizing influences, they see local social life—in its dynamic unpredictability—as an impediment. The local Sri Lankans, on their part, are reluctant to inhabit an artificial paradise controlled by the expatriates. They thus counter-exoticize the foreigners in an attempt to regain some sense of control. Exoticization and counter-exoticization here generate competing narratives in a context where local and foreign actors exoticize each other.

Urmi Bhattacharyya further explores the interrelationship of exoticization and self-exoticization as mutually constituted processes. In West Bengal, the referents of the exotic represent an outsider's point of view, emerging originally from a colonial gaze and more recently from images propagated by a postcolonial global economy. A colonial version of the exotic India became apparent in a particular Western discourse of superiority that attempted to redefine the Orient as the subject of imperial control. The representation of the colonized population as an exotic category played a legitimizing role for the colonial project: it concealed the vicious inequalities of domination behind the civilizing quest of the exotic Other. Colonial rule created the exotic in India, a discriminating category of naturalized inferiority, argues Bhattacharyya.

Nonetheless, the exoticization of India as a process externally imposed did not remain unopposed. In West Bengal, a community of artists who paint scrolls of cloth or paper has engaged in a form of counter-exoticization, using as a medium their pictorial art (*patachitra*), and the narratives that explain this art to local audiences. In colonial times, this distinctive local art followed wider anti-colonial trends that resisted discrimination, contributing to the re-articulation of a reviving Bengali identity—an act of indirect resistance. In the twentieth century, *patachitra* scrolls became commodified as popular souvenirs for pilgrims and tourists. By self-exoticizing their art form—following, in part, the exotic referents of a globalized market—the local artists have ensured that *patachitra* is now aesthetically significant at the global level.

A common feature in all these examples of self-exoticization is that bottom-up renegotiations of the exotic articulate with old and new exoticized imagery, although this time, in terms controlled by the exoticized subject. The sense of control that emanates from this process is of paramount importance to peripheral actors: their counter-exoticizing narratives can be conceived as a form of resistance. In this respect, seeing the Self from a position of exteriority involves a reclaimed sense of authorship in identity making. But it also engenders a new variety of grassroot or 'indigenous essentialism' (Howe 2009): the old exoticism is merely replaced, not eliminated. In an effort to de-pathologize the primitivism of colonial exoticization, counter-exoticizing narratives often reproduce and perpetuate the caricaturing referents of the top-down exoticization they try to repudiate.[7]

Conclusion

Steve Nugent, in chapter 3, argues that the burdensome nature of the exotic is related to "the fact that anthropological usages of the exotic are embedded in a loose conceptual repertoire that anthropologists are at pains to police."

We have tried here to shed some light to this loose conceptual repertoire. For this purpose we have taken a decisive step toward redefining anthropology's engagement with the exotic, highlighting not merely its burdensome Orientalist side but also the opportunities for acquiring new knowledge, the challenge that the exotic—as the outside—poses for reconfiguring previous registers of understanding (see also Kapferer 2013). In many respects, both the exotic (in its colonial vision) and self-exoticization (as a bottom-up readjustment or correction of a colonial vision) depend upon and recycle previous referents of alterity—romanticizing, patronizing, caricaturing. We can easily detect a variety of Orientalizing exoticizations—intellectualist, structuralist, allochronic—and a variety of essentializing self-exoticizations—nostalgic, defensive, or self-idealizing.

But we can also detect a variety of local attempts to reconfigure previous exoticizing stereotypes, which strive to reverse the exoticizing gaze or to counter-exoticize. It remains to be seen how future generations of anthropologists will handle the possibilities that emerge from this bottom-up (self-)exoticization. Will they avoid confronting the exotic—for example, by distancing themselves from the culture concept, universalizing, or confining the exotic in the particularity of ontological models? Will they rush into redefining the exotic in term of preexisting knowledge, previous classifications nostalgically reenacted as typologies of exteriority? Or will they grasp the opportunity provided by the challenge of the exotic—the unique perspectives that emerge from the unexpected, and occasionally subversive, points of view made available by exteriority?

Irrespectively of the trajectories outlined above, the exotic—as the outside, or the familiar seen from the outside—will remain a central concern in anthropology. Exteriority is a defining feature of 'sameness'—the anthropological axiom that "all societies embody the same cultural value worth" (Argyrou 2002: 1). We may even argue, that exteriority—as a demand for the elsewhere, far away or closer to home—has created the broader discourses that defined anthropology. The dialectic of 'the here and the elsewhere' have premised each other to create the West (and its vision of order) (Trouillot 1991: 29, 32). And as Trouillot (2003) has argued, anthropology inherited the conceptual 'slots' that accommodate such previous categorizations. The lessons gained from our confrontation with the exotic indicate that conceptualizations of exteriority that predicate the 'savage slot' are not inescapable or binding. Anthropology can take the opportunity provided by the exotic, conceived not as confirmation of existing hierarchies but as a challenge to well-trodden paths of acquiring knowledge: the new has always been exotic to the old.

Acknowledgments

Bruce Kapferer thanks the European Research Commission for support in the writing of his contributions to this book.

Bruce Kapferer is Director of an ERC Advanced Grant on Egalitarianism at the University of Bergen. He was the Foundation Professor of Social Anthropology at the University of Adelaide and later James Cook University. He was the Professor and Chair of Anthropology at University College London, where he is now also Honorary Professor. He is the author of several monographs, including *Legends of People, Myths of State* (2011) and *2001 and Counting: Kubrick, Nietzsche, and Anthropology* (2014), and editor of many volumes, among which are *Beyond Rationalism* (2003) and *In the Event* (2015, with Lotte Meinert). He has conducted ethnographic research in Zambia, Sri Lanka, Australia, India, and South Africa.

Dimitrios Theodossopoulos is Professor of Social Anthropology at the University of Kent. He has conducted research in Panama and Greece, focusing on processes of resistance, exoticization, authenticity, tourism, and environmentalism and on the politics of cultural representation and protest. He is the author of *Exoticisation Undressed* (2016) and *Troubles with Turtles* (2003), and editor of *De-Pathologising Resistance* (2015), *Great Expectations* (2011), *United in Discontent* (2010), and *When Greeks Think about Turks* (2007).

Notes

1. The term shares the same etymological route with the noun *exotika* (in plural), which in modern Greek refers to supernatural beings that occupy a spatial position of exteriority, clustering "around marginal areas" that "lie beyond the safe confines of the village" (Stewart 1991: xv).
2. A point that similarly applies to Viveiros de Castro's perspectivist approach.
3. Strathern's perspective also could be viewed as returning to a dominant Eurocentric perspective. Her approach (as does that of Bruno Latour with whom Strathern's is connected) can be conceived as relevant to current transitions in the contemporary state form from that of the territorially sovereign nation-state to that of the more deterritorialized corporate state. Strathern's rhizomic relational dynamic of the Melanesian person has some degree of fit with that of corporate state formations. In other words, as much sociological thought once corresponded with the milieu of the nation-state (most modernist theory), so do the poststructuralist orientations of Latour and Strathern express aspects of the contemporary corporate state formations that are integral to what is frequently described as globalization.
4. For example, Michael Herzfeld (1997) has introduced 'structural nostalgia' to capture the yearning for an irrevocable time of balanced perfection in social relations, evident in discourses that compare an idealized past of reciprocal sociality with a less perfect present, while Arjun Appadurai (1996: 77–78) discussed an 'imagined' nostalgia without lived experience—which he calls 'armchair nostalgia'—to highlight how mass merchandising supplies memories of loss that one may never have suffered.
5. Imperialist nostalgia relates to the paradoxical grief of the colonizer for what colonialism has destroyed, which is conveniently expressed after the realization of the colonizing process (Rosaldo 1989).

6. For example, a nostalgic engagement may even encourage a committed ethno-graphic pursuit of continuities with the past that will inevitably lead to the realiza-tion that such continuities may very well be artificially construed.

7. And in this respect, counter-exoticization positions itself ambivalently in between the two most common distortions of resistance: the pathologization and exoticiza-tion of the resisting subject (Theodossopoulos 2014).

References

Angé, Olivia, and David Berliner. 2015. "Introduction: Anthropology of Nostalgia—Anthropology as Nostalgia." Pp. 1–15 in *Anthropology and Nostalgia,* ed. Olivia Angé and David Berliner. New York: Berghahn Books.

Appadurai, Arjun. 1996. *Modernity at Large: Cultural Dimensions of Globalization.* Minneapolis: University of Minnesota Press.

Argyrou, Vassos. 2002. *Anthropology and the Will to Meaning: A Postcolonial Critique.* London: Pluto Press.

Bruner, Edward M. 1993. "Epilogue: Creativity Persona and the Problem of Authentic-ity." Pp. 321–334 in *Creativity/Anthropology*, ed. Smadar Lavie, Kirin Narayan, and Renato Rosaldo. Ithaca, NY: Cornell University Press.

Clifford, James. 1986. "On Ethnographic Allegory." Pp. 98–121 in Clifford and Marcus 1986.

Clifford, James, and George. E. Marcus, eds. 1986. *Writing Culture: The Poetics and Politics of Ethnography.* Berkeley: University of California Press.

Comaroff, John L., and Jean Comaroff. 2009. *Ethnicity, Inc.* Chicago: University of Chi-cago Press.

Descola, Philippe. 2013. *Beyond Nature and Culture.* Trans. Janet Lloyd. Chicago: Uni-versity of Chicago Press.

Dumont, Louis. 1980. *Homo Hierarchicus: The Caste System and Its Implications.* Chi-cago: Chicago University Press.

Fabian, Johannes. 1983. *Time and the Other: How Anthropology Makes Its Object.* New York: Columbia University Press.

Fardon, Richard. 1990. "General Introduction—Localising Strategies: The Regionalisa-tion of Ethnographic Accounts." Pp. 1–35 in *Localising Strategies: Regional Tradi-tions of Ethnographic Writing,* ed. Richard Fardon. Edinburgh: Scottish Academic Press.

Fernandez, James. 1986. *Persuasions and Performances: The Play of Tropes in Culture.* Bloomington: Indiana University Press.

Geertz, Clifford. 1980. *Negara: The Theatre State in Nineteenth-Century Bali.* Princeton, NJ: Princeton University Press.

Geertz, Clifford. 1984. "Anti-Anti-Relativism." *American Anthropologist* 86, no. 2: 263–278.

Gluckman, Max. 1965. *Politics, Law and Ritual in Tribal Society.* Oxford: Basil Blackwell.

Gluckman, Max. 1966. *Custom and Conflict in Africa.* Oxford: Basil Blackwell.

Hallam, Elizabeth, and Tim Ingold. 2007. "Creativity and Cultural Improvisation: An Introduction." Pp. 1–24 in *Creativity and Cultural Improvisation*, ed. Elizabeth Hal-lam and Tim Ingold. Oxford: Berg.

Harman, Graham. 2016. *Immaterialism: Objects and Social Theory.* Cambridge: Polity Press.

Henriksen, Georg. 2008. *I Dreamed the Animals: Kaniuekutat: The Life of an Innu Hunter*. New York: Berghahn Books.

Herzfeld, Michael. 1997. *Cultural Intimacy: Social Poetics in the Nation-State*. New York: Routledge.

Hobsbawm, Eric. 1983. "Introduction: Inventing Traditions." Pp. 1–14 in *The Invention of Tradition*, ed. Eric Hobsbawm and Terence Ranger. Cambridge: Cambridge University Press.

Holbraad, Martin. 2012. *Truth in Motion: The Recursive Anthropology of Cuban Divination*. Chicago: Chicago University Press.

Holbraad, Martin, and Morten Axel Pedersen, eds. 2016. *The Ontological Turn: An Anthropological Exposition*. Cambridge: Cambridge University Press.

Howe, James. 2009. *Chiefs, Scribes, and Ethnographers: Kuna Culture from Inside and Out*. Austin: University of Texas Press.

Kapferer, Bruce. 2011. "Louis Dumont and a Holist Anthropology." Pp. 187–208 in *Experiments in Holism: Theory and Practice in Contemporary Anthropology*, ed. Ton Otto and Nils Bubandt. Malden, MA: Wiley-Blackwell.

Kapferer, Bruce. 2013. "How Anthropologists Think: Configurations of the Exotic." *Journal of the Royal Anthropological Institute* 19, no. 4: 813–836.

Kapferer, Bruce. 2014. "Back to the Future: Descola's Neostructuralism." *Hau: Journal of Ethnographic Theory* 4, no. 3: 389–400.

Lévi-Strauss, Claude. 1962. *The Savage Mind*. London: Weidenfeld & Nicolson.

MacClancy, Jeremy. 2002. "Introduction: Taking People Seriously." Pp. 1–14 in *Exotic No More: Anthropology on the Front Lines*, ed. Jeremy MacClancy. Chicago: University of Chicago Press.

MacCormack, Carol P., and Marilyn Strathern, eds. 1980. *Nature, Culture and Gender*. Cambridge: Cambridge University Press.

Marcus, George E. 1986. "Contemporary Problems of Ethnography in the Modern World System." Pp. 165–193 in Clifford and Marcus 1986.

Marcus, George E., and Michael M. J. Fischer. 1986. *Anthropology as Cultural Critique*. Chicago: University of Chicago Press.

Marriott, McKim. 1976. "Hindu Transactions: Diversity without Dualism." Pp. 109–142 in *Transaction and Meaning: Directions in the Anthropology of Exchange and Symbolic Behavior*, ed. Bruce Kapferer. Philadelphia: Institute for the Study of Human Issues.

Miner, Horace. 1956. "Body Ritual among the Nacirema." *American Anthropologist* 58, no. 3: 503–507.

Pina-Cabral, João de. 2014a. "World: An Anthropological Examination (Part 1)." *Hau: Journal of Ethnographic Theory* 4, no. 1: 49–73

Pina-Cabral, João de. 2014b. "World: An Anthropological Examination (Part 2)." *Hau: Journal of Ethnographic Theory* 4, no. 3: 149–184.

Ramos, Alcida R. 2012. "The Politics of Perspectivism." *Annual Review of Anthropology* 41: 481–494.

Rio, Knut Rio, and Olaf H. Smedal, eds. 2010. *Hierarchy: Persistence and Transformation in Social Formations*. New York: Berghahn Books.

Rosaldo, Renato. 1989. "Imperialist Nostalgia." *Representations* 26: 107–122.

Sahlins, Marshall. 1999. "Two or Three Things That I Know about Culture." *Journal of the Royal Anthropological Institute* 59, no. 3: 399–421.

Salazar, Noel, and Nelson Graburn. 2014. "Toward an Anthropology of Tourism Imaginaries." Pp. 1–28 in *Tourism Imaginaries: Through an Anthropological Lens*, ed. Nelson Graburn and Noel Salazar. New York: Berghahn Books.

Sax, William S. 1998. "The Hall of Mirrors: Orientalism, Anthropology, and the Other." *American Anthropologist* 100, no. 2: 292–301.

Stewart, Charles. 1991. *Demons and the Devil: Moral Imagination in Modern Greek Culture.* Princeton, NJ: Princeton University Press.

Theodossopoulos, Dimitrios. 2013. "Laying Claim to Authenticity: Five Anthropological Dilemmas." *Anthropological Quarterly* 86, no. 2: 337–360.

Theodossopoulos, Dimitrios. 2014. "On De-Pathologizing Resistance." *History and Anthropology* 25, no. 4: 415–430.

Trouillot, Michel-Rolph. 1991. "Anthropology and the Savage Slot: The Poetics and Politics of Otherness." Pp. 17–44 in *Recapturing Anthropology: Working in the Present,* ed. Richard G. Fox. Santa Fe, NM: School of American Research Press.

Trouillot, Michel-Rolph. 2003. *Global Transformations: Anthropology and Modern World.* Basingstoke: Palgrave Macmillan.

Turner, Terence S. 2009. "The Crisis of Late Structuralism. Perspectivism and Animism: Rethinking Culture, Nature, Spirit, and Bodiliness." *Tipití* 7, no. 1: 3–42.

Viveiros de Castro, Eduardo. 1998. "Cosmological Deixis and Amerindian Perspectivism." *Journal of the Royal Anthropological Institute* 4, no. 3: 469–488.

Viveiros de Castro, Eduardo. 2004. "Perspectival Anthropology and the Method of Controlled Equivocation." *Tipití* 2, no. 1: 3–22.

Willerslev, Rane. 2007. *Soul Hunters: Hunting, Animism, and Personhood among the Siberian Yukaghirs.* Berkeley: University of California Press.

Chapter 1

On Ethnographic Nostalgia
Exoticizing and De-exoticizing the Emberá, for Example

Dimitrios Theodossopoulos

Ethnography is an inherently nostalgic exercise because it emulates a previous experience, a memory of fieldwork, articulated in dialogue with a previous ethnographic record or the narratives of others. In recent work (Theodossopoulos 2016), I have used the term 'ethnographic nostalgia' to refer to the inclination of ethnographers—and in general, authors who try to record cultural practices—to pursue nostalgic connections between a present social reality and what other people (previous authors or key informants) have said about a particular society before. Ethnographic nostalgia emerges from the comparison of the ethnographic object as encountered in the present with previous written or oral descriptions, for example, the ethnographic literature or local lore. According to this definition, most theories that attempt to uncover structural patterns—for example, most types of structuralism—flirt with the possibility of generating a certain nostalgic view. This is often predicated in the analytical attempt to identify an underlying structure by comparing an imperfect present with an increasingly idealized past.

When one's thoughts and observations are committed to paper, it is very hard to follow up the rhythm of social transformation. By the time a description of social life has been articulated—published, formalized, accepted as representative—society has already changed in numerous unanticipated and

Notes for this chapter begin on page 40.

as yet unaccounted for ways. It is to here that we can trace the roots of ethnographic nostalgia: the present ethnographic reality does not always fit, and often compare unfavorably, with the more perfect, well-articulated picture of the ethnographic record. The latter may be polished, already idealized, selective, often legitimized as a standard of authenticity. And this is why so many ethnographers relate to the present social reality in 'allochronic' terms, placing the peoples they study in another, distant, and safer time (see Fabian 1983), which generates nostalgia and a desire to salvage "ethnography's disappearing object" (Clifford 1986: 112; see also Berliner 2015).

'Ethnographic nostalgia' has an affinity with two other types of nostalgia identified by Renato Rosaldo (1989, 1993) and Michael Herzfeld ([1997] 2005). Rosaldo's 'imperialist nostalgia' focuses on the paradoxical lament of the colonizer for what colonization has already destroyed (1989). The Western observer longs for what the Western civilizing mission has radically transformed, romanticizing Otherness—which is seen as lost and therefore unthreatening—seeking absolution in the presumed innocence of such a nostalgic longing, as if domination could be erased. Herzfeld's 'structural nostalgia' uncovers a nostalgia that emerges from a comparison with the past, an idealized and irrevocable age of reciprocal sociality (2005). It is to be found both in official and local discourses—not only colonial narratives—when idealized narratives about the perfection of relationships in a previous, more sociable and authentic era are evoked to frame commentary for a less perfect present. The longing for former, better times, representative of 'structural nostalgia', may inform a desire to salvage what is perceived to be disappearing, which is so representative of 'imperialist nostalgia'.

Imperialist and structural nostalgia together substantiate 'ethnographic nostalgia'. The Western ethnographer—or the auto-ethnographer who adopts a Western epistemology—longs for what Westernization has transformed, seeking connections with an authentic representativeness found in narratives about society in the past—for example, the previous ethnographic record. The ethnographic record is imagined as a lost social world, idealized and purified in its written articulation, and therefore works as a standard of authentication, framing nostalgia and exoticizing the present in comparison with an imagined, well-structured, and articulated past. The ethnographer—or culture writer, more generally—may identify this artificially structured and, ultimately, imagined past in old cultural patterns that emerge spontaneously in the present; which often stimulate a sense of nostalgic recognition.

It is in this respect that the ethnographic process engenders a certain degree of nostalgic exoticization. My aim here is not to merely identify this danger but also to provide a more constructive message. Ethnographic nostalgia, despite its patronizing and idealizing proclivity, can generate the conditions of its own demise. It may lead—through reflexive self-questioning—to the recognition of intentionality in social life, leading to a confrontation with the essentialisms of the exoticizing nostalgic view. Nostalgia may also "engender its own ironies" (Battaglia 1995: 78), play a role in social life as a transformative force (Ange and Berliner 2015b), and be used by local actors as a discursive tool to subvert or highlight contradictions (see Herzfeld 2005). As such, vernacular—locally expressed, non-authorial—nostalgia can stimulate the revitalization or readaptation of older cultural themes in the present, produce new arguments about cultural representation, and breed creativity in unpredictable ways (Bruner 1993; Hallam and Ingold 2007)—a transformation of what is seen as tradition which may be conceived to be 'inventiveness' (Sahlins 1999: 399).

But let us return to the nostalgia experienced by authors who write about society. To the degree that their—'ethnographic'—nostalgia inspires the pursuit of what has been previously described or said about the past in the present, it paves the way for confronting complexity and the possibility that the present is not exactly like the past. Such contradictions may complicate previous authenticating ethnographic accounts or expose their incompleteness. Or, on the contrary, they may attract attention to reemerging cultural patterns that may unite the past with the present, in recognition that what was recorded before—and structured as the object of ethnographic nostalgia—is now part of a new configuration of knowledge. Bruce Kapferer has recently refigured the anthropological use of the exotic by directing attention to the moment of exotic recognition: the search for new possibilities "at the edge of or beyond knowledge," the exotic as a "challenge to understanding" (2013: 818). Such moments of exotic recognition may challenge and undermine one's attachment to a previous nostalgic view, destabilize the established pathways of authentication, and engender a de-exoticizing, de-essentializing awareness of complexity.

In this chapter I will highlight some of the obstacles that academic analysts confront when they attempt to contain their proclivity to exoticize, which is inherent in the practice of writing about societies. To avoid offending any particular colleague, or the broader academic community, I will focus my analysis on my own exoticizing tendencies during my struggle to understand the cultural practices of the Emberá, an Amerindian indigenous group. I believe the lessons I learned from this exercise will interest a broader academic audience, primarily academics engaged in ethnographic research, but also, indirectly, indigenous leaders and writers who produce narratives that inform cultural representation. Many authors who write about cultural practices—of their own people or others—are tempted to exoticize, to a greater or lesser degree, in a nostalgic manner. As with ethnocentrism, the distorting lenses of nostalgia and exoticization represent a constant challenge: the more biases we uncover, the more we are bound to discover.

Nostalgia about Emberá Clothes

My first gaze of the Emberá, dressed in their traditional attire, elicited a type of nostalgia very common among audiences of Westerners who visit indigenous groups (cf. Bruner 2005; Salazar 2010): a desire to encounter indigeneity uncontaminated by modernity, representative of a hidden, isolated, and authentic world. This is a naïve, romanticizing, but crypto-colonial nostalgia, 'imperialist' in Rosaldo's (1989) words. When I saw the Emberá welcoming me decorated

FIGURE 1.1 A first view of the Emberá of Parara Puru

Sketch © Dimitrios Theodossopoulos

in full traditional garb, wearing loincloths, colorful *paruma* skirts, beaded necklaces, and body paint designs, my mind stopped for a fleeting moment, as if I wanted to embrace and hold onto this image of quintessential, uncomplicated indigeneity, as if it was possible to stop the clock, reverse time, and experience what I had read about the Emberá in books.

The first Emberá I met were the residents of Parara Puru, one of a small number of Emberá communities close to the Panama Canal that receive regular visits from Western tourists. Parara is in all respects an organic, inhabited community—not a tourist enclave (Edensor 1998)—home to around 20 Emberá families, organized along the lines of the available system of political representation in Panama.[1] Its inhabitants nowadays work full time in indigenous tourism. Every other day—for the greater part of the year—they welcome and put on performances for tourists, and, after the tourists depart, they carry on with the usual chores of their everyday life. As a result, their compelling 'traditional' attire, I soon realized, was a temporary dress, a costume to wear during part of the day, before putting on, as all other Emberá in Panama, their 'modern' (as they call them) clothes.

Many tourists who visit the community seem to be surprised at the extent to which Parara Puru and its inhabitants closely match Western expectations of the appearance of indigenous Amerindians (see Theodossopoulos 2011). The tourists often describe the 'dignity' conveyed by the Emberá, who present their culture without begging for money or hustling their visitors. However, a few tourists, after recovering from their first overwhelming surprise, question the authenticity of the community (see Theodossopoulos 2013a) or express some reservations: "Is this really a real community?" "It looks too good to be true." "Are the Emberá dressed like this all the time?" "They look so much like real Indians!"

This suspicion of inauthenticity on the part of several Western visitors led me to return to Parara, after visiting many other 'non-touristy' Emberá communities in Eastern Panama. And I kept on returning, for the next decade, to conduct anthropological fieldwork and participate in the life of the community, an experience I have described in detail elsewhere (Theodossopoulos 2015, 2016). In the meantime, the issue of Emberá clothing kept on emerging and reemerging as a central theme, uniting different parts of my research. I have taken careful notes on what the Emberá describe as 'traditional' or 'modern' clothes, compared current practices with the ethnographic record, and provided my own neat and clearly outlined description of Emberá clothes (cf. Theodossopoulos 2012, 2016)—all of which have structured, and continue to inform, my ethnographic nostalgia.

But let me return to my first sight of the Emberá, since I now see that it played a trick on my exoticizing imagination. My nostalgia was more unforgivable than that of the tourists, considering I had already spent a good portion of my life teaching anthropology. Having persistently advocated the importance of resisting the temptation to see society in static terms, I myself was not prepared to surrender without a fight to my desire to see the Emberá in indigenous clothes. But the embarrassing realization was that such a nostalgic desire had indeed emerged. Was I the same person who had previously criticized the old-fashioned anthropologist, preoccupied with the 'tribal' peoples of faraway lands? In European anthropology, on which I had previously worked, this exoticizing perspective had been seriously questioned and destabilized (see Goddard et al. 1994; Just 2000). It was precisely because of my firm commitment to this critical perspective that I was so disappointed every time I caught myself longing for cultural difference untouched by modernity. This nostalgic feeling was in fact unredeemable in a double sense: unforgivable, despite the redeeming illusion conveyed by nostalgia (see Clifford 1986; Rosaldo 1989), but also inescapable—the more I tried to get rid of it, the more nostalgia I discovered within myself.

As soon as I realized it was impossible to kill my nostalgia once and for all, I decided to ignore it, focusing instead on the task at hand: documenting the subtle nuances of the Emberá clothing practices. This plan seemed to work at the outset, because the complexity I encountered worked as an antidote to nostalgia's essentializing vision. For example, I was soon able to recognize that the dichotomy between the traditional Emberá attire and their modern dress codes was not as impermeable as I had first thought. In fact, there was significant scope for accommodating modern as well as indigenous elements in the dress of the Emberá, which produced original combinations. Take, for example, the women, who combine in their everyday life their *paruma* skirts, which are mass manufactured but conceived of as indigenous, with a variety of modern tops. This practice has resulted in a distinctive indigenous—Emberá-Wounaan[2]—dress code, used extensively both inside and outside Emberá and Wounaan communities. Similarly, to offer another example, traditional or non-traditional *jagua* body paint designs—the old and diverse indigenous practice of body painting (cf. Ulloa 1992)—are matched with modern clothes in a variety of unpredictable ways, by young Emberá and Wounaan men and women.

Having recognized that various mixed modern and indigenous elements were incorporated into contemporary Emberá dress codes, I was able to appreciate the fluidity of Emberá cultural practices: that there was no deep, unyielding distinction between 'tradition' and 'modernity', no dichotomies, painful rifts, or a sense of irrevocable loss (the type of discontinuity so sharply underlined by imperialist nostalgia). Several Emberá clothing fashions in the past and present have emerged as transformations of previous transformations (Gow 2001) that have developed organically as the Emberá combine what they see as old (traditional and/or indigenous) with what they see as new (modern and/or exogenous). It is this fine balancing act that engenders the various Emberá 'micromodernities' that become in time "a synonym for current custom or personal performance" (Knauft 2002: 20). If we accept that neither modernization nor change are "incompatible with being indigenous" (Conklin 2007: 25), we are much more likely to agree with the Emberá when they insist that they remain distinctively Emberá in spite of the clothes they wear—modern, traditional, or mixed.

Such a fluid and processual view of modernity—that focuses on what can be seen from a local point of view as alternatively modern (Knauft 2002)—can be seen as another antidote for nostalgia and the vision of the vanishing cultures it perpetuates. Indigenous groups all over the world may choose to strategically resort to the visual exoticism (Conklin 1997) of their 'traditional' attire to communicate with wider audiences of potential sympathizers (see Bruner 2005; Conklin 1997, 2007; Ewart 2007; Faris 2007; Gow 2007; Knauft 2007; O'Hanlon 2007; Santos-Granero 2009; Turner and Fajans-Turner 2006; Veber 1992, 1996). In this respect, the Emberá of Parara Puru and other Emberá communities that entertain tourists are not exceptional. However, their use of the full traditional attire during cultural presentations should not be seen as a reassertion of what has been lost, as the nostalgic perspective implies. Instead of contradicting modernity, the full Emberá attire as used in the present is another expression of modernity's many faces: a new representational strategy (Bruner 2005).

The tourists who suspected inauthenticity on the part of the Emberá of Parara Puru were correct in assuming that the Emberá wear full traditional attire only for cultural presentations. It must be noted, however, that even in the time of their grandparents—which the Emberá attire, in its contemporary use as a costume, represents—the Emberá only wore the full complement of their adornments for special occasions and celebrations, including visits from Western outsiders (see Howe 1998; Marsh 1934; Taussig 1993; Verrill 1921). When the tourists depart, the Emberá of Parara Puru carefully stow away their adornments—various types of necklaces, belts, and bracelets[3]—to carry on with their daily chores, very much as their ancestors did, once their celebrations were over. What has changed therefore is not so much the dress code for special occasions but rather the daily clothes of the Emberá, which are nowadays modern (e.g., shorts and T-shirts, for the men), or modern-and-indigenous combinations (e.g., *paruma* skirts matched with a top, for most women).

The implications of these transformations in Emberá clothing practices are undoubtedly countless. Particular dress choices relate to particular intentions—for example, a wish to either accentuate or temporarily deemphasize their indigeneity as the Emberá move between ethnically homogenous and multicultural contexts; relationships that the Emberá choose to pursue (with lovers, partners, relatives, indigenous or nonindigenous neighbors); subtle messages that can be only understood on culturally intimate terms, in spaces of collective introspection or mutual embarrassment (Herzfeld 2005). The negotiation of such varied potential intentions may satisfy an anthropologist's insatiable desire to uncover underlying cultural patterns, more or less nostalgically reconstructed to formulate structures of meanings.

However, it is important to stress here that clothing practices, as made visible in everyday life, may also result from accidental dress combinations—the outcome of coincidences such as the availability of clothing items at a particular moment—with no subtext or further reflection. Or they may be related to the materiality of the particular items of clothing, the properties that make them convenient for certain tasks, or their distinctive 'feel' (Banerjee and Miller 2003; Miller 2005a, 2005c). Hence, the overall ethnographic picture—for example, of a people's clothing practices—can be made intelligible or unintelligible by further layers of complexity. The interaction of intentions with unintentional coincidences may or not reemerge in terms of culturally meaningful processes and patterns. It is this interplay of intentions, meaning, and pattern that a nostalgic predisposition may distort by overintellectualizing or reading an underlying structure where there is in fact only coincidence.

As Nostalgia Reemerges, Again and Again

Ethnographic nostalgia sprouts like an unwelcome weed—unremarkable, at first, and inconspicuous—and makes itself known only at the moment that the old form, pattern, or process reemerges spontaneously in contemporary practices. The accumulation of expertise in a given ethnographic field may encourage a deeper sense of engagement that leads the ethnographer to recognize similarities with previous descriptions of social life in the ethnographic record. This ability of the ethnographer—or any other author of culture—to recognize patterns of the past in the present yields fertile grounds for nostalgia to sprout from. I offer an example from my fieldwork among the Emberá and in particular the stage when I had already deceived myself into believing that my ethnographic nostalgia was firmly contained.

As I have already described, at the end of their cultural presentations for tourism, the residents of Parara Puru put their adornments aside and dress in modern clothes or, in the case of most women, mixed modern and indigenous clothes. This particular shift in Emberá dress codes—I noticed after comparing notes and observations from different years—may in some cases take place in a rather gradual manner. In the early afternoon, when the tourists have already departed, some Emberá keep elements of their old 'traditional' dress code for a bit longer to complete certain (mostly) labor-intensive jobs. So they may delay putting on a fresh set of clean modern clothes and carry on working in the community wearing, for example, a loincloth (in the case of men) or only a *paruma* skirt (e.g., leaving their torso uncovered as in the old times, in the case of women).

Such in-between dress transformations occur in Parara Puru spontaneously, triggered by practical considerations or the material properties of the clothes in question; for instance, the fabric of the loincloth or the *paruma* skirt make them particularly versatile and convenient clothing items for many jobs. There are usually several chores to finish, such as cleaning or maintaining the reception area, cooking, cutting wood, repairing houses and canoes, or clearing the areas around family houses. As the Emberá are already dressed in loincloths and *parumas* to participate in the cultural presentations, they find it convenient to free themselves from the formal adornments of the full attire—beaded necklaces or belts and stainless iron bracelets—and remain for a while dressed in the minimal dress code of their grandparents and great-grandparents.

The recognition of such spontaneous instances during which the Emberá were dressed very much like in the past—not to entertain, but to carry out their daily activities—worked as an irresistible impulse for my ethnographic nostalgia. It triggered the sentimental recognition of an older Emberá practice in the present, which, in turn, prompted me to rejoice at the resilience of Emberá culture in the face of modernization: "Emberá cultural patterns keep on reemerging despite the discrimination that the Emberá have experienced by the nonindigenous majority," I wrote in my field notes. What was important for me to realize, however, beyond recording the reemergence of an old pattern in a new context, was my idealized preference and enthusiastic identification with what had previously seemed to have vanished: an old code of dress emerging, due to a conspiracy of many different coincidences, once more.

But was I accepting as more authentic what the Emberá had framed as 'traditional' themselves, or what I had framed as 'traditional' in my own ethnographic writing? In truth, I should answer 'yes' to this question. I had fallen, as I had done before (see Theodossopoulos 2013a, 2013b), into authenticity's trap: victim to the dualisms it propagates (cf. Bendix 1997; Fillitz 2013; Lindholm 2008, 2013) and accepting something as more or less authentic than something else—a deeper, innermost authentic reality, hidden beyond, and privileged over, an external superficial reality (Miller 2005c; with respect to clothes, see Keane 2005; Küchler 2005; Miller 2005a). And when I saw the Emberá wearing once more fewer clothes than before, as their ancestors did, I was tempted to celebrate the recapitulation of the old ways, as if I could separate what I saw from its current context and meaning.

But, I should also acknowledge, without expecting to redeem myself, the contribution of the ethnographic project both in perpetuating and potentially demystifying such nostalgic temptations. I never would have been able to trace the details of past Emberá patterns, processes, and ideal forms without a committed engagement to the existing ethnographic record and/or a serious investment in keeping notes and comparing practices over the years. In this respect, my ethnographic nostalgia made me realize what I would have otherwise failed to notice: a complexity identified, and simultaneously obscured, by my own expertise—an imagined Emberá past reconstructed in terms of what had previously been recorded, little bricks of interesting information held together by a certain amount of nostalgia.

Beyond the attractive synergies of the ethnographic detail—enacted and reenacted in harmony or contradistinction with a vanishing past—I had some reason to rejoice, however unforgivably nostalgic the cause. Until recently, almost all Emberá men avoided wearing a loincloth in everyday life to escape the mockery of nonindigenous neighbors. The loincloth was caricatured as the dress of 'uncivilized' men who live in the jungle, uneducated, unaware of polite manners and the wider world. Yet nowadays, the Emberá of Parara Puru dare to wear the loincloth, aware that nonindigenous neighbors know that wealthy tourists from economically powerful nations admire Emberá culture. In this respect, wearing a loincloth may nowadays paradoxically signify a certain connection with the wider world that brings rewards nonindigenous neighbors cannot attain.

More broadly, participation in tourist presentations and the frequent practice of dressing according to the normative 'traditional' dress code has equipped the Emberá of Parara Puru with a certain degree of representational confidence (cf. Theodossopoulos 2011, 2014, 2016). It is this representational confidence—reinforced by the admiration of tourist audiences and the authenticating legitimacy of emerging narratives about the value of tradition (mostly delivered by Emberá leaders)—that has empowered the men of Parara Puru to wear a loincloth again, and the women to take off their T-shirts and appear in public with their chests uncovered, at least for the duration of the tourist presentations, sometimes a bit longer. So men and women in Parara Puru nowadays may choose to complete some of their daily chores wearing fewer clothes than before, resurrecting dress codes that were employed by their grandparents.

As we have seen so far, more than one process and set of coincidences have conspired to encourage this particular reemerging dress combination. One is the overarching context of an emerging representational self-confidence, that—as with another Panamanian group, the Kuna (Howe 2009)—has stimulated the circulation of new narratives and an emerging sense of pride in upholding indigenous identity. Another is the confidence that emerges from the reenactment of the past in cultural presentations, which has made the Emberá of Parara Puru more accustomed to the relative freedom of keeping their upper bodies uncovered, as their grandparents once did. Within their ethnically homogenous community—which has followed a pattern that emerged from a long-term struggle to enhance political representation in Eastern Panama (Herlihy 1986; Kane 1994; Velásquez Runk 2012)—they now feel comfortable enough to get dressed as they please, in modern and traditional clothes.

To the interpretative complexity that has emerged so far, we may add a couple of considerations that emerge from the material used for certain types of clothes, such as the loincloth and the *paruma*. These two items of clothing are comfortable, water resilient, easy to clean and dry, and versatile enough to accommodate a wide range of jobs and practical requirements. Considering the residents of Parara own a good number of these 'indigenous' clothes and already use them for tourist presentations, it is easy to understand why they sometimes prefer to wear them a bit longer to finish the odd job. It was this that deceived me into nostalgically seeing the past reenacted in the present. But sometimes I wonder: would I ever have problematized the complex considerations that inform these clothing practices without my ethnographic nostalgia leading the way? I will offer further examples in the following section.

As If Social Life Reemerges from the Pages of a Book

The more we read about a people's social life, the more narratives we collect about how things used to be, and the more likely we are to notice and appreciate—often with some degree of idealization—an old cultural pattern when it reappears in the present. In this respect, our awareness of the previous ethnographic record may lead to the nostalgic deception that social life reemerges from within the pages of a book. To elucidate how such a nostalgic mood can be generated, I will refer to a particular nostalgic image in my mind—that of an axe-wielding Emberá man making a canoe. Let me first contextualize my example further.

The Emberá dugout canoe represents important qualities of what it means be an Emberá man. According to the old tradition, making and owning a canoe qualifies a man to live with a woman and start a family (Kane 1994: 69). Canoes provide good topics of conversation—usually but not exclusively among men—that elicit memories of the past, organize time, or excite narratives that unravel personal histories. For example, an elderly Emberá man can lay eyes on a canoe and nostalgically contemplate the past: the canoes that he has made, in different periods of his life, the canoes of other important Emberá men, created in certain locations, at certain times, after cutting certain trees, which provided wood that lasted for a certain number of years. Unsurprisingly, several ethnographers have noted the central role of the canoe in Emberá life (Isacsson 1993, Kane 1994, Pineda and Gutiérrez 1999, Reverte Coma 2002; Torres de Araúz 1966,). Sven-Erik Isacsson discusses their symbolic associations in spiritual and family life (cf. Isacsson 1993: 92), while Stephanie Kane (1994: 66–82) has used the stages of the construction of a particular canoe to structure one of her chapters, using it as a story that allows her to tell more stories. In her captivating ethnographic style she provides information about the gendered symbolism of the Emberá canoe and the transformations that affect its spiritual essence and its material form.

Kane's and Isacsson's accounts together shaped my nostalgic admiration for the Emberá dugout canoes. This was, in turn, strengthened by my actual experience of living with the Emberá, traveling in their canoes, observing their exceptional skill in navigating them, and relying on them as a means of transportation. With respect to canoes, their use, and their importance in Emberá life, my fieldwork experience matched quite closely the picture I had already formed in my mind while reading ethnographies of the Emberá. This initial view was enriched over time, through fieldwork, with additional information, most of which verified a certain sense of continuity with previous established 'ways of life'; proof that despite the overwhelming transformations effected by modernization, traditional Emberá culture was alive, strong, and, in some respects, just as recognizable as before. For example, "canoe construction," writes Kane, "is part of a tradition that continues in the context of changing historical conditions, persisting and transforming according to varying definitions of competence, function, and value" (1994: 82).

During my time in the field, I enjoyed the recognition of such continuities with a sense of contentment. I did try hard, I must admit, to redeem my nostalgic feelings and deconstruct my previously static or 'armchair' view of Emberá culture, so I forced myself to embrace the modernizing preferences of the Emberá and the dynamism of social transformation. This deconstructive practice inflicted wounds on my ethnographic nostalgia, wounds that a part of me desired to heal. When I was not *en garde*, my nostalgic spirit would spontaneously reemerge in instances that provided a connection with the Emberá past. Sometimes I placed myself in such instances, for example, when I entered a canoe without a motor, navigated only by poles and paddles, listening to the sounds of water, sensing the rainforest, the rhythm of rowing. In an ethnographic passage drawn from my field notes, I wrote the following description:

> Three days later I joined … the family of [my neighbors] for a pre-Easter vigil at the neighboring settlement. We boarded the family's canoe at dusk, but we did not use a motor engine. Claudio steered a course with his traditional Emberá oar, while his two sons took turns punting at the bow. In full idealizing mood, I felt as if that particular moment was cut and pasted from the Emberá past, before the Emberá started to rely extensively on outboard motors. As I enjoyed nightfall on the tropical river and the rhythmic splash of the oar, I kept thinking about what Kane (1994) would have called an authentic discontinuity: an Emberá family going down the river—in the ancient Emberá way—this time not to join a shaman's ceremony, but to attend the vigil of an evangelical Church.

In the course of the incident described above, my nostalgic predilections were interrupted by a sudden splash of water, as Claudio's old canoe was particularly narrow and unstable. It was in fact very representative of a canoe of the old times, as they were made before the Emberá started transferring large quantities of plantains to sell at market in wider, longer, and more stable canoes. I would not have been in a position to notice and appreciate such fine details—including the experience of getting wet in a representatively unstable canoe—without the systematic structuring of knowledge I had gained by reading previous ethnographies. So, as I mentioned above, my ethnographic nostalgia was predicated on the pursuit of continuities with what I had read in the previous ethnographic literature or with the local narratives I had recorded about the Emberá past.

This leads me back to the image of the axe-wielding Emberá man making a canoe, on which I would like to focus more closely. One afternoon while walking along the riverbank, like many other afternoons that particular month, I came across Francisco, an Emberá friend working on his new canoe. He had been sculpting the trunk of a large tree washed by the river in a recent flood, and he had by that time already transformed its wooden bulk into the

FIGURE 1.2 Francisco working on his new canoe, dressed like the grandparents

Sketch © Dimitrios Theodossopoulos

recognizable shape of an Emberá canoe. He had been using, at least for the rough cuts, a chainsaw as most Emberá do nowadays, but also an axe and a machete, as in the old days. What triggered my ethnographic nostalgia that day was an additional detail—or rather, a coincidence: Francisco was dressed in a loincloth, wielding his axe very much like a sketch in Kane's book that portrays her key informant with the caption "Dzoshua wielding an axe" (1994: 68).

In the 1980s—when Kane conducted her fieldwork, in the most inaccessible communities of eastern Panama—it was still common to see an older man working in a loincloth. By 2010 and in the fringes of the Emberá society, where I worked, it was only imaginable. So, since what I saw was too close to how I had indeed imagined the Emberá past, I briefly wondered: was I presented with a figment of my imagination? This was, of course, one of many similar instances in the everyday life of the community that challenged my ethnographic nostalgia but also encouraged me to pay further attention to detail and process. The combination of all constituent elements that presented me with a sense of continuity with the past—the axe, the loincloth, the canoe constructed from a fallen tree—had occurred spontaneously, rather than in the context of a tourist performance. In fact, Francisco had put on his loincloth earlier that morning to prepare for the daily tourist presentations, but when the tourists had departed he had decided to finish some chores, while still wearing his loincloth, which saved him from sweating in and dirtying a clean set of clothes. Only after he finished his work and washed did he dress in a smart T-shirt and a pair of shorts, as most Emberá men do nowadays.

That I was filled with optimism to see Francisco wielding an axe dressed in a loincloth—"Ha! Just like the grandparents," he reflected while catching his breath—represented for me a revelatory moment. This enabled me to confront the nostalgic feeling upon which my optimism was founded: my yearning for the return of what was gone, lying hidden and silent behind my deconstructed awareness of social change and my desire to see Emberá culture subverting the homogenizing tendencies of modernity, resisting alterity, reemerging as a rec-ognizable continuation of a past I imagined as recorded before me or narrated to me—a vision of vanishing Emberá culture. Or had it not all disappeared forever? It was in terms of an engagement with such predilections—and pages of self-critical caricaturing in my field notes—that the particular revelatory moment framed my view of the contradictions that engender Emberá social life—"in the light of which life is lived" (Fernandez 1986: 62).

Conclusion

How deeply can our scholarly engagement with a people's culture and history instill a nostalgic connection with this people's past? To what degree does our systematic ethnographic engagement generate nostalgia? And to what degree is our nostalgia an obstacle that impairs our judgment? Undeniably, the collec-tion and organization of knowledge, as this is structured by the ethnographic endeavor, enables one to recognize certain details of social life that bear a resemblance with previous eras: an identification of a recorded past in the present that stimulates nostalgia. In this respect, the accumulation of ethnographic information invites a nostalgic pursuit of continuities that only experts can fully recognize—shamans, indigenous leaders, anthropologists and historians, among others. Such a nostalgic predisposition emerges from the comparison of current cultural practices with an idealized, already articulated view of cultural identity—for example, indigeneity conceived in allochronic terms (Fabian 1983), frozen in an ever-present static universe. Western historicism accentuates the contours of this comparison by perpetuating "the assumption that the past is disconnected from the present" (Hirsch and Stewart 2005: 265; Hodges 2013: 491–497).

So we keep on collecting information about particular cultural practices, what was previously said or recorded about them. In fact, the more expertise we build about such practices, the more likely we are to recognize their repetition in the rhythm of contemporary social life. This may lead to the impression that the past is repeated in the present, as if it has emerged from the pages of a book. The sight of an Emberá man making a canoe and dressed in a loincloth—to use my previous example—may signify a deeply embedded Emberá pattern, one that can be corroborated through scholarly study and comparison. But what can this tell us about the pattern in the present? On its own, very little, as the identified pattern may merely highlight some continuity in process but not necessarily a continuity of intentions. The Emberá canoe builder may use an axe or a chainsaw to transform a canoe from a tree trunk following an 'ancient' process, technique, or ideal form, but the canoe and its construction may not necessarily subscribe to the same 'ancient' meaning. It is the broader overarching context that sets the parameters of meaningfulness.

So ethnographic nostalgia may lead us to read the repetition of certain processes as evidence of a deeper culturally embedded meaning, which may not in fact exist. To the degree that we rush into theorizing about such meaning—as this emerges from the repetition of previous pattern and form—we risk separating action from its intentionality, thus exoticizing our ethnographic object. The anthropology of the early and middle twentieth century has been criticized for its predisposition to distance the ethnographic present from the ethnographer's reality (Fabian 1983), a deeply entrenched tendency that has survived the deconstructive wave of the 1980s. For example, recent variations of structuralism reproduce comparable allochronic slipups, which generate the nostalgic impression that anthropology's past is repeated in the present (cf. Fisher 2014; Nugent, chapter 3; Ramos 2012).

In this respect it is as if anthropology has not learned enough from previous critiques, such as James Clifford's (1986) attempt to expose the anthropological proclivity to idealize a vanishing social world. The redemptive dimension of such an idealization is further encapsulated by Rosaldo's (1989) 'imperialist nostalgia': Westerners exoticizing what Western domination has already transformed. No amount of nostalgic idealizing can redeem the violence of domination and colonialism, and this point must be foregrounded. But there is another dimension to nostalgia, which, I believe, deserves some attention.

It connects the reminiscence of the past with present action and intentionality, and is very well captured by Herzfeld's (2005) notion of 'structural nostalgia'. It emerges in official but also vernacular narratives that attempt to legitimize "deeds of the moment by investing them with the moral authority of eternal truth," the "collective representation of an edenic order—a time before time" (Herzfeld 2005: 147). The articulated perfection of such an ideal time is often set as the standard for shaping a less perfect present.

As I explained earlier, ethnographic nostalgia is constituted by elements of both 'imperialist' and 'structural' nostalgia. It legitimizes an imperfect ethnographic reality by juxtaposing it with a previous record of well-articulated depictions, sanitized of undesirable themes, and postcolonial inequalities. It is this exoticizing predisposition that makes ethnographic nostalgia a burden but also an opportunity for the ethnographic project. Like ethnocentrism, ethnographic nostalgia keeps on reappearing in concentric layers that distort social representation. Yet, as with ethnocentrism, ethnographic nostalgia presents an opportunity for deconstruction, which may potentially lead to the recognition of complexity—the ultimate de-exoticizing trajectory. It is important to note that ethnographic nostalgia itself cannot be fully redeemed, as it is predicated on the interplay of biases and distortions that spontaneously regenerate themselves. Yet, it is the very recognition of such biases and distortions that can make the notion of ethnographic nostalgia a useful analytical tool.

Our confrontation with the exotic, argues Kapferer (2013), may trigger a spark of recognition that challenges our previous understandings and provide a new perspective. In this regard, a self-critical engagement with the exoticizing misrepresentations of ethnographic nostalgia can encourage an appreciation of the entanglement of the past with the present. And more precisely, it may also make visible the contribution of what has already been articulated in shaping what has not yet been represented. In this manner, an experience of the past that is merely imagined—structured as it has been written or told, recorded ethnographically—can be construed as an experience of loss (Berliner 2015): a nostalgia for what, to paraphrase what Arjun Appadurai (1996: 77) said about advertising, has not yet been experienced or lost.

And finally, from the point of view of local actors, an angle that I did not closely pursue in this chapter, the nostalgic approach may after all have something interesting to contribute. For example, it may inspire a desire to accumulate knowledge (Battaglia 1995) or redirect attention to the destructive effects of various Westernizing forces on vulnerable peripheral communities (Werbner, chapter 2). This may encourage a refocusing onto wider processes, or a move in the opposite direction: to pay greater attention to the local nuances of the politics of memory. For example, apart from establishing continuities, nostalgia may also emphasize "distance and disjuncture, utilizing these diacritics of modernity as a means of critically framing the present" (Bissell 2005: 216). For all these reasons, it would be wise not to blind ourselves to nostalgia's "plasticity and mutability" (Howe 2009: 250).

A concern about the point of view of local actors may also lead us to ask the following question: what have we learned about the people in question—in my case, the Emberá—through deconstructing the nostalgia of the anthropological author? What is there that we wouldn't otherwise have learned? To the degree that problematizing ethnographic nostalgia confronts the allochronic tendencies inherent in the anthropological endeavor, a reflexive battle with nostalgia is likely to produce a slightly less exoticized account. In my ethnographic investigation of the Emberá clothes, for example, my identification of older dress codes in the present entailed their misrecognition as mechanical reproductions of the past. Here, my scholarly knowledge of detail and pattern obscured the complexity and dynamism of the indigenous relationship with the global audience (and the re-signification of Emberá attire through this relationship). As I explained in the previous sections, the contemporary use of the Emberá traditional attire is not simply the mechanic evocation of a lost cultural pattern, but a new representational strategy: an expression of an emerging Emberá modernity, an authentic tourist production (Bruner 2005: 5).

Let me conclude by returning to the image of the Emberá canoe maker wielding an axe dressed in a loincloth; nostalgia is, after all, predicated on the idea of returning. And the particular image as captured by ethnographers before me (e.g., Kane 1994) and as depicted in my own writing is likely to generate further waves of nostalgic engagement: among the Emberá who are becoming increasingly interested in their past (Theodossopoulos 2011, 2013a, 2014, 2016), or in my future fieldwork encounters and those of other ethnographers. It can be compared with the image of the Emberá canoe maker holding a chainsaw dressed in a T-shirt and shorts, and many other similar variations on the same theme—transformations of previous transformations (Gow 2001: 17) and 'authentic discontinuities' (Kane 1994: 41) that constitute Emberá social life. These became somewhat more visible to me through the embarrassment caused by my ethnographic nostalgia: how can one rescue a vanishing past that has never been lost? How can one return to where one has never before visited? Ethnographic nostalgia teaches through contradiction.

Acknowledgments

I would like to thank the ESRC (research grant RES-000-22-3733) for supporting my fieldwork among the Emberá.

Dimitrios Theodossopoulos is Professor of Social Anthropology at the University of Kent. He has conducted research in Panama and Greece, focusing on processes of resistance, exoticization, authenticity, tourism, and environmentalism and on the politics of cultural representation and protest. He is the author of *Exoticisation Undressed* (2016) and *Troubles with Turtles* (2003), and editor of *De-Pathologising Resistance* (2015), *Great Expectations* (2011), *United in Discontent* (2010), and *When Greeks Think about Turks* (2007).

Notes

1. The Emberá lived in dispersed settlements until the middle of the twentieth century. They started to form concentrated communities in the 1950s and 1960s, and by the 1980s the majority lived in villages with primary schools and elected representatives (see Herlihy 1986; Kane 1994). These transformations were followed by the foundation of a semiautonomous reservation, the Comarca Emberá-Wounaan, in 1983. There are almost as many Emberá in Eastern Panama who live in communities outside the Comarca as those living inside (see Colin 2010: 106). Communities without recognized land titles, such as Parara Puru, participate in the wider political initiative of *Tierras Colectivas* (see Velásquez Runk 2012).

2. The Wounaan are a separate ethnic group with a related but distinct language (see Velásquez Runk 2001, 2009). The Emberá and the Wounaan have been referred to collectively as "the Chocó" (or Chocoes, in plural), a generic term used extensively in Panama as a negative ethnic stereotype to accentuate the Colombian origins of the Emberá and Wounaan. Until the 1960s, ethnographers used Chocó extensively as a more inclusive category for analysis and comparison, but this use has now been abandoned in favor of the more politically correct alternatives, Emberá and Wounaan.

3. For a detailed description of these clothing items, see Theodossopoulos (2012).

References

Angé, Olivia, and David Berliner, eds. 2015a. *Anthropology and Nostalgia*. New York: Berghahn Books.

Angé, Olivia, and David Berliner. 2015b. "Introduction: Anthropology of Nostalgia—Anthropology as Nostalgia." Pp. 1–15 in Angé and Berliner 2015a.

Appadurai, Arjun. 1996. *Modernity at Large: Cultural Dimensions of Globalization.* Minneapolis: University of Minnesota Press.

Banerjee, Mukulika, and Daniel Miller. 2003. *The Sari*. Oxford: Berg.

Battaglia, Debbora. 1995. "On Practical Nostalgia: Self-Prospecting among Urban Trobrianders." Pp. 77–96 in *Rhetorics of Self-Making*, ed. Debbora Battaglia. Berkeley: University of California Press.

Bendix, Regina. 1997. *In Search of Authenticity: The Formation of Folklore Studies.* Madison: University of Wisconsin Press.

Berliner, David. 2015. "Are Anthropologists Nostalgists?" Pp. 17–34 in Angé and Berliner 2015a.

Bruner, Edward M. 1993. "Epilogue: Creativity Persona and the Problem of Authenticity." Pp. 321–334 in *Creativity/Anthropology*, ed. Smadar Lavie, Kirin Narayan, and Renato Rosaldo. Ithaca, NY: Cornell University Press.

Bruner, Edward M. 2005. *Culture on Tour: Ethnographies of Travel*. Chicago: University of Chicago Press.

Clifford, James. 1986. "On Ethnographic Allegory." Pp. 98–121 in *Writing Culture: The Poetics and Politics of Ethnography*, ed. James Clifford and George E. Marcus. Berkeley: University of California Press.

Colin, France-Lise. 2010. "'*Nosotros no solamente podemos vivir de cultura*': Identity, Nature, and Power in the Comarca Emberá of Eastern Panama." PhD diss., Carleton University.

Conklin, Beth A. 1997. "Body Paint, Feathers, and VCRs: Aesthetics and Authenticity in Amazonian Activism." *American Ethnologist* 24, no. 4: 711–737.

Conklin, Beth A. 2007. "Ski Masks, Veils, Nose-Rings and Feathers: Identity on the Frontlines of Modernity." Pp. 18–35 in Ewart and O'Hanlon 2007.

Edensor, Tim. 1998. *Tourists at the Taj: Performance and Meaning at a Symbolic Site.* London: Routledge.

Ewart, Elizabeth. 2007. "Black Paint, Red Paint and a Wristwatch: The Aesthetics of Modernity among the Panará in Central Brazil." Pp. 36–52 in Ewart and O'Hanlon 2007.

Ewart, Elizabeth, and Michael O'Hanlon, eds. 2007. *Body Arts and Modernity.* Wantage: Sean Kingston Publishing.

Fabian, Johannes. 1983. *Time and the Other: How Anthropology Makes Its Object.* New York: Columbia University Press.

Faris, James C. 2007. "Body Art and Modernity: South-east Nuba." Pp. 72–87 in Ewart and O'Hanlon 2007.

Fernandez, James W. 1986. *Persuasions and Performances: The Play of Tropes in Culture.* Bloomington: Indiana University Press.

Fillitz, Thomas, and A. Jamie Saris. 2013. "Introduction." Pp. 1–24 in *Debating Authenticity: Concepts of Modernity in Anthropological Perspective*, ed. Thomas Fillitz and A. Jamie Saris. New York: Berghahn Books.

Goddard, Victoria A., Josep R. Llobera, and Cris Shore, eds. 1994. *Anthropology of Europe: Identities and Boundaries in Conflict.* Oxford: Berg

Gow, Peter. 2001. *An Amazonian Myth and Its History.* Oxford: Oxford University Press.

Gow, Peter. 2007. "Clothing as Acculturation in Peruvian Amazonia." Pp. 53–71 in Ewart and O'Hanlon 2007.

Hallam, Elizabeth, and Tim Ingold. 2007. "Creativity and Cultural Improvisation: An Introduction." Pp. 1–24 in *Creativity and Cultural Improvisation*, ed. Elizabeth Hallam and Tim Ingold. Oxford: Berg.

Herlihy, Peter H. 1986. "A Cultural Geography of the Emberá and Wounaan (Choco) Indians of Darien, Panama, with Emphasis on Recent Village Formation and Economic Diversification." PhD diss., Louisiana State University.

Herzfeld, Michael. 1987. *Anthropology through the Looking-Glass: Critical Ethnography in the Margins of Europe.* Cambridge: Cambridge University Press.

Herzfeld, Michael. [1997] 2005. *Cultural Intimacy: Social Poetics in the Nation-State.* New York: Routledge.

Hodges, Matthew. 2013. "Illuminating Vestige: Amateur Archaeology and the Emergence of Historical Consciousness in Rural France." *Comparative Studies in Society and History* 55, no. 2: 474–504.

Howe, James. 1998. *A People Who Would Not Kneel: Panama, the United States, and the San Blas Kuna.* Washington, DC: Smithsonian Institution Press.

Howe, James. 2009. *Chiefs, Scribes, and Ethnographers: Kuna Culture from Inside and Out.* Austin: University of Texas Press.

Isacsson, Sven-Erik. 1993. *Transformations of Eternity: On Man and Cosmos in Emberá Thought.* Göteborg: University of Göteborg.

Just, Roger. 2000. *A Greek Island Cosmos: Kinship and Community on Meganisi.* Oxford: James Currey.

Kane, Stephanie C. 1994. *The Phantom Gringo Boat: Shamanic Discourse and Development in Panama.* Washington, DC: Smithsonian Institution Press.

Kapferer, Bruce. 2013. "How Anthropologists Think: Configurations of the Exotic." *Journal of the Royal Anthropological Institute* 19, no. 4: 813–836.

Knauft, Bruce M. 2002. *Exchanging the Past: A Rainforest World of Before and After.* Chicago: University of Chicago Press.

Knauft, Bruce M. 2007. "From Self-Decoration to Self-Fashioning: Orientalism as Backward Progress among the Gebusi of Papua New Guinea." Pp. 88–107 in Ewart and O'Hanlon 2007.

Küchler, Susanne. 2005. "Materiality and Cognition: The Changing Face of Things." Pp. 206–230 in Miller 2005b.

Lindholm, Charles. 2008. *Culture and Authenticity.* Oxford: Blackwell.

Marsh, Richard Oglesby. 1934. *White Indians of Darien.* New York: Putnam.

Miller, Daniel. 2005a. "Introduction." Pp. 1–19 in *Clothing as Material Culture,* ed. Susanne Küchler and Daniel Miller. Oxford: Berg.

Miller, Daniel, ed. 2005b. *Materiality.* Durham, NC: Duke University Press.

Miller, Daniel. 2005c. "Materiality: An Introduction." Pp. 1–50 in Miller 2005b.

O'Hanlon, Michael. 2007. "Body Arts and Modernity: An Introduction." Pp. 1–17 in Ewart and O'Hanlon 2007.

Pineda, Roberto, and Virginia Gutiérrez de Pineda. 1999. *Criaturas de Caragabí: Indios Chocoes, Emberáes, Catíos, Chamíes y Noanamaes.* Medellín: Editorial Universidad de Antioquia.

Ramos, Alcida R. 2012. "The Politics of Perspectivism." *Annual Review of Anthropology* 41: 481–494.

Reverte Coma, José Manuel. 2002. *Tormenta en el Darien: Vida de los Indios Chocoes en Panama.* Madrid: Museo Profesor Reverte Coma.

Rosaldo, Renato. 1989. "Imperialist Nostalgia." *Representations* 26: 107–122.

Rosaldo, Renato. 1993. *Culture and Truth: The Remaking of Social Analysis.* London: Routledge.

Sahlins, Marshall. 1999. "Two or Three Things That I Know about Culture." *Journal of the Royal Anthropological Institute* 59, no. 3: 399–421.

Salazar, Noel. 2010. *Envisioning Eden: Mobilizing Imaginaries in Tourism and Beyond.* New York: Berghahn Books.

Santos-Granero, Fernando. 2009. "Hybrid Bodyscapes: A Visual History of Yanesha Patterns of Cultural Change." *Current Anthropology* 50, no. 4: 477–512.

Taussig, Michael T. 1993. *Mimesis and Alterity: A Particular History of the Senses.* London: Routledge.

Theodossopoulos, Dimitrios. 2010. "Tourism and Indigenous Culture as Resources: Lessons from Emberá Cultural Tourism in Panama." Pp. 115–133 in *Tourism, Power and Culture: Anthropological Insights,* ed. Donald V. L. Macleod and James G. Carrier. Bristol: Channel View.

Theodossopoulos, Dimitrios. 2011. "Emberá Indigenous Tourism and the World of Expectations." Pp. 40–60 in *Great Expectations: Imagination and Anticipation in Tourism,* ed. Jonathan Skinner and Dimitrios Theodossopoulos. New York: Berghahn Books.

Theodossopoulos, Dimitrios. 2012. "Indigenous Attire, Exoticization, and Social Change: Dressing and Undressing among the Emberá of Panama." *Journal of the Royal Anthropological Institute* 18, no. 3: 591–612.

Theodossopoulos, Dimitrios. 2013a. "Emberá Indigenous Tourism and the Trap of Authenticity: Beyond In-authenticity and Invention." *Anthropological Quarterly* 86, no. 2: 397–426.

Theodossopoulos, Dimitrios. 2013b. "Laying Claim to Authenticity: Five Anthropological Dilemmas." *Anthropological Quarterly* 86, no. 2: 337–360.

Theodossopoulos, Dimitrios. 2014. "Scorn or Idealization? Tourism Imaginaries, Exoticization and Ambivalence in Emberá Indigenous Tourism." Pp. 57–79 in *Tourism*

Imaginaries: Anthropological Approaches, ed. Noel B. Salazar and Nelson H. H. Graburn. New York: Berghahn Books.

Theodossopoulos, Dimitrios. 2015. "Sharing Anthropological Knowledge, Decolonizing Anthropology: Emberá Indigeneity and Engaged Anthropology." Pp. 33–54 in *Indigenous Studies and Engaged Anthropology: The Collaborative Moment*, ed. Paul Sillitoe. Surrey: Ashgate.

Theodossopoulos, Dimitrios. 2016. *Exoticisation Undressed: Ethnographic Nostalgia and Authenticity in Emberá Clothes*. Manchester: Manchester University Press.

Torres de Araúz, Reina. 1966. *La Cultura Chocó: Estudio Ethnológico e Historico*. Panama: Centro de Investigaciones Antropológicas, University of Panama.

Turner, Terence, and Vanessa Fajans-Turner. 2006. "Political Innovation and Inter-ethnic Alliance." *Anthropology Today* 22, no. 5: 3–10.

Ulloa, Astrid. 1992. *Kipará: Dibujo y pintura: Dos formas embera de representar el mundo*. Bogotá: National University of Colombia.

Veber, Hanne. 1992. "Why Indians Wear Clothes: Managing Identity across an Ethnic Boundary." *Ethnos* 57, no. 1–2: 51–60.

Veber, Hanne. 1996. "External Inducement and Non-Westernization in the Uses of the Ashéninka Cushma." *Journal of Material Culture* 1, no. 2: 155–182.

Velásquez Runk, Julie. 2001. "Wounaan and Emberá Use and Management of the Fiber Palm *Astrocaryum standleyanum* (Arecaceae) for Basketry in Eastern Panama." *Economic Botany* 55, no. 1: 72–82.

Velásquez Runk, Julie. 2009. "Social and River Networks for the Trees: Wounaan's Riverine Rhizomic Cosmos and Arboreal Conservation." *American Anthropologist* 111, no. 4: 456–467.

Velásquez Runk, Julie. 2012. "Indigenous Land and Environmental Conflicts in Panama: Neoliberal Multiculturalism, Changing Legislation, and Human Rights." *Journal of Latin American Geography* 11, no. 2: 21–47.

Verrill, A. Hyatt. 1921. *Panama Past and Present*. New York: Dodd, Mead & Co.

Chapter 2

BETWEEN *TRISTES TROPIQUES* AND CULTURAL CREATIVITY
Modern Times and the Vanishing Primitive

Pnina Werbner

Against Critical Nostalgia

When and why do people abandon or revive valued rituals or customs? And how does anthropology's valorization of diversity and local knowledge mesh with its commitment to study contemporary societies in their encounter with the state, globalization, Western consumerism, or the media and entertainment industry? What ethical issues are at stake in our anthropological endeavor to record this encounter? In this chapter I consider the exotic not only from the modernist anthropologist point of view but also from the point of view of the actors themselves. What value does the exotic have for them? And is it merely a project of nostalgic romanticism for anthropologists to try to record for posterity, 'salvage' as it were, the vanishing customs of the people we study?

Reviewing the history of anthropology as a discipline, George Marcus and Michael Fischer (1986: 24) tell us that beyond the sense of romance and discovery, "the main motif that ethnography as a science developed was that of salvaging cultural diversity, threatened by global Westernization, especially during the age of colonialism."[1] This salvage operation ensured that the world's

Notes for this chapter begin on page 62.

disappearing cultures could be entered into the "great comparative project of anthropology," to support the Western goal of "social and economic progress." Why salvaging a lost cultural diversity would enable social and economic progress is not spelled out by the authors, but in any case, as they go on to point out, that project of cultural salvage is no longer viable since, as they suggest optimistically, "the cultures of world peoples need to be constantly *rediscovered* as these people reinvent themselves in changing historical circumstances" (24). Therefore, a (new) ethics of critical ethnography, it would seem, must respond to the fact that "[d]ifference in the world is no longer discovered, as in the age of exploration, or salvaged, as in the age of colonialism or high capitalism, but rather must be redeemed, or recovered as valid and significant, in an age of apparent homogenisation and suspicion of authenticity, which, while recognizing cultural diversity, ignores its practical implications" (167).

Citing Bronislaw Malinowski's ironic comment about modern anthropology, that "at the very moment when it begins to put its workshop in order, to forge its proper tools ... the material of its study melts away with hopeless rapidity," James Clifford critiques the image of the doomed, disappearing primitive (Malinowski 1922: xv; cited in Clifford 1986: 112). Once again, the counter to this narrative of cultural entropy and, indeed, as Clifford admits, of violent rupture and even 'elimination', is the hopeful invocation of people 'reinventing' themselves. According to Clifford, this proves that ethnography's 'disappearing object' is a 'rhetorical construct', invented to legitimate 'salvage' ethnography, an 'ethnographic pastoral'. It assumes an essentialized notion of culture and, moreover, that non-Western societies are so weak that they can only be represented by an outsider. Hence, as Clifford puts it so elegantly, the implicit presumption is that "[t]he recorder and interpreter of fragile customs is custodian of an essence, unimpeachable witness to an authenticity" (1986: 113). Indeed, he adds, even today the allegory of salvage or critical nostalgia is inescapable in the very process of anthropological textualization or inscription. It places the people anthropologists study in a set-apart, non-Western past rather than recognizing them, in his words, as "resilient, enormously varied" societies of the *future* (113). Similarly, Marcus distinguishes between two modes of 'fixing' ethnographies historically: salvage and redemptive—the former referring to the salvaging of a cultural state on the verge of transformation, the latter celebrating the survival of cultural authenticity in out-of-the way places (Marcus 1986: 165n).

Elsewhere, writing about New York City, museums, and ethnographic collections, Clifford sees in the juxtaposing of different cultural shreds and fragments "humanity's entropic future" so that the "jumble of humanity" can "be grasped simultaneously in all its precious diversity and emerging uniformity" through a chronotope that sees modern anthropology salvaging "consultable archives for thinking about the range of human invention." Hence, the jumble of New York's collectable ethnographic artifacts becomes "a global allegory of fragmentation and ruin" (Clifford 1988: 244). Such a chronotope is necessarily 'blind' to the 'inventive present', the 'present-becoming-future' (248), caught as it is in a narrative of 'critical nostalgia'.[2]

Such critiques of ethnographic writing and practice clearly rest on an optimistic belief in the inventiveness and creativity of indigenous cultures in the face of global homogenization, on the one hand, and on a reading of culture as a kind of symbolic gloss on social life akin to fashion or lifestyle, to be discarded and replaced with new, culturally hybrid, delightfully inventive alternatives, without radical rupture, on the other hand. While critiquing the tendency to see 'culture' as a kind of gloss, Marshall Sahlins (1998) too supports the optimistic narrative of 'indigenous modernity' according to which native cultures adapt and evolve inventively without losing their cultural distinctiveness.

Such conceptualizations, however, risk deflecting criticism away from the very real destruction that capitalism, religious proselytizing, and modern education may inflict on small, vulnerable communities and on their capacity to achieve autonomous self-dignity. Equally saliently, the culture-as-lifestyle approach underestimates the embeddedness of cultural practices in significant social relations. These configure gendered and generational relations in unique, embodied ways. Their displacement is thus socially destructive as well. Third, through an imperceptible sleight of hand, a single customary practice, a ritual, or a symbolic complex, is equated with the whole 'culture' of a 'society' so that anthropological analyses of ritual or symbolic complexes on the edge of extinction are read as tantamount to arguing for the disappearance of a whole people, tribe, nation, or culture, which in turn provokes accusations of cultural essentialism and nostalgia for the vanishing primitive. Indeed, any attempt to analyze a present-day ritual performance in its full symbolic complexity—given the modernizing forces affecting the far corners of most contemporary societies—may be read as capitulation to such essentialist or nostalgic tendencies. This induces anthropological guilt at the intellectual curiosity and excitement inspired by signs of a lost cultural past (see, e.g., chap. 1).

These reflections arise out of my own dilemmas in representing and analyzing the Tswapong female puberty ritual, the *mothei*, in its full symbolic, figurative, and social elaboration at a time when the ritual appears to be in rapid decline. Until recently, girls' puberty rites in Moremi, a small village in the foothills of the Tswapong hills in Eastern Botswana, have been practiced in their full symbolic elaboration despite villagers embracing Western education and Christianity. As a cultural form, the *mothei* ritual, I have argued (Werbner 2009, 2014a), empowers women and girls, the social group most vulnerable to sexual exploitation and harm, particularly in the face of the HIV/AIDS pandemic in Botswana. Hence, the abandonment of the ritual may arguably have very real negative social implications. But beyond such contestable practical considerations, the dilemma is more serious. Genuine (dare one say, authentic?) inventiveness as a valued feature of culture is far more likely to occur, I propose, *within* such indigenous rituals than it is through assimilation into a semi-Westernized, anglicized, and Christianized mass underclass, a point I return to below.[3]

Indigenous sources of wealth and voluntary labor are mobilized in the Tswapong puberty ritual to create a viable 'society of women', beyond the reach of the state, and to constitute a women's counter-public within the village arena.

The playfulness in the ritual—its sheer fun and enjoyment and the rich variety of interpretations given by actors to its symbolic actions and paraphernalia—attest to this inventiveness. Until recently, puberty rites among Tswapong continued to be practiced in their full symbolic elaboration alongside two other modes of knowledge practices—Christianity and Western education—and yet the ritual is being gradually abandoned under pressure from a modernizing state and, increasingly, young girls' understanding of themselves as modern subjects.[4]

To the extent, however, that recognizing one's worth means recognizing one's distinctiveness, uniqueness, self-mastery, ethical subjectivity, and autonomy, rituals such as the *mothei* may be said to dignify women as individuals, despite their poverty and marginality, and to establish their place in a society of women. Among Tswapong, the *mothei* ritual signifies the achievement of *seriti* (dignity) and is characterized by mutual help and sociability. It is a ritual that deploys nonviolent physical ordeals and dramatizes respect through humor, fun, and transgressive enactments of sexuality, drawing on a local lore of songs, dances, stylized burlesque, and parody, as well as on substantive cosmetic bodily treatment, in order to fashion a woman and endow her with fertility, strength, and moral authority.

Nevertheless, young teenage girls attending local high schools who aspire to be 'modern' are quickly discarding the *mothei* in favor of *sesha* (modern times). In the past, a family's status in the village was enhanced by the size of its *mothei* feast, but now the celebration is an expense few can easily afford. For older women, for whom the ritual encapsulated a world of knowledge and experience, the loss of the ritual is deeply painful, as one woman elder lamented: "In the past, we liked this culture ... we lived with it. Now when they throw it away like this ... it is not good ... The country has changed ... [people are dying] because of jumping over the culture ... We are living in modern times (*sesha*)." Women elders who feared the ritual would soon vanish, with dire consequences, allowed me, a non-initiated outsider, to 'enter' the hut and film the ritual.

Tristes Tropiques and the Quest for the Vanishing Primitive

On the surface, it seems unproblematic and self-evident that the 1980s new ethnographic criticism reflected increasing doubts—a 'crisis' of representation—about how we know, and write about, 'the Other'. Yet there is an underlying, and quite different, concern animating these texts: the impossibility of representing not simply the 'Other' but the *authentic* Other. Claude Lévi-Strauss remarks on the fact that authenticity is a felt quality when he writes, referring to the Bororo people in *Tristes Tropiques,* "there are societies so vividly alive, so faithful to their traditions, that their impact is disconcertingly strong" ([1955] 1970: 198).

Like many cultural works, *Tristes Tropiques* has a surface message and a deep structure. The author quite explicitly presents the surface message, which has also been appreciated by critics, while the more radical project remains somewhat buried in the pages of the book, perhaps not fully and self-consciously intended. In the author's own words, "true reality is never the most obvious of realities ... its nature is already apparent in the care it takes to evade our detection" ([1955] 1970: 61). The surface message is one, to use Clifford's (1986: 112; 1988: 14) phrase, of 'cultural entropy': "[A]ll that is over: humanity has taken to monoculture, once and for all, and is preparing to produce civilization in bulk, as if it were sugar-beet. The same dish to be served to us every day ... And that is how I see myself: traveller, archaeologist of space, trying in vain to repiece together the idea of the exotic with the help of a particle here and a fragment of debris there" (Lévi-Strauss [1955] 1970: 39, 44).

The paradox of anthropological inquiry is described as follows:

> The less one culture communicates with another, the less likely they are to be corrupted, one by the other, but, on the other hand, the less likely it is that the respective emissaries of these cultures will be able to seize the richness and significance of their diversity. The alternative is inescapable: either I am a traveller in ancient times, and faced with a prodigious spectacle which would be almost entirely unintelligible to me and might, indeed, provoke me to mockery or disgust; or I am a traveller in my own day, hastening in search of a vanished reality. In either case I am the loser ... for today, as I go groaning among the shadows, I miss, inevitably, the spectacle that is now taking shape. (45)

Lévi-Strauss is, of course, the master of surrealism (see Clifford 1988: 242, 244–245), juxtaposing debris, bits, and pieces from here and there. And, as Clifford Geertz (1988) perceptively reminds us, his book has a reformist message: Lévi-Strauss rejects the filth, squalor, ugliness, and degradation that civilization has brought into the new world. But is *Tristes Tropiques* (apart from being a travel book, an ethnography, and a philosophical and symbolist text) simply an expression of "aesthetic repugnance" as Geertz (1988: 40) would have it? Is it simply about cultural entropy? Is the hidden quest in the book that of Ulysses, hopelessly seeking his home among the islands, or is it not, more tragically, that of Orpheus descending to Hades, wandering hopelessly among the shadows?

The key to *Tristes Tropiques*, perhaps to the whole of Lévi-Strauss's quest, lies, I believe at the beginning and end of the book. Not in the first chapter, which aims to throw us off the scent, but in the second, third, and penultimate chapters of the book. The events described in the rest of the book happened during a four- or five-year stint in Brazil from 1935 onward. But the book really begins much later, during a different journey that is not really a journey at all but a flight: the escape of the author, together with a large number of other eminent Jewish scholars, from France to the United States in 1941 after the fall of France to the Nazis and the establishment of the Vichy government. These scholars and intellectuals, including the author himself, were fleeing certain personal extermination, in the knowledge that they were leaving behind them a Europe in which an ancient civilization—two millennia of Jewish culture, history, literature, music, whole communities—was in the process of being physically destroyed (on this in detail, see Wilcken 2010: 111–142).

Tristes Tropiques's deep structure is 'really' about destruction—wanton, senseless, evil, physical, human, and ecological destruction. Yet only once, toward the very end of the book, does Lévi-Strauss mention the Holocaust, and then he focuses on the victims: "We must set aside those cases in which people eat one another for lack of any other meat—as was the case in certain parts of Polynesia. No society is proof, morally speaking, against the demands of hunger. In times of starvation men will eat literally anything, as we lately saw in the Nazi extermination-camps" (Lévi-Strauss [1955] 1970: 385).

Instead, we are constantly reminded throughout his journey in the interior of Brazil of the devastation wrought by conquest, disease, ecological destruction, and sheer physical domination. As others have recognized: "A slow-burning pessimism, a lament at the progressive loss of our links—sensual, intellectual and cultural—to the world around us pervades the book. Its pathos caught the post-war mood perfectly, particularly in France. For Lévi-Strauss, globalization was creating a bleak world of architectural and cultural uniformity" (Wilcken 2010: 202). Lévi-Strauss's conclusion is deeply pessimistic:

> The societies which we could study today, in conditions which it would be a great illusion to compare to those four centuries ago, were *enfeebled in body and mutilated in form*. Distant as they were from the western world, and weird as had been the intermediaries between themselves and it … they had been *pulverized* by the development of western civilization. For them, as for so large and so innocent a fraction of the human race, this development has come as a *monstrous and unintelligible cataclysm*. (Lévi-Strauss [1955] 1970: 318; emphasis added)

And finally:

> To be a man means, for each of us, membership of a class, a society, a country, a continent, and a civilization. For those of us who are earth-bound Europeans, our adventurings into the New World have a lesson to teach us: *that the New World was not ours to destroy, and yet we destroyed it; and that no other will be vouchsafed to us*. (392; emphasis added)

Tristes Tropiques is, quite simply, a book about racism. In the light of this, Geertz's interpretation of the book is deeply flawed, missing as it does the heart of the matter: "As a reformist tract, *Tristes Tropiques* is an outburst, less of *moraliste* rage—which is one of the things that divides him from Sartre, who is rather more worried that people are dominated than that they are degraded—than of aesthetic repugnance. Like Swift's, Lévi-Strauss's deep social disgust seems to rise out of an even deeper disgust with the physical and the biological. *His radicalism is not political. It is sensory*" (1988: 41; emphasis added).

If there is a shred of hope in the book, a kind of question mark, it is in the undying creativity of the *bricoleur*, that tribal craftsman who "builds ideological castles out of debris" and, we are told, "builds up structured sets, not directly with other structured sets but by using the remains and debris of events: … odds and ends in English, fossilised evidence of the history of an individual or a society" (Lévi-Strauss [1955] 1970: 21–22). Here, then, is one survivor, the anthropologist, collecting bits and pieces, odds and ends, the remains and debris, from the mutilated survivors of extinct societies, in the hope, perhaps, that new ideological castles will magically reappear to reconstitute these groups.

Richard Fardon rightly criticizes the 1980s new ethnographic critics for stressing the overriding historicity and contextuality of truth and knowledge, while sometimes ignoring it in their own interpretations of anthropological texts (Fardon 1990: 20, in particular). Nowhere is this more evident than in Geertz's analysis of *Tristes Tropiques*. The 1980s new critics ignore not only the terrible pre- and postwar trauma of fascism and its wholesale destruction but also the general sense of outrage that continues to prevail among regional students of Brazilian Indians, as well as missionaries and ecologists in that country, against the total, rampant, uncontrollable, and wanton annihilation of fragile, defenseless cultural groups and their habitats (see Taussig 1984). Lévi-Strauss is really only one among the many who protest in vain. You cannot study Brazilian Indians, it seems, without wondering whether they will even exist the following year.

Which brings us to the final puzzle of *Tristes Tropiques*: why, when he finally reaches the Munde—'his' savages, the apotheoses of his quest—does Lévi-Strauss abandon them so quickly? He says, rather lamely, that he "could not put aside the time that was indispensable if I were to hope to know them properly," claiming he only had a few days and reflecting that, in any case, "no sooner are such people known, or guessed at, than their strangeness drops away and one might as well have stayed in one's own village" (Lévi-Strauss [1955] 1970: 326). Instead, he spends the next two or three weeks chasing after a group of Tupi on the very point of liquidation. Why? And what does this tell us about his 'real', not fully acknowledged quest?

One part of the answer can be found, I suggest, in the final pages of the book: "When we make an effort to understand, we destroy the object of our attachment, substituting another whose nature is quite different. The other object requires of us another effort, which in turn destroys the second object and substitutes a third—and so on until we reach the only enduring Presence, which is that all distinction between meaning and the absence of meaning disappears" (394). He does not want to be the 'advance guard' of this process of revelation and destruction meted upon those "delightful people whom no white man had seen before me, and none would ever see again" (326)—*if*, that is, he leaves them *before they* get to know *him*!

There is also, however, a far more compelling reason why he abandons the Munde so fast. His quest is a different one: repeatedly, wherever he goes, he compares what he finds with the historical records about the groups he visits written by earlier missionaries, travelers, and explorers. Abandoning the Munde, inspired by historical records of ancient travelers, he believes he is about to encounter the Tupi:

> known, at the time of their apogee, to the European travellers of the sixteenth and seventeenth centuries whose narratives laid the fuse for the anthropological studies of our own time; for it was under their unknowing influence that the

political and moral philosophy of the Renaissance set out the road which was to lead to the French Revolution. To be, as seemed very possible, the first man to penetrate a still-intact Tupi-Kawahib village was to *go back more than four hundred years and join hands with Lery, with Staden, with Soares de Souza, with Thevet, and even with Montaigne*, who ruminates in one of his essays (the one on cannibals) on a conversation with Tupi Indians whom he met in Rouen. What a temptation! (329; emphasis added)

The Tupi turn out to be a pitifully small group on the point of extinction, about to give up their central symbol, the eagle, recorded long ago by Cândido Rondon, as a safe-passage offering to 'civilization'. They are afflicted by illness:

> Was it poliomyelitis, or some other virus, which had gone on ahead of any real contact with civilization? ... it was heart-rending to think back to the page on which Thevet speaks with such admiration of the Tupi whom he visited in the sixteenth century: "A people," he says, "made of the same stuff as ourselves, who has never as yet been afflicted with leprosy, or paralysis, or lethargy, or chancres, or other bodily ailments which are apparent to the eye." He had no idea that he and his companions were the advance guard of these evils. (341)

But it is among the Tupi, the author tells us, that he is "destined to re-live the misadventures familiar four centuries earlier to Yves d'Evreux and Jean de Lery ... [to witness] a strange and exclusive association, many centuries old, between a species of insects and a group of human beings" (346–347).

This, then, is the key to *Tristes Tropiques*. It is a book about violence, racism, and destruction, but not only that—a book, also, about survival in the face of these violations, a deeply historical book seeking to answer how, and if, human cultures can survive on the point of extinction.

Culture and Violence

To a European traveler in the United States, what is most striking is not cultural *difference* but rather the amazing sameness of this vast subcontinent. From McDonald's to Pizza Hut, Holiday Inn to Hilton, Safeway to Sears; from the leafy suburbs of Washington, DC, to the leafy suburbs of Chicago, Austin, or Los Angeles; from the skyscrapers of Manhattan to the skyscrapers of Detroit or Philadelphia; from IBM and Apple to Nintendo and Microsoft, this land of many immigrants seems to be less a cultural mosaic and more a vast green desert, peopled by nomadic travelers who pitch their tents in one oasis after another, sure to find the same palm trees, dates, and delightful hospitality wherever they go as they spiral socially. Cultural difference thus becomes a very personal creation, a bit of this and a bit of that, with which to adorn the very tasteful houses of the vast middle classes—all the more so in a neoliberal age of inventive consumerism: cultural pluralism and 'culture' itself understandably have, in this context, an elusive quality, an incompleteness, a self-consciousness. There is little that is violent, destructive, or violating about 'culture'. Obsolescence is a requirement of the market, inexorably propelled forward by the products of inventive cultural originality and authenticity (Hutnyk [1997] 2014). There is, of course, urban violence and racial violence, but culture is, at most, 'hegemonic'.

Thus, it seems possible for US anthropologists to separate cultural pluralism from racism and wanton destruction (or communalism or nationalism); so too are they able to think about colonialism or postcolonialism as a matter of cultural 'hegemony' and creolization, as a movement of commodities and 'ideas'. For European and commonwealth anthropologists, however, racism is as much a matter of 'cultural violation' as of terror and physical destruction (see P. Werbner [1997] 2014). Similarly, the issue of colonialism and postcolonialism is not simply one of 'hegemony' but rather of powerful material and physical interventions, of dispossessions, of communal destruction and terror.

I propose to argue here that the new 1980s critics' deconstructions of the works of early anthropologists, mainly European, are fundamentally informed by their own present-day cultural sensibilities, especially the concern with cultural image, inventiveness, and hegemony. They thus fail to see, as in the case of Lévi-Strauss, that issues of racism and colonialism implicitly determined the way pre- and postwar British and Commonwealth anthropologists wrote, as well as the theoretical frameworks they adopted. The new 1980s critics' own writing, in other words, lacks attention to the very historicity they advocate.

The rise of fascism in Europe in the 1920s occurred at the very time that 'realist' anthropological texts were first being produced. European powers were gearing up for another war. In Africa, there were German and Italian invasions of North and East Africa and present-day Namibia. De facto apartheid in South Africa was increasingly entrenched, while the Afrikaner Nationalists openly supported the Nazis. British and French colonialism was at its most developed, having taken over vast areas of the Ottoman Empire. Mining, labor migration, cash cropping, land appropriation, and European settlement had all become established movements throughout the continent. In this unfolding historical drama, it is no exaggeration to say that the very *raison d'être* of social anthropological writing was antiracist and anticolonialist, *not* romanticist and pastoral.

The concern with the right and ability of colonized people to govern themselves led, perhaps, to an exaggeration of the closure of what have always been, in some respects, open societies. In explaining this relative autonomy, however, two key sociological analytic concepts were identified by Evans Pritchards in his study of the Azande and the Nuer, and were developed by the Manchester School, to deal with problems of labor migration, urbanism, economic and political development, and social process. These concepts continue to have important bearings on current discussions of hybridism and authenticity.

Cultural ideas, beliefs, and values were sustained and perpetuated, it was argued, through a process of 'situational selection'. Azande demonstrated the way conflicting 'facts' or external interventions did not necessarily modify cultural ideas embedded in particular social contexts. Developing this point, members of the Manchester School argued that by the same token, 'culture contact' with the West did not inevitably lead to 'acculturation', 'assimilation', or even hybridism. Secondary elaborations were mobilized to preserve cultural practices in different social situations. These 'social situations' were specific events enacted by a particular set of actors, enabled by particular material and social conditions, and conducted in a familiar (but sometimes 'invented', 'created', or 'improvised') cultural idiom. A social situation was thus less than a 'whole' society or 'culture'. It was, in effect, a particular and unique instance of that culture in action.

It was thus possible for a tribesman to be a townsman in town, a tribesman at home; a miner to be involved in trade union activities one day and a kinsman during the next, competing in a bitter struggle for the village headmanship. Marxist theorists were later to call this oscillation economic 'articulation' and to build a theory of capitalist exploitation upon it, but their descriptions lacked the cultural sophistication of this earlier model.

New social situations created new cultural forms, often hybrid. The building of a bridge in modern Zululand, dance groups on the Copperbelt, sorcery accusations on the shop floor. The new 1980s American cultural critics use notions of contestation, authenticity, hybridism, historicity, globalism, and identity without recognizing their anthropological antecedents. This illusory 'newness' of their 'discovery' obviates for them the necessity of grappling with the toughness of cultural practice embedded in the taken-for-grantedness of everyday social interaction, their resilience, and the violence this very oppositional resilience could unleash. The gentle cultural pluralism achieved by third-generation European immigrants in the United States seems to bear little resemblance to destructive communalism in India or Sri Lanka, intertribal slaughter in Eritrea, or the apparently irresoluble conflict between Israelis and Palestinians in the Middle East.

It is evident that an uncritical use of terms such as 'global homogenization', 'cultural entropy', or the quest for 'authenticity' obscures the different ways societies and their modes of living are affected by their incorporation into wider collectivities. One aspect of this incorporation is the way people's cultural understandings lose their implicit, taken-for-granted quality in the course of cultural encounters and the passionate battle for cultural recognition. Indeed, it is the distinction between culture as a set of natural, taken-for-granted ways of living and culture as a taken-out-of-context, packaged, or reified ideology or set of objects that lies at the heart the problem of 'authenticity'.

Writing the Exotic: The Vanishing *Mothei*

Botswana is not on the whole a violent country. It prides itself on its values of *kagiso* (peace) and *botho* (humanity). It also prides itself on being a developmental state: health and education are virtually free up to (and including) tertiary education, and rates of literacy are very high (around 95 percent for 15- to 24-year-olds). Nevertheless, just over half young people attend senior high school, while poverty rates and inequality are high and clearly marked by differences in home ownership and consumption.[5] The huge, new, shiny, shopping malls could be anywhere in the world, and increasingly teenagers in Botswana are computer literate, Internet savvy, and adept at using cellphones, much like their counterparts in the north. Botswana is said to have the highest rates of Facebook use in Africa.[6] But many young people remain marginalized and excluded from the country's growing wealth, all the more so in marginal regions like Tswapong.

When I arrived in Moremi in 2001 and asked about *mothei*, I was told that the schools had rejected the ritual, complaining that it took a girl out of school for a whole week. I wondered whether some sort of compromise could not be reached. Could the ritual not be held for a shorter period, say, over a weekend, or later? At the time people seemed shocked by the idea. After all, the ritual was prompted by *danger*, the danger inherent in the blood of first menstruation. How could it be held at some other time, or for a shorter duration? What would be the point?

By 2005, however, a more complex picture had emerged. If the ritual was fast being discarded in favor of *sesha* (modern times), there were multiple causes to this attrition. Moremi village is known to be one of the last strongholds of tradition in the Tswapong Hills, but even there, some girls or their parents had refused to have the ritual performed. All over the Tswapong region, many particulars of the ritual process were still known in detail, even by teenage girls, and women claimed it was still being celebrated in their villages. But I found, on digging deeper, that in some villages it had all but disappeared,[7] and in others it was celebrated so rarely that it was hard to mobilize the range of ages needed for the ritual. Where it had survived, it had done so through compromise and adaptation.

In public, when asked why it was important to preserve the ritual, women highlighted a key truth: that the neophyte is 'taught' proper sexual conduct. The laying of the law (*laola*) by the cult elders is whispered in hushed tones into the ear of the novice and her friends toward the very end of the ritual. But the persuasive power of this customary instructional episode derives its imperative, I suggest, from the overwhelming aesthetic and sensual impact of the cosmetic treatment of the neophyte's body and the constant drumming and dancing during sleepless nights throughout the seclusion period.

At the time of my study, between 2001 and 2005, the ritual was still being practiced, if intermittently, in its full symbolic complexity, and this allowed for a semiotic, structural analysis of the *mothei* (see fig. 2.1). The analysis makes evident that the ritual is framed by the rising sun. The girl is moved out of the hut in pitch darkness, just before dawn, surrounded by women. They guide her to a place outside the village, at a crossroads in the middle of the 'forest', where she is made to crouch on the ground, in almost complete darkness. She and her companion helper, by custom the most recent initiate to the cult, are covered entirely by a large blanket. At the very moment of sunrise, the blanket is lifted away from their heads as they raise their faces to look east, illuminated by the sun as it rises crimson on the horizon. The ritual ends seven days later when the neophyte exits the hut for the last time as the sun rises, this time to face west, in the shade of the hut, amid ululations. In these entries and exits, darkness and light are clearly alternated in the ritual. The hut is shrouded in complete darkness even during the daytime, with only a Tilley lamp burning.

FIGURE 2.1 The spiral of rebirth

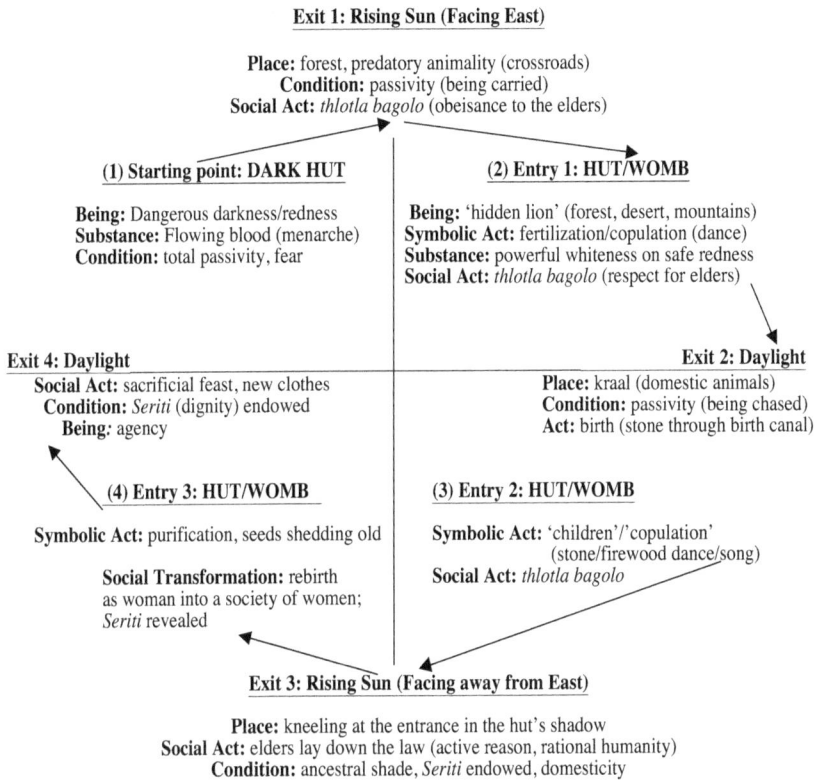

Exit 1: Rising Sun (Facing East)

Place: forest, predatory animality (crossroads)
Condition: passivity (being carried)
Social Act: *thlotla bagolo* (obeisance to the elders)

(1) Starting point: DARK HUT

Being: Dangerous darkness/redness
Substance: Flowing blood (menarche)
Condition: total passivity, fear

(2) Entry 1: HUT/WOMB

Being: 'hidden lion' (forest, desert, mountains)
Symbolic Act: fertilization/copulation (dance)
Substance: powerful whiteness on safe redness
Social Act: *thlotla bagolo* (respect for elders)

Exit 4: Daylight
Social Act: sacrificial feast, new clothes
Condition: *Seriti* (dignity) endowed
Being: agency

Exit 2: Daylight
Place: kraal (domestic animals)
Condition: passivity (being chased)
Act: birth (stone through birth canal)

(4) Entry 3: HUT/WOMB

Symbolic Act: purification, seeds shedding old

Social Transformation: rebirth
as woman into a society of women;
Seriti revealed

(3) Entry 2: HUT/WOMB

Symbolic Act: 'children'/'copulation'
(stone/firewood dance/song)
Social Act: *thlotla bagolo*

Exit 3: Rising Sun (Facing away from East)

Place: kneeling at the entrance in the hut's shadow
Social Act: elders lay down the law (active reason, rational humanity)
Condition: ancestral shade, *Seriti* endowed, domesticity

In one of the dances, enacting copulation with a firebrand as prop, even this is extinguished. The special fire on which the novice's food is cooked is located behind the hut. Ventures by the neophyte into the daylight are fleeting and marked by specific rites.

The entries and exits, as Victor Turner (1967) so perceptively recognized, enact the passage from the womb through the birth canal in menstruation and birth. As one woman put it, "when she comes out of the entrance, we want her to enter the hut" (*setse o dule ka kgoro*—coming through the door, an expression also for menstruation and ovulation).[8] In all, the neophyte enters and exits the hut four times, each episode containing specific symbolic rites or ceremonies. I present this in diagrammatic form to stress the symbolic integration and complexity of the ritual process.

The beginning of the ritual is marked as much by sound as by vision. Once the girl has revealed that she has had her first period, usually to her mother, she enters and is kept in the hut until the early morning. Meanwhile, the women of the household call a *morero*, a private consultative meeting, to discuss the ritual, whom to invite, and what their contributions of food, money, and labor will be.

By early morning these matters will have been settled. Just before dawn the women of the household begin their distinctive ululations, calling the women of the village to gather for the *mothei*. I asked what the ululation sounded like. Somewhat to my surprise, I was told that the sound most resembled that of an elephant trumpeting, or so several women thought. During the course of the ritual, the *mothei* ritual invokes and enacts a whole menagerie of wild animals,[9] remarkably so, given the long disappearance of big game from the vicinity of the village, although there are baboons and cape vultures in the hills, while the odd kudu or ostrich are sometimes sighted. Sound travels very great distances in the silence before dawn, and when they hear these distinctive ululations, people in the village know that a *mothei* is taking place. Men know they must stay away because women are moving around with a hidden, taboo creature that they must not see or come into contact with. Women know they are being called to gather.

Once enough women have gathered, the *mothei* is smeared with *phepa* (python dung),[10] said to come from a 'desert' (*sekaka*, a place with no vegetation). She is taken out of the hut, usually accompanied by a companion, by custom the girl initiated into the cult just before her. Covered entirely with a blanket she is led outside the 'village', that is, the compound, to a crossroads in the bush. The cross is another symbol that recurs repeatedly in the ritual. It represents the cardinal points and as such appears to be a symbol of encompassment, although women I asked seemed puzzled by its meaning. When the neophyte reenters the hut from the crossroad, white crosses, ideally of python dung, are drawn on her back and front, between and under her breasts.

Altogether, in the course of the ritual, the neophyte is moved in and out of the hut six times, making for a doubling up of the interlude period inside the hut, framed by her double encounter with the rising sun (fig. 2.1, and for a full analysis, see P. Werbner 2009, 2014a). The first interlude sees her treated with white python dung on *letsoko* (a red mixture of fat and of ochre from the Southern Tswapong hills). The second is defined by the healing and strengthening achieved by the switch smeared with *letsoko* (first by her young cousin as she runs to the kraal, and then by an elder women before her final exit from the hut), as well as by the singing and dancing. The ritual is thus highly structured symbolically. The overlaying of red with white is symbolically significant among Tswapong: in blowing away ancestral wrath, those of a 'white' heart blow water to mitigate the red anger of the aroused ancestors (R. Werbner 1989, 2015). But white and red are clearly also widely grasped as the colors of fertility, as Turner (1967) argued.

The move from east to west is from (crimson) exposure to shadowed protection. The entire ritual enacts and stresses respect and self-dignity, a quality of 'shade' endowed by the ancestors. The continuous stress is on seniority, and signs of respect follow the order of seniority. But the inverse is also true. The neophyte is the central focus of attention for the whole community. She is celebrated, taught to dance and sing, and ultimately feted in a new dress. As one neophyte told me when I asked if initiation gives a person dignity. "Yes," she said, "[because] you are never undermined" (*nyenyefadiwa*—looked down upon, made small, diminished, debased).

A sensory aesthetics is thus inaugurated in the *mothei* with ululations that pierce the night and continues over seven days with song, dance, drumming, ritual substances and objects, body decoration, gymnastics, dramatized spatial movement, darkness, and light—all choreographed in ritual performance to transform the neophyte bodily, cognitively, and ontologically. During the ritual, Tswapong women also implicitly appeal to ancestral divinities (*badimo*) to bless and protect the initiate and congregation present. The performances taking place in the hut, including the songs and dances, are very secret and are said to originate from the *badimo*. If revealed, I was told, this would bring calamity on the community. A mature woman who has never been initiated is not allowed into the initiation hut.[11] Any man daring to come close to the hut is chased away by women brandishing large sticks or whips.

Access to esoteric knowledge thus creates solidarities among Tswapong women and structures a gendered society, dramatized through the different ritual acts and phases (Young 1965). Significantly, the *mothei* focuses on an individual girl. Audrey Richards makes the important point that even in a supposedly premodern African society like the Bemba, initiation empowers an individual woman, she "gains confidence and she is now able to act on her own" (1956: 162). This is made very explicit among Tswapong: it is said that a girl who has had her *mothei* has *seriti*, denoting ancestral 'shade', personal dignity, public respect, and self-respect. The implication (and hope) is that such a girl will not just sleep around. She will not let men treat her with disrespect.

Nevertheless, the *mothei* appears to be rapidly vanishing. To me, it seemed astonishing that a tradition of such cultural and symbolic vibrancy, richness, and subtlety, so central to the society of village women, could be discarded. This sentiment, it emerged, was also one shared by some of the older women throughout the hills, and—as it turned out—by a few of the girls as well. These guardians of tradition were willing to make all sorts of compromises to ensure the *mothei*'s survival. One of these was to allow me to film the ritual despite its secrecy, to ensure that its customs were recorded for posterity. Another was to curtail the ritual's duration or shift it to school holidays. In the villages of Gootau, Majwaneng, and Gosekweng the ritual was still frequently held but during school vacations. The month of December in particular had become a time of *mothei*. This was also the time, of course, when urban migrants returned home for Christmas. In Gosekweng, I was told, all of the novices were initiated at the same time, starting at the evergreen tree in the village, before scattering to individual family huts. In Gootau the ritual was staggered during the month of December so that each girl could still have her own special initiation. In Malaka, parents got permission from the school (as they do in Moremi) to hold the ritual. *Mothei* rituals may also be held in April, especially during the Easter public holidays, or during the school holidays in August.[12]

The aesthetic force, beauty, and mystery of the *mothei* ritual, its sheer fun and laughter as it brings together old and young in positive generational relations, are clearly not enough to assure its continuity. Anthropological valorization of such qualities may not be shared with young people.

It would be pointless to argue that a ritual such as *mothei* serves an important practical function in any simple, straightforward way. Women continue to cooperate with one another in churches and to help with funerals and other celebrations (on this cooperation and the emotional amity it generates, see in particular Klaits 2010). They express their worth through their active participation in elected village committees. Young girls are given status, seniority, and dignity at school. There is solidarity among school peers. Pupils are educated there about the risks of pregnancy, unprotected sex, and HIV/AIDS, as well as the dangers and hygiene surrounding menstruation. Many continue to respect their elders. Moreover, young high school leavers expect to leave the village and seek work in town. They anticipate that the village will no longer be the center of their social universe.

In the context of the gradual abandonment of the ritual, what value does 'writing' the *mothei* have? Why engage in what seems self-evidently to be an exercise in salvage anthropology? Why do we need to understand the rapidly disappearing *mothei* in all its exotic richness, given that the young teenage girls in remote villages in the Tswapong Hills, aspiring to be 'modern', are abandoning the ritual?[13] Why not study 'inventiveness' and 'creativity' instead, as recommended by the 1980s American critical anthropologists who reject the ethnographic pastoral?

'Creative' Anthropology

Although its overall intent may be serious, the *mothei* is a ritual of improvisation, creativity, and fun, as Audrey Richards also found in Chisungu. In particular, intergenerational relations are manifested in mock threats if neophytes raise their heads, talk, or fail to observe etiquettes of respect, while there is much laughter at the gaucheness of young, inexperienced dancers' clumsy attempts to dance. There is problem-solving improvisation: when the blanket covering the young neophyte carried on the back of her companion fell short in a ritual I observed, there was much tugging and joking; men approaching too close were threatened with a stick; women 'healing' each other with Moretwa switches clowned around.

But there was also creative accomplishment: dancers who master the difficult acrobatic dance moves are admired, lead singers improvise as they accompany the choir of girls singing in harmony or introduce new tunes, talented drummers beat the rhythm with special embellishments. Sexually explicit songs/dances enacting sexuality are greeted with laughter and applause.

Recent work in creative anthropology—on the 'inventive present', the 'present-becoming-future' invoked by James Clifford—stresses repeatedly that inventiveness arises from mastery of a culture or aesthetic genre more than from outside it. Rejecting the distinction between 'novelty' and 'improvisation', Tim Ingold and Elisabeth Hallam follow Edward Bruner (1993) in suggesting that people are compelled to improvise "not because they are *on the inside* of an established body of convention, but because no system of codes, rules and norms can anticipate every possible circumstance" (Ingold and Hallam 2007: 2). There is, in other words, no totally fixed culture; it is always a world 'in the making' (3), a 'living tradition' (Sahlins 1998: 409). Creativity or improvisation is a *collective* project while modernity, by contrast, celebrates the 'exceptional individual' (409). With regard to ritual, one might go even further to argue that it is the accomplished actors within a ritual, those who have truly mastered its customs, song, dances, and embodied traditions, who are also the masters of improvisation and creativity. Within an established, highly stylized high-cultural tradition, as Felicia Hughes-Freeland shows in her study of Javanese dance, "during the performance, the highly controlled and formalised movement ideally frees the dancer ... [so that] for individuals within the tradition, creativity, liberation and even immanent subversion were central to their understanding of the tradition in which they worked" (2007: 214).

More in line, perhaps, with critical anthropological invocations of 'inventiveness', James Fernandez's (1982) work on the 'argument of images' among the Fang in Gabon finds creativity in African religious movements, that work to overcome:

> social disorganization and culture denial or culture loss. The truly creative religious leader, in this context, was the unconventional one whose words and organization of ritual action offered amelioration—not to say transformation—of conventional yet anomic social relationships, and a vision of a world invested with meaningful cultural content—either traditional or acculturated or, as in most cases, a syncretism of the two. His or her challenges were the discredited conventions of the traditional life-world, on the one hand, and the disadvantageous and racist–colonialist conventions of the colonial and post-colonial world on the other. His creative power lay in such ameliorative or transformative power over convention. (Fernandez 1982: 25)

It is important to note, however, that the Fang leaders of Bwiti were, Fernandez shows, men at the center of their society who created an almost seamless *bricolage* ('argument of images') between Fang mythology and Christianity, in the face of the destructive ravages of colonialism and modernization. In other societies studied by anthropologists, former initiation rituals were rejected wholesale in favor of an all-enveloping Christianity, as among the Urapmin of Papua New Guinea, in the face of 'humiliation' by Christian neighbors (Robbins 2004: 15–27).

While creolization, hybridity, or syncretism may highlight ways peripheral societies resolve the encounter with colonialism, modernity, or Christianity, they also confront us once again, as in *Tristes Tropiques*, with issues of marginality, violence, and destruction. Paradoxically, perhaps, it has been the very marginality of Moremi village and of the Tswapong women who celebrate *mothei* that allowed for its 'survival' long after male initiation had been abolished by Tswana chiefs. Now that young women are being educated and exposed to modern ideas, they reject 'tradition' and 'custom' as out of step with the times, while men, still in authority, refuse to fund the considerable expenses of the ritual. Thus, there is no longer even the possibility of inventiveness within a tradition, now that that tradition is being abandoned wholesale.

Conclusion: Critical Nostalgia or a Ritual of Self-Dignity?

The abandonment of a local culture needs to be considered in the context of a people's location in the wider world. Tswapong live in an out-of-the-way place on the margins of Botswana, itself a small, peripheral nation in the family of nations. In an increasingly competitive job market, young school leavers are at a disadvantage. Many village women are single mothers, 'destitutes', living on state food rations. To the extent that recognizing one's worth is recognizing one's distinctiveness, one's uniqueness and autonomy, so too rituals such as *mothei* may be said to dignify women as individuals, despite their poverty, and to establish their place in a society of women. In a way, the question is one of ownership: to own a culture, ritual, or symbolic performance is to possess riches unavailable to dominant groups, beyond their reach, and thus to challenge their dominance. Deprived of sovereign control of what is theirs alone exposes communities to a crushing sense of inferiority, failure, and dependency.

Echoes of rituals long abandoned do live on, incorporated into other cultural performances. During the 2011 two-month public sector strike in Botswana, dancing and singing in daily worker assemblies under giant shade trees drew on ritually licensed songs of rebellion, in this instance directed at politicians, while in their forays beyond the strike grounds workers carried shade branches, as in southern Tswana women's puberty rituals. This sort of vernacular cosmopolitanism, which creatively combines a demand for workers' rights, grounded in International Labor Organization conventions, with local cultural forms, reflects I think the intimate cultural knowledge of modern urban workers of their still vibrant cultural roots in the countryside (see Werbner 2014b).

Another performance echoing the *mothei*, which I encountered on a trip to Botswana in 2006, also highlighted the potential for cultural creativity and improvisation invested in apparently lost symbolic forms. In a three-week festival held throughout Botswana in the days around 1 December, World AIDS Day, organized by the Youth Health Organization (YOHO) and Ghetto Artists—two youth NGOs promoting safe sexual practices, especially abstention—young dancers of all ages were encouraged to perform on temporary stages, alongside actors and professional groups. Sound systems blaring, dancers displayed incredible feats in a variety of indigenized styles, mainly inspired by black American hip-hop: break dancing, freestyle, kwaito (the Johannesburg variation on hip-hop; see Magubane 2006), and Jamaican limbo, as well as sexually expressive bushman 'traditional' dancing by local stars. Gyrating pelvises, bottoms, and bellies, mock displays of sexual intercourse, and incredible acrobatic feats of suppleness and agility reminiscent of *mothei* dancing communicated a message of bodily empowerment and sexuality, which unconsciously seemed to subvert the show's overt verbal message preaching abstention and delayed sexuality.

Whether the dances, performed together by boys and girls, men and women, before mixed audiences, inscribe personal empowerment over sexuality as the *mothei* does, is unclear. Although not framed by ritual taboos like the *mothei*, the overt message of the performances—the need to control sexuality—is transmitted through melodramatic sketches, usually with tragic endings, in the educational dramas put on by YOHO and Ghetto Artists, and in their 'life skills facilitation'. The dances are glossed as mere entertainment, meant to draw the crowds and encourage audience participation.

In a recent book on the Bemba girls' *cisungu* ritual, Thera Rasing found that the ritual was still practiced among Catholics in 1995 and 1996, much as described by Richards, and with the same symbols and dances (Rasing 2001: 12). In the village where Richards had conducted her fieldwork, Rasing observed a *cisungu* that took place over a whole month, during which clay models were displayed every night (1). She recorded 490 short, mostly one-line songs, and describes 110 ritual Mbisa clay figures used in the ritual.

May we say, perhaps, that the aesthetic force, beauty, and mystery of a ritual, the sheer fun and laughter of its celebration as it brings together old and young, can make for its continuity? And paralleling this aesthetic continuity, could it be that the critical nostalgic tradition in anthropology does not arise merely from a desire to capture a vanished cultural 'essence' but as a lament of the forces that obscure the shadows of a local imagination in the mundane light of the everyday world?

Acknowledgments

This chapter was first presented at the 17th World Congress of the International Union of Anthropological and Ethnological Sciences at Manchester in 2013, and at the Satterthwaite Colloquium on African Ritual and Religion in the Lake District in 2015. I am grateful to the participants at these events and to the reviewers for their comments.

Pnina Werbner is Professor Emerita of Social Anthropology at Keele University. She is the author of *The Making of an African Working Class: Politics, Law, and Cultural Protest in the Manual Workers' Union of Botswana* (2014) and of the Manchester Migration Trilogy: *The Migration Process* ([1990] 2002), *Imagined Diasporas* (2002), and *Pilgrims of Love* (2003). She has edited several theoretical collections on hybridity, cosmopolitanism, multiculturalism, migration, and citizenship, including *Anthropology and the New Cosmopolitanism* (2008) and *The Political Aesthetics of Global Revolt: Beyond the Arab Spring* (2014). She currently holds a Leverhulme Emeritus Fellowship to study the 'changing Kgotla' in village Botswana.

Notes

1. Why colonialism is singled out is unclear, given that Westernization began in real earnest in many corners of the globe during the American hegemonic era.
2. 'Critical nostalgia' is a term taken from Raymond William (1973) to denote a textual narrative that laments a lost pastoral authenticity with the city as embodiment of the corrupt hegemonic present (see Clifford 1986: 114).
3. Roger M. Keesing, after first pointing to the cruelty of many Papua New Guinea initiation rituals, makes the point that it is unfortunate that 'the alternatives to participation traditional cultures have are marginal participation in the world capitalist economy' (1982: 37). Among Tswapong, where girls' puberty rites are gentle and humorous, this point seems doubly valid.
4. I first witnessed the performance of the ritual in 1973 and twice in 2005. In a trip around the Tswapong Hills in 2007, I found that the ritual was still practiced in some villages, often adapted to be performed in school holidays, while in others it had been abandoned it entirely.
5. See http://www.unicef.org/infobycountry/botswana_statistics.html (accessed 7 August 2014).
6. *Sunday Standard*, 29 March 2016, http://www.sundaystandard.info/botswana-has-highest-rates-facebook-use-africa (accessed 26 August 2016).
7. For example, in Mauntlala, Lesenepola, Mosweu, Mokukwane, Ratholo, and possibly Lecheng. In other villages such as Lerala, Malaka, Matolwane, Gootau, and Moremi some families celebrate it but others have ceased to do so. These were the villages I visited in 2007.
8. As translated by my assistant.
9. This is typical of initiation songs elsewhere as well. See Willoughby 1909 on southern Tswana.
10. I did not witness this smearing, only the smearing when the neophyte returns to the hut, but several informants assured me it had indeed been done before going to the crossroads.
11. A concession was made to allow me in on the occasion of several rituals, but local uninitiated women would normally be excluded.
12. In August 2007 I visited ten villages, six in southern Tswapong, to ascertain the extent to which the ritual was still held. In the small village of Gosekweng, the whole village apparently continued to hold the ritual.
13. Paradoxically, as I point out elsewhere (Werbner 2014a), the abandonment of the *mothei* is occurring at the very time that southern Tswana women are massively and enthusiastically embracing a rather tame, invented/imagined *bojale*, the long-abandoned Kgatla puberty ritual, despite being modern women, in the name of tribal identity and female solidarity (see also Setlhabi 2014).

References

Bruner, Edward M. 1993. "Epilogue: Creative Persona and the Problem of Authenticity." Pp. 321–334 in *Creativity/Anthropology*, ed. Smadar Lavie, Kirin Narayan, and Renato Rosaldo. Ithaca, NY: Cornell University Press.

Clifford, James. 1986. "On Ethnographic Allegory." Pp. 98–121 in Clifford and Marcus 1986.

Clifford, James. 1988. *The Predicament of Culture.* Cambridge, MA: Harvard University Press.

Clifford, James, and George E. Marcus, eds. 1986. *Writing Culture: The Poetics and Politics of Ethnography.* Berkeley: University of California Press.

Fardon, Richard. 1990. "General Introduction—Localising Strategies: The Regionalisation of Ethnographic Accounts." Pp. 1–35 in *Localising Strategies: Regional Traditions of Ethnographic Writing*, ed. Richard Fardon. Edinburgh: Scottish Academic Press.

Fernandez, James W. 1982. *Bwiti: An Ethnography of the Religious Imagination in Africa.* Princeton, NJ: Princeton University Press.

Geertz, Clifford. 1988. *Works and Lives.* Stanford, CA: Stanford University Press.

Hallam, Elizabeth, and Tim Ingold, eds. 2007. *Creativity and Cultural Improvisation.* Oxford: Berg.

Hughes-Freeland, Felicia. 2007. "'Tradition and the Individual Talent': T.S. Eliot for Anthropologists." Pp. 207–222 in Hallam and Ingold 2007.

Hutnyk, John. [1997] 2014. "Adorno at Womad: South Asian Crossovers and the Limits of Hybridity-Talk." Pp. 106–136 in Werbner and Modood [1997] 2014.

Ingold, Tim, and Elizabeth Hallam. 2001. "Creative Arguments of Images in Culture, and the Charnel House of Conventionality." Pp. 17–30 in *Locating Cultural Creativity*, ed. John Liep. London: Pluto Press.

Ingold, Tim, and Elizabeth Hallam. 2007. "Creativity and Cultural Improvisation: An Introduction." Pp. 1–24 in Hallam and Ingold 2007.

Keesing, Roger M. 1982. "Introduction." Pp. 1–43 in *Guardians of the Flutes: Idioms of Masculinity*, ed. Gilbert H. Herdt. New York: McGraw-Hill.

Klaits, Frederick. 2010. *Death in a Church of Life: Moral Passion during Botswana's Time of AIDS.* Berkeley: University of California Press

Lévi-Strauss, Claude. [1955] 1970. *Tristes Tropiques: An Anthropological Study of Primitive Societies in Brazil.* Trans. John and Doreen Weightman New York: Atheneum.

Magubane, Zine. 2006. "Globalization and Gangster Rap: Hip Hop in the Post-Apartheid City." Pp. 208–229 in *The Vinyl Ain't Final: Hip Hop and the Globalization of Black Popular Culture*, ed. Dipannita Basu and Sidney J. Lemelle. London: Pluto Press.

Malinowski, Bronislaw. 1922. *Argonauts of the Western Pacific.* London: Kessinger.

Marcus, George E. 1986. "Contemporary Problems of Ethnography in the Modern World System." Pp. 165–193 in Clifford and Marcus 1986.

Marcus, George E., and Michael M. J. Fischer, eds. 1986. *Anthropology as Cultural Critique.* Chicago: University of Chicago Press.

Rasing, Thera. 2001. *The Bush Burnt, the Stones Remain: Female Initiation Rites in Urban Zambia.* New York: Transaction.

Richards, Audrey I. 1956. *Chisungu: A Girl's Initiation Ceremony among the Bemba of Zambia.* London: Tavistock.

Robbins, Joel. 2004. *Becoming Sinners: Christianity and Moral Torment in a Papua New Guinea Society.* Berkeley: University of California Press.

Sahlins, Marshall. 1998. "Two or Three Things That I Know about Culture." *Journal of the Royal Anthropological Institute* 5, no. 3: 399–421.

Sahlins, Marshall. 1999. "What Is Anthropological Enlightenment? Some Lessons from the Twentieth Century." *Annual Review of Anthropology* 28: i–xxiii.

Setlhabi, Keletso G. 2014. "The Politics of Culture and the Transience of Culture in Botswana: Bakgatla-baga-Kgafela Women's Initiation in Botswana." *Journal of Southern African Studies* 40, no. 3: 459–477.

Taussig, Michael. 1984. "Culture of Terror—Space of Death: Roger Casement's Putumayo Report and the Explanation of Torture." *Comparative Studies in Society and History* 26, no. 3: 467–497.

Turner, Victor. 1967. *The Forest of Symbols*. Ithaca, NY: Cornell University Press.

Werbner, Pnina. [1997] 2014. "Essentialising Essentialism, Essentialising Silence: Ambivalence and Multiplicity in the Constructions of Racism and Ethnicity." Pp. 226–254 in Werbner and Modood [1997] 2014.

Werbner, Pnina. 2009. "The Hidden Lion: Tswapong Women's Initiation Cult and the Achievement of Dignity in Botswana at a Time of AIDS." *American Ethnologist* 36, no. 3: 441–458.

Werbner, Pnina. 2014a. "Between Ontological Transformation and the Imagination of Tradition: Girls' Puberty Rituals in 21st Century Botswana." *Journal of Religion in Africa* 44, no. 3–4: 355–385.

Werbner, Pnina. 2014b. *The Making of an African Working Class: Politics, Law, and Cultural Protest in the Manual Workers' Union of Botswana*. London: Pluto Press.

Werbner, Pnina, and Tariq Modood, eds. [1997] 2014. *Debating Cultural Hybridity: Multi-Cultural Identities and the Politics of Anti-Racism*. London: Zed Books.

Werbner, Richard. 1989. *Ritual Passage, Sacred Journey*. Washington, DC: Smithsonian University Press.

Werbner, Richard. 2015. *Divination's Grasp: African Encounters with the Almost Said*. Bloomington: Indiana University Press.

Wilcken, Patrick. 2010. *Claude Lévi-Strauss: The Poet in the Laboratory*. London: Bloomsbury.

Young, Frank W. 1965. *Initiation Ceremonies: A Cross-Cultural Study of Status Dramatization*. New York: Bobbs-Merrill.

Chapter 3

THE EXOTIC ALBATROSS
Exotic Indians, Exotic Theory

Stephen Nugent

This chapter is in two parts. The first is mainly a sketch of some general matters concerning the status and history of the notion of the exotic in anthropology. The second is primarily concerned with the exoticism associated with Amazonian Indians. The main aim in this section is to look at what underlies the particular kinds of Amazonian exoticism that have fed back into what has been widely and provocatively hailed as noteworthy advance in 'anthropological theory' (Latour 2009): perspectivism, multiple ontologies, neo-animism.

The chapter title alludes to the burdensomeness, and perhaps inevitability, of the concept of the exotic as a defining feature of the anthropological project, burdensome because the concept seems so obviously relevant (could there be an anthropology without a concept of the exotic?) yet also subject to such timeworn discussion as to appear ordinary and only marginally relevant. Sally Price's brilliant discussion of primitive art (in civilized places) opens with a question apposite for the exotic: "What do we mean when we talk about 'primitive art' [the exotic]? I am not aware of any other term in anthropology or art history that has come under such disgruntled attack by people who feel they should dissociate themselves from it but still on some level wish to believe its legitimacy. The result has been a large number of disclaimers" (1989: 1).

Notes for this chapter begin on page 79.

The exotic, on its own plinth in the museum of anthropological concepts, similarly evokes that odd combination of disgruntlement and legitimacy. The question of the degree to which the exotic continues to define or is essential to anthropology has prompted a number of well-known responses. These include what I take to be the equivocal, mainstream claim that anthropology may have once been focused on (or at least seen to be focused on) extreme examples of cultural expression—headhunting, fetishism, errant kinship practices—primarily outside of the West, but in the study's maturity it is equally at ease engaging in what is referred to as 'anthropology at home' (e.g., MacClancy 2002), finding in the shopping malls and gun clubs of the metropolitan West, for instance, suitable material for anthropological analysis.

Although this response is in part the expression of demands for 'relevant' material in an academic system in which scholarly pursuit has an increasing number of non-scholarly entailments, it is hardly novel. Margaret Mead's reputation, for example, is based largely on comparative Samoan and US material, long before the 'relevance' claims were widely articulated, and Hortense Powdermaker and Robert Park (and many others) early on had also clearly broken the archaic-exotic moorings. What is noteworthy about the catalogued 'exotic no more' position (e.g., MacClancy 2002) is that it doesn't actually represent a rejection of the archaic-exotic as much as it represents an extension of the anthropological remit[1] and authority in coding and decoding the exotic.

Another response is represented in historical anthropological approaches in which, taking Eric Wolf (1982) as the prime example, the emergence of the modern world system engages formulations of the primitive, other, savage—various versions of the archaic-exotic of diverse origin—locked into the classificatory needs of a field that exists because it is initially situated in the center. The title *Europe and the People Without History* is a concise rendering in which the exotic is not something outside the system but intrinsic to it. Michel-Rolph Trouillot's (2003) 'savage slot' commentary, although employing more of the language of post-social scientific anthropology than Wolf ('geographic imagination'), makes a similar point, as indeed, from a different perspective, does postcolonial discourse. For these, the archaic-exotic does not represent an object of analysis that must be tackled by anthropology but rather is implicated in the field's very definition. From this vantage the sensibility of 'exotic no more', far from making anthropology more relevant, ends the conversation (for if it is exotic no more, anthropology is no more).

The Exotic versus the Scientific

The emergent scientific anthropology of the early twentieth century tasks the concept of the exotic in two ways. First, it privileges social system as the object of analysis, not the exotic icons, objects, and practices that stand for such systems. Second, it explains away the exotic by revealing the cultural (or system) logic according to which the seemingly exotic is actually integral to the system overall. Head shrinking may seem odd when taken on its own, but once the system in which it is embedded is elaborated, it makes (a kind of) sense. The impulse in both early cultural and early social anthropological forays was to defuse the archaic-exotic and downplay it as the defining rationale of anthropological explanation.

This 'emergent scientific' take on the exotic overlaps to a considerable degree with the later 'exotic no more' proposal in as much as the practice of 'anthropology at home' often mimics, without great subtlety, what is perceived to be a traditional rendering of the relationship between traditional fieldwork and traditional/exotic subjects: in the core, metropolitan, ethnographic landscape, one finds analogues of the remote exotic, gypsies, junkies, sex workers, cult members, various species of marginal social types. The fixation on locally available versions of 'real' (i.e., remote, Orientalist) exotics reveals much of the albatross character of the exotic that adorns the anthropological neck: without the exotic, anthropological legitimacy is diminished, as is indeed the case with the widespread appropriation of ethnography by non-anthropological researchers. As a conservation strategy, acknowledgment of the exotic, and ethnography, has an obvious, and likely vital, role to play.

The active inclusion of exotic analogues within the 'anthropology at home' program also reveals another dimension of the relativity of the exotic concept: on one hand, the exotic in classificatory terms is infinitely malleable (the anthropology of electrical kitchen appliances, for instance, is wholly plausible and exotic), but what is more crucially revealed in the cultivation of the exotic is the difference in political power of those who research (abroad or at home) and those who are studied. The exotic, as a placeholder for 'studiable', repeatedly represents the position-that-can't-say-no—exotic dancers in crumbling strip malls, not Ivy League dining club members.[2] Beyond the anthropological domain, which is to say academia largely, the exotic is so widely distributed as to have lost much analytical utility.[3]

Two other linked and clearly expressed anthropological views on the archaic-exotic significantly challenge the centrality of concept as a platform for debate. One of these views, of which Maurice Bloch (2011) is an exemplary, longstanding, polemical spokesperson, argues that an original (modern scientific anthropology since the time of Malinowski) part of the anthropological project—with a distinctive theoretical/explanatory goal—should be sharply distinguished from the 'ethnography = anthropology' stance that has long prevailed. A concern for theories about the human species in general preserves no special place for the exotic—that is a task of comparative ethnography or ethnology.

Similarly, Dan Sperber is unsparing in his turn away from what he long ago characterized/caricatured as the *Conformist* view: "Anyhow, it is no longer the aim of anthropological theory to describe a so-called human nature: its aim is to understand how cultures and societies are structured, and how they change." Against that, (and pursued in much subsequent writing) he proposes an anthropological project that will "help outline an epistemology of anthropology [as against] a discipline which imposes on its practitioners great personal demands, only a loose methodology, and *no theoretical standards whatsoever*" (1985: 7; emphasis added).

From these latter two standpoints, the general question of the exotic is not a viable platform for the pursuit of anthropological explanation, yet the persistence of interest in the exotic and exoticization still seems to guarantee the plausibility of the anthropological project: if, as the ethnographists[4] would have it, there is an inductivist-relativist project to be maintained within the professional boundaries of academic anthropology, it can only claim coherence if it can be convincingly distinguished from any other disciplinary claims (say from cultural studies or another cognate field), and to secure those claims it must submit to some—even a mild—scientific orientation (ethnographers are not novelists or travel writers, after all—usually). On the other hand, those for whom human nature or a central concern with universals serve as primary objects of analysis in anthropology have also been methodologically shaped by fieldwork exposure to the exotic. For one camp, simplifying wildly, the exotic is a persistent feature of the enterprise; for the other, it is contingent.

To summarize some of the points raised thus far, the albatross aspect of exoticism consists in the fact that anthropological usages of the exotic are embedded in a loose conceptual repertoire that anthropologists are at pains to police. On one hand, and in terms of public culture, the expert claims of the field depend in large part on having overcome the ignorance of simplistic notions of the exotic and in having proposed instead a technical treatment. Skull shrinking may seem sine qua non exotic, but it can be—if not 'explained away'—made intelligible in context.[5]

On the other hand, however, if all sociocultural systems are merely different positions within a horizontal spectrum, if the exotic is just a matter of a perspective on unfamiliarity, what is the point of anthropology as more than comparative sociology, albeit a variant with a wider cultural remit? That version of anthropology, a discipline devoted primarily to describing different cultural systems and subsets of such systems without a fundamental analytic objective, is the notion criticized above as the mere ethnographic project. This dilemma, it might be suggested, has grown out of a fundamental change in the status of anthropologists as official, although hardly exclusive, interlocutors between, in that highly reductive phrase, the West and the Rest during the period since the 1920s.[6]

Two parallel processes have undermined the status of anthropological observation and analysis and have simultaneously created more of the exotic material that anthropologists were meant to command. The first process is the inexorable if uneven integration within the capitalist world economy: in the course of encouraging commodity production as normative economic activity throughout the world, the remoteness of the idealized anthropological terrain has receded (accessible air travel, the foreign holiday as a scheduled consumer event, mass media familiarity, etc.) and esoteric anthropological fieldwork experience becomes ordinary.[7]

The second, and related, process is the search for new assets. Included here are not only new sources of primary materials (including, of course, 'exotic' minerals and woods, etc.) and the, by now, traditional kinds of primitive accumulation but also new categories of cultural assets, in the course of which, for example, Maori tattoo/*tāmoko* patterns, whose cachet lies in a familiar version of the remote exotic, are transposed onto metropolitan white skins, a technical process unregulated by original exotic context. Similarly, Brazil nut oil hair conditioner sourced from Brazilian Amazonian Indians both valorizes the 'trade not aid' posture of Body Shop International and leaps cultural boundaries with by now familiar neoliberal grace. The exotic becomes a Janus-faced token of authenticity and counterfeit.[8]

This criticism of limited theoretical ambition, raised decades ago by Sperber, may indicate in part why the exotic still plays such a key role in anthropological discourse. How else could one include the diversity of subfields in sociocultural anthropology (the Open Anthropology Cooperative lists more than two hundred specialist groups—from paganism to recycling) without concepts of such flexibility and indeterminacy as the exotic?

The exotic, and its problematic status within the technical vocabulary of anthropology, also betrays something in its contradictory affiliation with both premodern and modern anthropology (something strongly revealed in current Amazonianist work). The notion of fetish, for example, which appears to date from early colonial period encounters in which European chroniclers identified exotic beliefs as breaching cause-and-effect protocols of the time, presents an early limiting case example of the exotic. Despite the numerous inflections that 'fetish' has since taken on—most notably the mistaking of relations between human subjects for relations between things—that early fetish/exotic equation is vigorously represented in very recent anthropological ventures (see, e.g., the proposal that objects have agency/intentionality).

That the exotic continues problematically to engage the anthropological project may reflect something about the effects of the limited overlap of professional anthropology (still largely confined to the academy) and public culture. That relative isolation has allowed anthropology to prosper as its own culture industry—witness the enormous publication output and apparent visibility and recognition of the medium/genre of ethnographic film—yet have a limited general readership confined to a few key titles.[9] While professional anthropologists might have thorough and considered views about those works that have achieved mainstream visibility (Mead, Lévi-Strauss, Turnbull, Geertz, Chagnon), there is a preoccupation with the way the concerns of 'the field' are meaningfully represented in work that achieves a kind of translation/communicability that for primary work in anthropology (from field notes to journal article) is so painfully achieved.[10]

If one achievement of modern anthropology was formally to de-exoticize the exotic (basically, relativize it), the prospect of its removal from the lexicon is still vexing. Bruce Kapferer (2013: 815), for example, in his Huxley Memorial Lecture, goes to some lengths to justify the continued usefulness of the term even within a mature anthropology where, he says, one "engages with the exotic as a methodology for discovery and understanding." In the same piece, however, the exotic also assumes quite a different character: "The scientific exotic challenges received wisdom and, as in Darwin's case, overturns theories and becomes the basis for new ones" (818). That dual role of the exotic, as method and as telos as well, seems to have a general appeal and applicability, but in looking at the concept not in general but rather at a level in which the concept has been applied to a restricted body of ethnographic material and within specific historical parameters, it is possible to see something quite different in the concept, something that seems to express less an interest in the exotic as a category that sustains anthropological interest in explaining things about the world and more in taking anthropological theory itself as the ground upon which anthropology walks. The Amazonian Indian has provided a medium for the growth of perspectivism, an involutional gesture in anthropology that reifies the baseline exoticism of the Amazonian Indian to an unprecedented degree.

The Exotic Amazonian Indian

The exoticism of the Amazonian Indian has a long history and durability. In crucial respects it resists prehistorical and historical contextualization and has achieved a sort of transcendental ahistoricity, invoked as convincingly and casually (and ignorantly) in World Cup 2014 media coverage as in sixteenth-century woodcuts, in the first as celebrant and symbol of national unity, in the second as inveterate cannibal.

As with many anthropological subjects, knowledge about and understanding of Amazonians have been substantially revised over the (relatively) brief career of modern anthropology, but what has been typically depicted as exotic about the Amazonian Indian should also be cast as exceptionalist: like Highland New Guinea peoples, Amazonians represent a limiting case of indigene as close as possible to, in the unfortunate cliché, the nature-culture cusp. An emphasis on exceptionalism as well as exoticism focuses attention on the repetitive stress injury of a representation of noble savagery emphatic enough to coexist with prehistorical, historical and ethnographic material that severely challenges the coherence of the cliché—and yet.

The main argument to follow is that it is the anthropological discourse about Amazonians that tends to be exotic, not the Indians themselves, or not the Indians themselves any more than any other cultural actors. What is particularly interesting about the Amazonian case is that there has emerged a super-exotic anthropologicism, an anthropology of the exotic that has reverted to prescientific anthropology: when an Amazonian Indian says he is an armadillo, he is not, as in terms—for instance—of the rationality debate, speaking metaphorically, or mistakenly or unintelligibly. He is an armadillo. Anthropologists who are able to grasp multiple ontologies (you are an armadillo as well as you are not an armadillo) assert that whereas the longstanding assumption has been that nature is unitary and culture diverse, the reality is that that nature is multiple and culture unitary. This trend within Amazonianist anthropology—and elsewhere—places older questions about the exotic on a different footing. Anthropology is not, even in the mainstream relativist view, basically about the mapping of cultural difference (and perspectivists tend to resist the idea that they are 'merely' radical relativists), and certainly not about the systematic analysis of universals/human nature, but is instead a rhetorical strategy of sublimation.[11]

Why Amazonian Indians Seem to Be Exotic

A number of factors account for the attention Amazonian Indians receive as exotic peoples. The ones discussed here are (1) the early and persistently influential conceptions of the noble savage; (2) a particularly powerful form of humid neotropical environmental determinism (an especially rigid form closely associated with 'green hell', a variant of what Blaut [1993] referred to as 'the doctrine of tropical nastiness'); (3) the contributions of Claude Lévi-Strauss; and (4) the photographic record that precedes anthropological codification of the Amazonian Indian by more than half a century.

The Amazonian Indians' early codification as exemplary noble savages, people whose natural state had yet to be corrupted by culture and society, has long been a touchstone for discussion and philosophical speculation inside and out of anthropology. That codification was pursued by many European commentators, but not on the basis of much knowledge about Amazonians. What was to become known about Amazonians was accreted through the accounts of conquerors, explorers, travelers, clerics, and others involved initially in the creation of a colonial apparatus primarily concerned with the extensive (rather than intensive)[12] extraction of natural resources (dismissively cast as *as drogas do sertão*) and control of Indian labor for transport and administrative purposes. There are observational accounts and official records from the period between the early-sixteenth-century European conquest of the Brazilian Amazon and the pioneering anthropology of the late nineteenth/early twentieth centuries (to which Curt Nimuendajú is the most important contributor), but in terms of archetypal features, the Indian of modern anthropology was very similar to that noble savage of the sixteenth century.

In the intervening period, however, and as is now well understood (as it was not in 1900), the dominant model of Amazonian Indian society underwent a radical change. The typical hunter-gatherer society of the twentieth century—low population, forest-dwelling, materially impoverished in many respects—had succeeded sedentary, riverine societies some would depict as proto-state (see Lathrap 1968 and Roosevelt 1991 for discussions that bookend late twentieth century ethnography, and Heckenberger 2005 and Schaan 2011 for more recent overviews).[13]

By the time anthropologists began to do research among Amazonian Indians, any examples of large-scale preconquest societies had long disappeared, as had most of the population. Conservative estimates of preconquest populations (5 to 6 million) against a current population of 400,000[14]—virtually all in small, fragmented polities—make the assumption that extant Amazonian Indian societies are significantly representative of their preconquest forms extremely unlikely, yet the image of the Amazonian Indian represented in the literature is emphatically one of an ur-condition: these are Indians as they were preconquest.

The point here is that this assumption of the representativeness of modern Indians in itself is an exotic conception. No one would dispute the reality of the modern, forest-dwelling[15] Indian (who, despite inclusion in Brazil's symbolic triumvirate of racial democracy, is in a parlous state), but that Indian—sharply distinguished from other social actors in Amazonia who despite Indian antecedents are classed as *mestiço* outliers—is very much a reflection of the exoticization routines of anthropology. Put another way: anthropology has chosen to focus on an exotic object of analysis, and the Amazonian Indian is, in Alcida Rita Ramos's (1994) celebrated formulation, very much a 'hyperreal' Indian as well as an Indian.

The two other noted factors in the exoticization of the Amazonian Indian both represent the influence of a powerful nature-culture binary: notions of humid neotropical environmental determinism and the familiar Lévi-Straussian models. The work of Betty J. Meggers and Clifford Evans (especially Meggers 1971), a standard in the literature, represents an obdurate reinforcement of the view that the evolution of social complexity is highly constrained/impossible in Amazonia because of rigid limits imposed by nature (against the evidence adduced in Roosevelt 1991 and Schaan 2011, to name but two, both of whom worked, like Meggers, on Marajó). Whatever the precariousness of the evidential basis of the standard view, the image of the exotic, marginal, forest Indian is paramount as a point of reference for discussion and debate within Amazonian studies, a testimony to the power of exoticization.

Lévi-Strauss's influence on the exoticization of the Amazonian Indian is, perhaps somewhat confusingly, both extremely obvious and extremely covert. *Tristes Tropiques*, *The Savage Mind*, and *Les Mythologiques* have in different ways foregrounded a hyper-idealized Amazonian Indian with derivative, exoticizing effects. *TT* portrays the melancholy landscape of interior/Indian Brazil just before World War II. The material can hardly be described as ethnographic in a fulsome sense (periodic forays, assisted by guides, little/no linguistic facility), yet the journeys produced much evocative and imaginative material (as well as vast amounts of material culture conveyed back to Paris; see Wilcken 2011). *SM* was a dramatic intellectual intervention in which the standard portrayal of Amazonian societies (e.g., Steward and Faron 1959), as bundles of traits and practices was supplanted by a model of concrete science that contributed much to the promotion of the anthropologist as hero (Hayes and Hayes 1970; Sontag 1963) as it did also to the native-as-thinker. Finally, *LM* consolidated an impression that Amazonian Indians (and their North American precursors) occupied a mental-myth world of staggering intellectual complexity.[16]

Despite the fact that Lévi-Strauss's direct engagement with the Indian-in-the-field was limited to a few short visits from 1935 to 1939, his work was of sufficient influence to shape if not prevail over much of subsequent Amazonian Indian ethnology (the symbolic/structural) that was not nakedly culturally materialist (how many bananas does a hunter need on a trek?).

The fourth and final, for this discussion, factor in the anthropological exoticization of the Amazonian Indian concerns the role of photographic imagery sustaining durable stereotypes. There are two aspects of the role of photography to be considered here. One concerns the actual record of images; the other concerns the way images have been employed in anthropological literature.[17]

Early (mid-nineteenth-century) photographic resources continue to emerge (see, e.g., the recent Schmidt collection in Bossert and Villar 2013 and material from the Nimuendajú 2004 collection in Gothenburg), but there are sets of well-known images from Albert Frisch, for example, and other commercial photographers (see especially the work of Huebner in Schoepf 2000) that consolidate features of the noble savage stereotype established much earlier. One of the first photo-centric commentaries from within the then-emergent ranks of modern professional anthropology, that of E. F. im Thurn (1893) in a critique of the anthropometric photographic offerings from the Torres Straits expedition, bears down heavily on a 'native-captured-at-his-ease' prescription for modern anthropology.[18]

One of the most extensive early twentieth century collections that contributed to the noble savage–inflected portrayal of 'the original Brazilians' was provided by the soldier Cândido Rondon, appointed by the state to be the bureaucratic Indian in Chief. Prior to creating the federal Indian Protection Service (SPI) in 1910, Rondon led expeditions (1900–1915) into the interior, a primary task of which was the laying of telegraph lines, and images from which were collected in three volumes, *Indios do Brasil* (1953). By this point, of course, there were no longer complex riverbank societies, so the photographic record of forest-dwelling Amazonian Indians comprised by default an unchallenged vision.

While Amazonian exoticization no doubt shares much with other ethnographic areas (and in the case of New Guinea there are also similarities in the development of hyper-theorization, as in the parallel work of Marilyn Strathern and Eduardo Viveiros de Castro), and one could no doubt generalize about processes, two unique features of the Amazonian situation deserve attention. One of these is the way the exoticization of the Indian also represents and is reflected in an exoticization of nature. The second is the way the Amazonian Indian has lent weight to the exoticization of anthropological theory itself, in the form of perspectivism.

Claims for the exoticism of Amazonia-the-natural-sphere are based on an extravagant biodiversity,[19] abundance of toxic plants, presence of attention-grabbing animals (piranha, electric eel, sloth, tapir, giant armadillo, blind pink dolphin), river network, short nutrient cycle, and so on. In terms of scientific understanding, none of this is terribly exotic: effectively insulated from the impact of the last ice age, speciation carried on unimpeded for longer than was the case elsewhere, resulting in high species diversity, low species density, efficient cycling of limited nutrients, and the emergence of an oligarchic (or senile) forest. The complexity of the humid neotropics, however, has been the basis of hyper-exoticization (the biggest this, the most poisonous that) through the reports of explorers and natural historians, especially through the nineteenth century, and realized in such long-echoing work as Arthur Conan Doyle's *Lost World* (1912) and its derivatives (e.g., the *Jurassic* Park series). Yet on a day-to-day basis there is nothing terribly exotic about timber extraction and milling, mineral extraction (iron, bauxite), fishing, and those forms of extraction and economic activity through which the region has been integrated in the global economy for centuries. Those prosaic economic activities tend to be subsumed under a mask provided by açaí, guaraná, curare, ayahuasca, and aromatic plants that command more exotic cachet.

The special powers attributed to the tropical environment in shaping the possibilities for social complexity in Amazonia have long been of overwhelming, and confusing, significance. Until the relatively recent acknowledgment of demographic revisionists, it has been widely taken for granted that the low population of the region is in an unproblematic sense 'a natural outcome', that is, the tropics simply do not tolerate much in the way of carrying capacity much less sociocultural development. This misperception strongly supports the view of Indians as exotic-to-hyper-exotic, for they seem to represent the limits of human intervention in an untoward setting. Beyond that, the exotic status of natural Amazonia appears extreme enough that those who maintain a social landscape may be included as just one more exotic feature/species. The continued and wearisome press interest in 'lost' and 'undiscovered' tribes[20] underscores the persistence of a naturalistic mythologizing/exoticization.

A contemporary portrayal of Amazonian Indians that meshes particularly well with the vigorous exoticization of nature is represented in the formulation of the 'wise forest manager'.[21] On one hand this concept is little more than a market/neoliberal-inflected version of an oft-repeated anthropological discovery: people who live and work in an environment often have a better grasp of social system-biosystem interfaces than would-be modernizing outsiders. This is not to say this portrayal is inaccurate or that it has not served at times some indigenous interests, but on the other hand, that Indian, as Ramos (1994) has noted, bears the weight of others'—non-Indians'—expectations of what an Indian is and isn't, what she characterises as the hyperreal Indian.[22]

Much of the exoticism attributed to Amazonia and Amazonians recedes in the face of prehistorical and historical material—some of which has long been available, if overlooked, and other of which is quite recent—but many of the ways Amazonians were first codified as imperial and, later, scientific subjects has persisted,[23] and the hyperreal designation provides another ideological layer. Ramos's critique of this categorization of the Indian is mainly directed at NGOs for whom the Indian has become the subject of routinized heroism, the Indian whose effective agency actually lies in the bureaucracy that takes it upon itself to advance the Indian's interests, "the perfect Indian whose virtue, sufferings and untiring stoicism have won for him the right to be defended by the professionals of indigenous rights" (Ramos 1994: 161).

This perfect—hyperreal—Indian is, of course, a construct, and it might be said, a kind of exotic one. It excludes, for example, on the grounds of 'insufficiency of exotic' the many compromised Indians assimilated into the diverse Amazonian peasantries,[24] the ignobles who no longer qualify for inclusion as proper Indians, as well as those such as the Tukano 'collaborators' whom Ramos (1994: 153) takes as her starting point in her original her original hyperreal article. Within Amazonianist anthropology it has long been clear that if an anthropological subject is designated 'Amazonian', that is taken to mean 'Indian'. Other Amazonian subjects are *campesinos* (peasants) or *caboclos* (racial term with connotation of assimilated Indian), and there are many other kinds of Amazonians, but the point is that Amazonian-as-Indian is for many a pure, untrammeled category despite the fact that in overviews of the ethnographic literature, 'the Amazonian Indian' is actually represented by numerous case study examples that resist meaningful encapsulation except as a shorthand (and one that is strikingly similar to that held in nonspecialist and folk versions). Anthropology may resent popular versions of the exotic wrenched from the authoritative grasp of experts, but the versions of the Amazonian Indian often seem indistinguishable.

From the Anthropology of the Exotic to Exotic Anthropology

As suggested above, the reasons for the persistence of a questionable reliance on the concept of the maximally exotic in Amazonian research lie partly in the history of the discipline itself—the localized impact of Lévi-Strauss, for example, whose highly abstract work provided an opening for the idea of *theory* as an end in itself—partly in the particular unfolding of colonial society (massive early demographic collapse; marginal, frontier relationship with the state) and partly in the array of geo-environmental features of the humid neotropics.

The exoticism of Amazonian Indian societies has long rested on the assumption that extant societies are significantly representative of their preconquest predecessors, although that assumption has come under increasing pressure. Nonetheless, the focal, exotic Amazonian Indian society has long been the primary object of analysis of anthropological investigation. The exoticism of the Indian has also proved useful to other interests. In terms of the Brazilian state, for example, the Indian is subject to continuous and cynical manipulation— 'protected' by the state while being 'assimilated' into national society, and the use of Indians and Indian iconography is evident at many other political and commercial levels, highlighted to a perverse degree—given the actual material conditions of the Indians and their marginal status within Brazil—in the context of World Cup and Rio Olympic celebrations. Ramos's critique of NGO interest in Indian clientage has provided an important commentary on the costs of 'national integration', and the trope of uncontacted, lost peoples is regularly invoked in the press. While the exotic characterization of the Indian is well and widely established, in a narrow context of Amazonian anthropological inquiry, the Indian has recently also come to serve as the basis for exotic theory in the form of perspectivism.[25] If cultural relativism à la Clifford Geertz (which is to say a multiculturalist reaction to a 'reductionist' scientism) domesticated 'the exotic' by making the ordinary task of anthropological investigation the iterative interpretation of interpretation such that the exotic became normalized in context, perspectivism raised (or aspires to raise) the interpretive game by an order of magnitude. If the discussions in Bryan Wilson (1970) turned around the question of translating rationality cross-culturally, Viveiros de Castro moved the discussion onto an ontological footing.[26] Questions of causality—as in the case of sorcery, for example, or shamanic trans-species activity—are subsumed under two radical claims: one, that Amazonian Indians are ontologically different from their anthropological observers; and two, that anthropologists are in the privileged position to understand and access both ontological positions.[27]

Perspectivism is approached gingerly, in the same way one might advance on a bizarre (exotic?), never-before-seen creature cast up on the beach. Unlike the mysterious sea creature, however, this new specimen may well have been seen before: casual inspection reveals it to be the long-thought-extinct species of primitive mentality. What is different, although opinion varies enormously about whether that difference is interesting or consequential or significant, is that the proponents' claims—first, that "I am a human; that is an anteater" and "I am human and I think like an anteater" and, second, that "Anteater thinks like me"—are accessible to human consciousness (multiple ontologies). The most concise expression of this radical perspectivist move lies in the claim that whereas the Western anthropologist conceives of a single nature and multiple cultures, the Amazonian Indian conceives of one culture and multiple natures (Viveiros de Castro 2004: 6).[28]

It sounds an exotic claim, yet may have more prosaic origins than the evident Lévi-Straussian influences: the speculations of Lucien Lévy-Bruhl. A sketch of the movement between Lévy-Bruhlian primitive mentality and its new version might be the following:

- Modern anthropology disposed of the claims of Lévy-Bruhl by putting aside both concepts of primitive and mentality.
- Instead, the new position argued, there were holistic social systems (for some, glossed as cultures as well) within which seemingly implausible beliefs were not evidence of defective rationality (which is really a different-species claim), but were expressive of a culture-logic according to which such beliefs made a kind of (local) pragmatic, contextual sense.
- Subsequent to modern anthropology's achieving academic respectability, the cognitive revolution begun in the late 1950s saw the cultural relativism-in-holism model challenged by a universalist/innatist/hard-wired[29] project agnostic (or hostile) to the idea that cultural difference defied a shared rationality. The hermeneutic/symbolic/interpretive insistence on a social constructionist project became, and remains, the mainstream (see Sperber 1975, 1985, 1996).
- And lo and behold, armadillos are human because an anthropological subject claims as much.

That is, I hope clearly, a broad-brush caricature, although it does concisely track the fall and rise of 'primitive mentality', first wrested from prescientific speculation and]then accounted for within the terms of an aspirationally scientific analysis of culture-sociologic but finally re-instated as an artifact of a branch of social science extremely nervous about the science (and materialism, naturalism, and physicalism).

Both critics and proponents of perspectivism place Lévi-Strauss firmly in the story despite a diffidence in both quarters about whether he has been built upon (there is hardly a discernible theoretical edifice, albeit much architectural prototyping) or superseded, but there is no question that perspectivism requires Lévi-Strauss, not least because of the exploitability of his heuristics (nature : culture :: raw : cooked; transformation; homologous structures), but also because he solves the problem of Lévy-Bruhl: where Lévy-Bruhl saw the change from primitive to not-primitive as evolutionary/progressive, Lévi-Strauss proposed that different kinds of thinking may coexist (*bricolage* + scientific-expert, famously). Those tendencies in anthropology that pursued, broadly, those kinds of cognitive issues found theoretical support and interest elsewhere (in linguistics, psychology, philosophy), not so much in anthropology. The perspectivist return to Lévy-Bruhlian notions shows a very odd operation: whereas Lévi-Strauss made a suggestive universalist claim (humans in general are multimodal), the perspectivists seem to confine their arguments to Amazonians alone (although Inner Mongolia and PNG provide candidates as well).

Two responses by Amazonianists—Alcida Rita Ramos and Terence S. Turner—offer salutary and some might think, devastating critiques, although at times moderate and respectful to a degree. One is by Ramos (2012), who transposes or redirects her hyperreal arguments from bureaucratic idealization to a new target, mainly Viveiros de Castro. Two points of hers in particular lend weight to the claim of an anthropological exoticism overtaking the anthropology of the exotic. The first of these concerns the bald claim that 'Amazonian' is a useful notion. As Ramos notes, in the face of 'an impressive collection of monographic works on Amazonian Indians' (482), in fact 'there are no Indians in general' (283), rather a diverse set with different linguistic affiliations and historical paths. The idealized 'Amazonian Indian' is itself an exotic artifact of anthropological theorizing, not of societies in 'their specific historical trajectories' (283). The second vital point of criticism from Ramos concerns Viveiros de Castro's (2004) use of the ventriloquism trope to claim that perspectivism amounts to an anthropology from within: "If perspectivism is an indigenous anthropology, it is so only vicariously, through the ethnographers' writings" (Ramos 2012: 490).

Turner (2009), in a long and focused piece, is intermittently critical of Viveiros de Castro (as well as Philippe Descola on the animist wing), but the extended attention he grants to perspectivist discussion offers a mitigating legitimation, the title itself ("The Crisis of Late Structuralism") conferring a questionable a gravity on the proceedings. The crisis is that the Lévi-Strauss Amazonian project did not produce the expected fruits—"unviability of his approach," "never able to define invariant constraints," "failure to find the structure of myth," "failure of the structuralist quest" (3). But then, "Perspectivism proceeded by turning Lévi-Strauss' reductionist propositions inside out through an equally radical but opposite reduction of nature to culture, achieved through the elevation of subjective perspective over objective associationism as the determining constituent of the "spiritual" identities of all creatures, animals and humans alike. The foundational claim of perspectivism is that indigenous

Amazonians believe that animals, as the archetypal "natural" creatures, sub-jectively identify themselves as humans, the archetypal cultural beings" (11). If the challenge taken by Lévi-Strauss' successors, and pursued in detail by Turner, seems particularly fraught, and the very premise of an interspecies theory of mind more a matter of wild and fruitless speculation, why examine it at such length?

This is the exoticism of an anthropological theory that seeks solace in rhe-torical play. In the same way that the headline exoticism of the Amazonian Indian stereotype can be peeled way by attending to the historical circum-stances of the emergence of that characterization, so may the exotic theory of perspectivism be peeled away. Anthropology, as a culture industry in which the validation of result is largely—not exclusively—achieved through internal regu-lation, matters of focal disciplinary concern tend to become more esoteric. The longish term shift of sociocultural anthropology away from a four-field context (however implausible full synthesis was) toward a social science and then toward an overtly hermeneutic framework has reduced intelligibility (transla-tion prospect) outside the field (as defined by dominant practitioners, depart-ments, publishing outlets). A foundational exotic is unavoidable in a field ostensibly looking outside its natal settings, and anthropology has contended with the contradictions generated by the uncertainty of the anthropological project from the outset. With perspectivism, the modicum of respectability guaranteed by some kind of affiliation with argument based on evidence that may be appraised outside the regulatory framework of anthropology itself seems to have waned. Anthropology has always been pretty ambitious and pro-miscuous (or just wide-ranging) in pursuing the 'science of humankind' brief, but as that (attenuated) 'science' is now to include all other animal subjectivi-ties, that is exotic indeed. I think I'll just have a word with my dog.

Stephen Nugent is Professor of Social Anthropology at Goldsmiths, University of London. He is the author of several books on Amazonian themes, including *Big Mouth* (1990), *Amazonian Caboclo Society* (1993), and *Scoping the Ama-zon: Image, Icon, Ethnography* (2007), and the editor of *Critical Anthropology: Foundational Works* (2012). For a number of years he has convened the film-making program in the Department of Anthropology at Goldsmiths..

Notes

1. Similarly, one might wonder about an 'anthropology of the South'. If anthropology is a historical product of the expansion of capitalism from a European core, is not an anthropology of the South qualitatively quite a different project, not just an extension? 'Exotic no more' may also be a paraphrase of Latour's claim that "we have never been modern."

2. 'Studying up' continues to be an exotic goal. What is actually achieved, more often, is only access to kitsch exotic, such as *Lifestyles of the Rich and Famous*.

3. As a euphemism in common parlance, exotic now has such a range of connotations that merely being 'outside' indicates little that can stand without further explication. The exoticism of pets, plants, dancing, haircuts, underwear, and minerals—to mention but a few—does not necessarily acknowledge the priority of the authoritative, anthropological rendering.

4. An ugly but necessary neologism for present purposes.

5. While shrunken heads used to be widely found in museum displays, this is no longer the case, mainly in recognition of the personhood of what were previously held to be exotic material objects. (And the same pertains for other human remains.) Not all such interventions of anthropological expertise into public spheres are as straightforward. FGM, for example, provokes conflicted commentary from professional anthropologists.

6. It is now well recognized that many exotic peoples themselves were and are active in the process of exoticization in advance of the exotic's achieving its current problematic status within professional anthropology. Jewelry manufacturing by Southwestern Indian groups and Inuit carving are but two well-documented examples. In Evans and Glass's (2014) *Return to the Land of the Head Hunters*, the extent of Kwakitutl collaboration with Curtis in the cinematic portrayal of their lives raises interesting questions about the linked processes of documentation and exoticization.

7. Bruce Parry's *Tribe* television series embodies, for some anthropologists, an outstandingly abusive appropriation. Disney's 1957 *Perri* achieved a similar effect in transforming the natural history documentary into an entertainment format.

8. Jonathan Crary's *24/7* provocatively suggests that only sleep remains beyond reach of commodification.

9. One could look, for example, at what anthropology is reviewed in the *LRB* or *NYRB*.

10. Witness the reception of Tierney's *Darkness in El Dorado* (2000) and the professional preoccupation with the impact the book was likely to have on public perceptions of anthropology. For an account by a non-anthropologist, see historian Dreger's (2011) report.

11. In the past, when fieldworkers—anecdotally, at least—chose to remain with their subjects they were regarded as having lost their anthropological perspective—gone over to the other side, gone 'native', in unreconstructed parlance. From the vantage point(s) of a multiple ontology position, presumably, the other side is both a reasonable place to be and one that can coexist happily with not being on the other side. A familiar objection to this is that if one can tolerate two ontologies, there must be a commonality that permits such a bifurcated stance, in which case there must be some translation possibility, i.e., synthetic effacing of ontological breach. The standard response to that objection takes the form of (1) you just don't get it, or (2) we're just playing with ideas here. The informal appropriation of the exotic in graduate departments of anthropology in the 1970s, in London, included homeopathic and sometimes slightly ridiculous statements of alliance with exotic others (a fellow fresh from Papua New Guinea would stick a match through his nose at

parties; one department, it is said, had an annual gathering at which attendees would appear in the garb of their field exotics). And few can resist including in their domestic space tchotchkes from the field.

12. It was not until the introduction of soya in the late twentieth century that intensive agriculture succeeded. Previous attempts—cacao and rubber among them—succumbed to forms of predation characteristic of this environmental regime.

13. The 'revisionist' literature is extensive and authoritative. In terms of demography, Denevan has been most influential. For an extensive summary, see Roosevelt (2014).

14. All census figures are open to dispute: Ribeiro (1967) predicted that the Brazilian Indian would be extinct by the end of the twentieth century; the Aborigines Protection Society Report of 1972 (Brooks et al. 1973) provided an estimate of 50,000; the Instituto Socioambiental is currently the source with most likely accurate estimates.

15. 'Forest-dwelling' may contain a greater connotative load than is at first apparent: until the construction of the Trans-Amazonian Highway network (commencing 1970), access to the Brazilian Amazon was fluvial, and even in that respect impeded on many major tributaries by rapids. Hence, Indians already in the interior or who fled there were more insulated from the depredations of white societies. The carrying capacity of upland forest (see Fearnside 1986).

16. See Turner (2009) for an insightful discussion of Lévi-Strauss's theoretical development in relation to Amazonian materials.

17. For an extended discussion, see Nugent (2007).

18. The images he provides for illustration purposes are more than faintly ridiculous given his naturalistic claims: natives lounging on frond-decorated plinths.

19. One of the associated features of Amazonian biodiversity is the appearance of a generalized 'tropical regime' as a result of low species density/high species variety. While there is discernable variation in the concentrations of species, overall there is a relative uniformity, unlike, say, the case in landscapes occupied by North American indigenes. As a consequence, there is a predisposition to stereotypical representation of the 'nature-culture' contrast as it applies to 'green hell' and the 'noble savage' in Amazonia.

20. Compare, for example, mainstream reporting on actual condition of Indians that provided sightings of naked Indians shooting arrows at overflying airplanes.

21. Closely associated with the work of the late Darrell Posey, the concept now looks more aspirational than actual.

22. The 'wise forest manager' characterization makes a claim for distinctive knowledge embedded in a 'pure' indigenous actor (as distinguished from the peasant-with-a-chainsaw). See see Balick and Posey (2006) for a variety of contributions to this discussion. In relation to the idealization of 'native knowledge' evident in some Amazonian material, Atran et al.'s (1999) study of the association between indigeneity and 'management' skills among Mayan groups in Guatemala challenges crucial assumptions about the culture-knowledge link.

23. This is hardly to deny the importance that the notion of the exotic continues to play in anthropological discourse as well as more general realms. When Chico Mendes, for instance, joined the Environmental Defense Fund in fundraising in the United States in the 1980s, he was presented as a green man from the forest, which indeed he was, not as a Communist trade union organizer, which he also was said to be.

24. In Brazil, in contrast to the United States and Canada, commonly invoked for comparative purposes, it is generally the view that one can remain 'properly' Indian only if one lives in an Indian society. Mario Juruna, the first (Akwe-Xavante) Indian to hold the elected office of federal deputy in the National Congress Brazil, was initially denied a passport to travel to the Netherlands to attend the Russell Tribunal

in 1980 on the grounds that he represented Indians (and even then, only his own group) and not Brazil. For more discussion, see Ramos (1998).

25. This discussion is justifiably, to my mind, brief. It might even be said to be prophylactically brief in the belief that many of the perspectivist claims do not justify as much attention and that, indeed, criticism has already has gone too far in legitimating the premises of such claims. While there is a seduction in the complex language employed to mount the mutually sympathetic perspectivist/animist/ontological claims, the evidence required to proceed much beyond the claims of an interspecies theory of mind simply does not exist.

26. Latour (2009) provides a guide to the relative contributions of Viveiros de Castro and Descola, the two most prominent contributors to the perspectivist/multiple ontologies intervention in anthropology (alongside Latour himself and, it might be said, Strathern).

27. One might imagine that if one were capable of maintaining/coexisting in/tolerating two different ontologies, there must be the capacity to recognize that difference, in which case one might wonder about an ontology accessible from another ontology.

28. In this early, programmatic account of perspectivism, there is an uneasy equation of 'cosmology' and 'ontology'. Cosmological difference—as between an anthropologist's understanding of subjective agency and that of an Amazonian Indian—is a familiar territory (one doesn't have to believe in witches in order to appreciate how someone else might), but the ontological claim is far more severe and bears the weight of the claim that Amazonian Indians represent a different kind of human species. Viveiros de Castro writes (2004: 7): "Therefore, the aim of perspectivist translation—translation being one of shamanism's principal tasks, as we know (Carneiro da Cunha 1998)—is not that of finding a 'synonym' (a co-referential representation) in our human conceptual language for the representations that other species of subject use to speak about one and the same thing. Rather, the aim is to avoid losing sight of the difference concealed within equivocal 'homonyms' between our language and that of other species, since we and they are never talking about the same thing. This idea may at first sound slightly counterintuitive, for when we start thinking about it, it seems to collapse into its opposite."

29. A crude gloss, but such is the gap between cultural/constructivist and cognitive/materialist that the designation will suffice here.

References

Atran, Scott, Douglas Medin, Norbert Ross, Elizabeth Lynch, John Coley, Edilberto Ucan Ek', and Valentina Vapnarsky. 1999. "Folkecology and Commons Management in the Maya Lowlands." *Proceedings of the National Academy of the Sciences* 96, no. 13: 7598–7603.

Balick, Michael J., and Darrell Addison Posey, eds. 2006. *Human Impacts on Amazonia: The Role of Traditional Ecological Knowledge in Conservation and Development.* New York: Columbia University Press.

Blaut, J. M. 1993. *The Colonizer's Model of the World.* New York: Guilford Press.

Bloch, Maurice. 2011. "The Blob." *Anthropology of This Century* 1. http://aotcpress.com/articles/blob/.

Bossert, Frederico, and Diego Villar. 2013. *Hijos de la Selva | Sons of the Forest.* Ed. Viggo Mortensen. Santa Monica, CA: Percevel Press.

Brooks, Edwin, Rene Fuerst, John Hemming, and Francis Huxley. 1973. *Tribes of the Amazon Basin in Brazil 1972: Report by the Aborigines Protection Society*. London: Charles Knight.

Crary, Jonathan. 2013. *24/7: Late Capitalism and the Ends of Sleep*. London: Verso.

Denevan, William M. 1992. "The Pristine Myth: The Landscape of the Americas in 1492." *Annals of the Association of American Geographers* 82, no. 3: 369–385.

Doyle, A. Conan. 1912. *The Lost World*. London: Hodder & Stoughton.

Dreger, Alice. 2011. "Darkness's Descent on the American Anthropological Association: A Cautionary Tale." *Human Nature* 22, no. 3: 225–246.

Evans, Brad, and Aaron Glass, eds. 2014. *Return to the Land of the Head Hunters: Edward S. Curtis, the Kwakwaka'wakw, and the Making of Modern Cinema*. Seattle: Bill Holm Center for the Study of Northwest Coast Art & University of Washington Press.

Fearnside, Philip M. 1986. *Human Carrying Capacity of the Brazilian Rainforest*. New York: Columbia University Press.

Hayes, E. Nelson, and Tanya Hayes, eds. 1970. *Claude Lévi-Strauss: The Anthropologist as Hero*. Cambridge, MA: MIT Press.

Heckenberger, Michael J. 2005. *The Ecology of Power: Culture Place and Personhood in the Southern Amazon, A.D. 1000–2000*. London: Routledge.

im Thurn, E. F. 1893. "Anthropological Uses of the Camera." *Journal of the Anthropological Institute of Great Britain and Ireland* 22: 184–203.

Kapferer, Bruce. 2013. "How Anthropologists Think: Configurations of the Exotic." *Journal of the Royal Anthropological Institute* 19, no. 4: 813–836.

Lathrap, Donald W. 1968. "The 'Hunting' Economies of the Tropical Forest Zone of South American: An Attempt at Historical Perspective." Pp. 23–29 in *Man the Hunter*, ed. Richard B. Lee and Irven Devore. Chicago: Aldine.

Latour, Bruno. 2009. "Perspectivism: 'Type' or 'Bomb'?" *Anthropology Today* 25, no. 2: 1–2.

Lévi-Strauss, Claude. [1955] 1973. *Tristes Tropiques*. Trans. John and Doreen Weightman. New York: Atheneum.

Lévi-Strauss, Claude. [1962] 1966. *The Savage Mind*. London: Weidenfeld & Nicolson.

Lévi-Strauss, Claude. [1964] 1969. *The Raw and the Cooked*. London: Harper & Row.

Lévi-Strauss, Claude. [1966] 1973. *From Honey to Ashes*. New York: Harper & Row.

Lévi-Strauss, Claude. [1968] 1978. *The Origin of Table Manners*. New York: Harper Colophon.

MacClancy, Jeremy, ed. 2002. *Exotic No More: Anthropology on the Front Lines*. Chicago: University of Chicago Press.

Meggers, Betty J. 1971. *Amazonia: Man and Culture in a Counterfeit Paradise*. Chicago: Aldine.

Nimuendajú, Curt. 2004. *In Pursuit of a Past Amazon: Archaeological Researches in the Brazilian Guyana and in the Amazon Region*. Compiled and trans. S. Rydén and P. Stenborg. Gothenburg: Världskulturmuseet.

Nugent, Stephen. 2007. *Scoping the Amazon: Image, Icon, Ethnography*. Walnut Creek, CA: Left Coast Press.

Price, Sally. 1989. *Primitive Art in Civilized Places*. Chicago: University of Chicago Press.

Ramos, Alcida R. 1994. "The Hyperreal Indian." *Critique of Anthropology* 14, no. 2: 153–171.

Ramos, Alcida R. 1998. *Indigenism: Ethnic Politics in Brazil*. Madison: University of Wisconsin Press.

Ramos, Alcida R. 2012. "The Politics of Perspectivism." *Annual Review of Anthropology* 41: 481–494.

Ribeiro, Darcy. 1967. "Indigenous Cultures and Languages of Brazil." Pp. 77–165 in *Indians of Brazil in the Twentieth Century*, ed. Janice H. Hopper. Washington, DC: Institute of Cross-Cultural Research.

Rondon, Cândido. 1953. *Indios do Brasil*. 3 vols. Rio de Janeiro: Conselho Nacional de Proteção aos Indios.

Roosevelt, Anna C. 1991. *Moundbuilders of the Amazon: Geophysical Archaeology on Marajo Island, Brazil*. New York: Academic Press.

Roosevelt, Anna C. 2014. "The Amazon and the Anthropocene: 13,000 Years of Human Influence in a Tropical Rainforest." *Anthropocene* 4: 69–87.

Schaan, Denise P. 2011. *Sacred Geographies of Ancient Amazonia*. Walnut Creek, CA: Left Coast Press.

Schoepf, Daniel. 2000. *George Huebner, 1862–1935: Un photographe a Manaus*. Geneva: Musée d'ethnographie.

Sontag, Susan. 1963. "A Hero of Our Time." *New York Review of Books*, 28 November. http://www.nybooks.com/articles/1963/11/28/a-hero-of-our-time/.

Sperber, Dan. 1975. *Rethinking Symbolism*. Cambridge: Cambridge University Press.

Sperber, Dan. 1985. *On Anthropological Knowledge*. Cambridge: Cambridge University Press.

Sperber, Dan. 1986. *Explaining Culture: A Naturalistic Approach*. Oxford: Blackwell.

Steward, Julian H., and Louis C. Faron, eds. 1959. *Native Peoples of South America*. New York: McGraw Hill.

Tierney, Patrick. 2000. *Darkness in El Dorado: How Scientists and Journalists Devastated the Amazon*. New York: W. W. Norton.

Trouillot, Michel-Rolph. 2003. *Global Transformations: Anthropology and the Modern World*. London: Palgrave Macmillan.

Turner, Terence S. 2009. "The Crisis of Late Structuralism, Perspectivism and Animism: Rethinking Culture, Nature, Spirit, and Bodliness." *Tipití* 7, no. 1: 3–42.

Viveiros de Castro, Eduardo. 2004. "Perspectival Anthropology and the Method of Controlled Equivocation." *Tipití* 2, no. 1: 3–22.

Wilcken, Patrick. 2011. *Claude Lévi-Strauss: The Poet in the Laboratory*. London: Bloomsbury.

Wilson, Bryan R., ed. 1970. *Rationality*. New York: Harper & Row.

Wolf, Eric R. 1982. *Europe and the People Without History*. Berkeley: University of California Press.

Chapter 4

LIVING THE LI(F)E
Negotiating Paradise in Southern Sri Lanka

Maurice Said

Toward the end of my first year of doctoral fieldwork in 2012, I had just moved into Sunil's[1] house in the village of Po in the southern Sri Lankan district of Matara. Sunil ran a guesthouse that in part also served as his home where he lived with his wife and daughter. One day at the end of October 2012, I decided to treat myself and brought home a bottle of wine I had purchased from an off-license store in the main town. Sunil picked up the bottle, surveyed it closely, brought it up, to his nose and asked, "This is wine, no? For women only?" I confirmed that it was indeed wine but that both men and women drank it. He gave me an unconvinced look and added, "But we drink this not to get drunk, no? This one only for the taste!" Sunil's brother Lasantha had given me a lift to town on his motorbike and now walked up behind me after placing his helmet on the ground. He chimed in, stating that it must be for women because it was very light in alcoholic content, had no acrid taste, and was very expensive (a bottle cost 1,500 rupees, or around 9 euros at the time of writing). This comment pointed to what the men often said about women with regard to alcohol, an association of women with being weak (like wine) and flamboyant with money—both Lasantha and Sunil had stated that women spend extravagant amounts on the upkeep of the house and clothes but on nothing

Notes for this chapter begin on page 98.

useful or worthwhile, like the men do. I told Lasantha that Peter *mahathmayā*,[2] a wealthy and powerful English man who lived in a beachside villa in the next village also drank wine. Both looked up in interest upon hearing this and asked if they too could try some wine. If Peter *mahathmayā* drank wine, then it must be a prestigious drink and one worthy of a man, and a man of status at that.

Peter, a British expatriate, had coordinated numerous relief projects from 2005 to 2007 in southern Sri Lanka in aid of those affected by the 2004 Asian tsunami. He had lived in his beachside villa in the south since the early 2000s and had been relatively unknown locally until the disaster struck. His generosity and deep involvement in the rehabilitation efforts in the immediate aftermath had made him a household name along the southern coastal strip yet also something of an enigma. He kept very much to himself, and locals in neighboring villages mythologized his wealth and power (see Salazar 2012). As Gilberto Velho (2001) has indicated, that which is in proximity to us is not necessarily familiar and may turn out to be more exotic than that which is at a greater distance to us.

In this chapter I analyze the relationships and interactions between expatriates, travelers, and local Sinhalese in southern Sri Lanka in the aftermath of the Asian tsunami of 2004. The disaster received unparalleled media attention, and millions of dollars in aid poured into the country. In the process, aid distribution altered the Sri Lankan landscape and reversed the power relations between locals and foreigners, where outsiders became gift givers and locals were beneficiaries of aid and relief (Gamburd 2014; Stirrat and Henkel 1997). Through the distribution of aid and the experience of the disaster, coastal Sri Lankans were depicted as vulnerable, poor, and unable to cope without help from the outside world, whereas foreigners were depicted as wealthy and powerful. I specifically explore the persistence of these latter perceptions and the misplaced expectations of the Other that emerge as a result of the experience of the tsunami aftermath. How is identity renegotiated in light of diverging expectations of the Other?

The experience of the Other is often preceded by a preconception and expectation of that experience (see Bruner 2005). Tourists traveling to exotic locations may expect to replicate preestablished imaginaries they have of the place and people they are visiting, or of themselves in that place. The case studies I present here illustrate two aspects of this type of exoticization and counter-exoticization. Following on the work of Edward Bruner, I highlight the ways "narratives are structures of power" (1986: 144) that emerge from dominant political processes, in this case post-tsunami recovery. In this respect, the case studies I present here highlight the ways post-tsunami narratives of the powerful foreigner and the vulnerable, uncivilized local versus the cunning local and gullible foreigner are utilized as both empowering and disempowering lacunae in the imaginary of the self. Thus, exoticization and counter-exoticization are seen here as a reciprocal process (Theodossopoulos 2014), as well as counter-reactions used both to empower and disempower.

As highlighted by Bruce Kapferer and Dimitrios Theodossopoulos in the introduction, Exoticization "presupposes an awareness of Otherness" or the creation of a category of difference (Bhattacharyya, chap. 6). In addition, I posit that exoticization and counter-exoticization constitute a mutual process between groups and individuals whereby identities of Self and Other are constantly being negotiated and renegotiated (see Lefkaditou, chap. 5). In this mutual process, individuals involved actively conceal aspects of themselves and build on imaginaries of the Other to redefine the Self in juxtaposition to Other. Thus, the interrelationality of counter-exoticization imposes conflicting imaginaries of both Self and Other.

Developing Paradise after the Asian Tsunami

Both the villages of Po and Thomale had suffered severe losses as a result of the Asian tsunami of 26 December 2004. More than 35,000 people were killed and more than half a million were displaced by the tsunami in Sri Lanka alone (Frerks and Klem 2005). In Matara District a total of 1,088 people were killed and 29,550 displaced by the disaster (Ruhuna University 2005). Although equally affected by the wave, both villages received unequal degrees of aid and assistance. Po, with its scenic coastline, wide-open spaces, and the odd remnant of the colonial era concealed within foliage-ridden nooks, represented a cradle for investment, especially 'outsider' investment, as a site imbued with all of the characteristics that might see those investments further developed. Thomale, on the other hand, was a stretch of intersecting broken pathways running along a crocodile-infested riverbank and flanked at its other end by a ridge of jagged rocks and murky brown sea frothing violently at their base. Half of the village is an extended fish market, a ground strewn with entrails, and air suffused with the lingering odor of fish and any other scents that the busy end of the river donated. The fact that the large majority of families in Thomale are composed of fishermen has allowed it to remain somewhat walled in as a community, geographically, and socially bounded and distinct. This is further aided by the dominant perception among Sinhalese in nearby localities, including the major towns, that fishermen are prone to violence and excessive drinking, and unpredictability, and thus to be avoided. It is taken as a given with certain forms of livelihoods, such as fishing, that drinking is an essential and inseparable social function, as even Michele Gamburd (2008), has noted. As a result, after the tsunami, most agencies and NGOs in the area that were looking to establish a base and projects turned their focus to Po at the expense of Thomale.

Many local families residing along the coast had lost their homes to the tsunami wave and had moved to IDP (internally displaced persons) camps further inland. In the weeks and months following the disaster, NGOs and aid started pouring into the affected areas. Some researchers and development practitioners (Gamburd 2014; Gunewardena 2008; Klein 2005; Leckie 2005; Stirrat 2006) have argued that the aftermath of the tsunami in Sri Lanka presented a unique opportunity for the further development of the tourist industry. This development was made possible, and allegedly encouraged, by a contentious policy laid down by the Government of Sri Lanka (GoSL), which imposed building restrictions within a 100 meter buffer zone along the coast of the disaster affected areas, restrictions from which tourism establishments were exempt (De Silva and Yamao 2007; Gamburd 2014; Gunewardena 2008; Kuhn 2010; Ruwanpura 2009). Apart from the buffer zone, a "duty free importation scheme" (Gunewardena 2008: 75) for materials required to restart or upgrade their businesses afforded the tourist industry uncontested claims to coastal space. Unable to utilize the housing aid available to them to rebuild their homes along the coast, many displaced families felt pressured to accept houses in housing projects outside of their villages, in many cases quite a distance from their original localities. Thwarted by the inability to rebuild their old homes, and in some cases owing to fear of another tsunami, numerous families sold their coastal land in the initial months following the disaster for much less than its actual worth. Much of this land was bought up and developed by entrepreneurs attached to the tourist industry. The increased availability of coastal land also saw an increase in the development of plots by foreigners for the construction of holiday properties and luxury homes.

The buffer zone was eventually reduced from 100 meters to 35 meters in early 2006 in the Matara District (Kuhn 2010: 46; Vaes and Goddeeris 2012: 4). Some locals who had accepted houses further inland had held onto their plots of land in their villages, in the hope that at some point in the future the government's policy would change, and maybe by then they would have the capital to rebuild their old homes (Gamburd 2014). In 2005 and 2006, I was working with an NGO in Po, a village of just over 600 households. By mid-2006 a foreign couple and an elderly Swedish man had purchased plots of coastal land in Po and began building houses. By the time I returned in 2008 for a six-month stretch of fieldwork, the number of foreign-owned houses had increased to five, and another four houses were being rented out by foreigners at exorbitant rates by Sri Lankan standards. Villagers who owned coastal land had identified the economic benefits of selling their land to foreigners searching for their piece of paradise. Boštjan Kravanja writing about conceptions of paradise in southern Sri Lanka states, "Paradise serves as a powerful trope for discovering and then experiencing the perfect place where one can escape from the banal existence we live on a daily basis" (2012: 180). He notes that many tourists travel to Sri Lanka in search of an ideal and 'unspoiled destination' but are quickly disappointed by the manufactured element of the exotic reproduced by locals for the benefit of the tourist, and travelers quickly take their search elsewhere. Similarly, Jeremy MacClancy (2010) notes that the search for paradise often results in disappointment for many tourists and backpackers seeking the authentic local setting, untouched by the outside world. While Malcolm Crick (1991: 12–13) states that in their search for the 'Other', the exciting, and the different, tourists still feel the need to keep that safe distance and have some control over the encounter. The development of tropical paradise homes in coastal Sri Lanka may be one way to affect that control. Unlike the typical traveler or backpacker described by Kravanja, the expatriates I encountered were considerably older and possessed enough capital to purchase land and design a home that adhered to their imaginary of what a tropical paradise should resemble. Thus, instead of searching for paradise, they attempted to create it, and by creating it, they controlled it. The post-tsunami scenario offered favorable conditions for the accomplishment of such projects.

By 2008 the sale of coastal land to foreigners had become a profitable business for some local entrepreneurs in Po. Most of these entrepreneurs were already inserted in the tourist industry in one way or another, either as guesthouse owners, diving instructors, or small tour operators. A number of local entrepreneurs acted as brokers between villagers who wanted to sell their land and the foreigners who wanted to purchase and develop that land. By 2008 they had also begun to engage local architects and masons to design and build homes for the foreigners they met. Through trial and error, local entrepreneurs learned to identify what foreigners were looking for in terms of a home and how to best promote their locality to them. In Po, villagers who owned guesthouses were in regular contact with foreigners and attempted to entice them into buying land in the village or one of the neighboring villages where their network of contacts extended. In many cases, potential buyers cultivated a close relationship with their local brokers, who even hosted them for free at their establishments or homes for the duration of their stay while they viewed the available plots of land. In other cases some foreigners were suspicious of their hosts and contracted outsiders to locate land for them. In this way they immediately alienated their future neighbors.

There were obvious advantages to having a local broker to aid in the acquisition of land. Under part 6 of the Finance Act (No. 11 of 1963), as amended in 2004 (Parliament of Sri Lanka 2004), approved foreign companies or individuals were allowed to purchase land in Sri Lanka subject to a 100 percent tax on the value of the property. While some foreigners had the capital and contacts available to purchase land under these conditions, most utilized the close friendships they developed with local brokers to register the property under their broker's name and avoid the taxes that came with the purchase. In the case of foreigners who built holiday homes, the property would be vacant for long periods of the year. Local brokers were allowed to rent out the property to tourists and keep the profits, in exchange for taking care of the maintenance of the properties. Since brokers in the context of Po were usually prominent local figures at the village level, registration of the property with them ensured its security from damage or looting. Brokers maintained close relationships with expatriates, recognizing that they would serve as character references for other foreigners intent on purchasing property in the same manner. Some villagers even partnered in business with their foreign friends.

Theodossopoulos notes that exoticization in the context of tourism can be a reciprocal process and states that "the host communities gradually develop their own versions of exoticization, as they categorize and stereotype the tourists" (2014: 57). His argument here is that recognizing this counter-exoticization by the hosts allows us to see them as more than passive agents, who instead utilize the encounter to renegotiate their own identities. In the context of post-tsunami coastal Sri Lanka, the disaster aftermath provided a platform for the enactment of different levels of exoticization and counter-exoticization. Theodossopoulos identifies two tropes to exoticization. The first is the view of the native as backward, uncivilized, and primitive. The second trope is that of the noble savage living in harmony with nature and their surroundings. In the context of post-tsunami Sri Lanka, the tendency I observed among expatriates and travelers was to adopt two adaptations to the first trope: (1) a view of villagers as vulnerable victims deserving empathy and friendship, and (2) a view of villagers as poor, uneducated, and savage, with whom one must always be on the alert—and in many cases a combination of these two views. The widespread contact with outsiders and the development post-tsunami had reduced the likely possibility of travelers or expatriates imagining an untouched paradise where villagers lived in harmony with their surroundings, oblivious to the outside world. In contrast I argue that villagers' interactions with expatriates reflect a counter-narrative to the stereotypes foreigners develop of them. These stereotypes emerged in no small way as a reaction to the publicity and media coverage surrounding the tsunami aftermath that portrayed locals as vulnerable and lacking agency (Gamburd 2014).

The competitive nature of aid distribution in the disaster aftermath (Stirrat 2006) motivated some villagers to develop elaborate narratives of personal loss and despair. In this way they appealed to charitable foreigners in the hope of receiving aid. Aid distribution also led many Sri Lankans to assume that all foreign visitors were wealthy and easily manipulated. Youths in Po would sometimes joke and boast with each other about who had come up with the most elaborate narratives to separate tourists and other foreigners from their money. A number of villagers in Po, particularly those attached to the tourist industry, disapprove of this deception and attribute the mounting distrust expressed by foreigners to its widespread practice. Thushara, a guesthouse owner in Po, claims that such actions are motivated by greed and a lack of shame and attributes this trend to the irresponsible distribution of aid post-tsunami. However, Thushara whose guesthouse was destroyed by the tsunami, regularly utilized photos of the damage he sustained to inspire sympathy in tourists and expatriates he conducted business with.

The context of the widespread distribution of aid has altered the nature of relationships between southern Sri Lankans and European visitors, such that the normally bounded tourist spaces of coastal Sri Lanka have been extended to incorporate previously untouched areas along the south coast. Rather than engaging fully with the villages they inhabit, expatriates who have moved into these localities develop their own version of an authentic tropical location as a way of consolidating their different perceptions of paradise. In response, villagers counter these perceptions through narratives of control.

In the following sections I illustrate some of the stereotypes that emerge out of this social distancing, as case studies in exoticization and counter-exoticization. A useful departure point in understanding the attempt by foreigners to create the ideal paradise, and their rejection of the native as a grotesque juxtaposition to the splendor of their environment, is to consider the narrative of Ovid's Pygmalion. Pygmalion was a Cypriot sculptor who, disgusted by witnessing the Propoetides reduced to prostitution, is put off women. He carves a statue out of ivory and names it Galatea, but so realistic is the statue that he falls in love with it. Ashamed of his desire for Galatea, he makes offerings to the goddess Aphrodite to grant him a woman in her likeness, and on returning home and clasping his sculpture he feels the ivory turn soft and into flesh. The story depicts Pygmalion's aversion to the immoral woman tainted by prostitution and leads him onto a search for the ideal, only the ideal comes from him, is controlled and shaped by him, and consumes him. Pygmalion, we are told, goes on to marry Galatea, has a son, and leads a happy life, but rarely does the myth become reality.

Modalities of Control

I was sitting in a cushioned wicker chair overlooking a garden teeming with color in a house located at the edge of a fishing village in southern Sri Lanka. At that moment, Marta stormed past the back porch, foaming at the mouth and spitting out curses in French. She paused as she reached the edge of the porch, turned her head, and glared at her husband. Switching to English, supposedly for my benefit, she told her husband, "Those fools! I told them not to block the road and now they come to lay the gravel—it's a small mountain in the middle, there is no way to go round it." Bertrand sighed as his wife made her way into the house and banged the door shut. He poured me another glass of beer and explained, "We knew they wanted to add gravel and make a section of the road, but we asked them to wait a few days. I told you we need to go to the airport to pick up some friends tomorrow morning, now the road is blocked so we surely cannot get out." He poured himself a beer and added, "They do this on purpose, you know, because we are the foreigners. You never see laborers on Sunday, and today they are working. It's a big coincidence. No? These people they are still so backward, they need some education. Why do they act like this with us?"

We were sitting on the patio leading to Bertrand's extensive garden, which was protected by a wall lined with a variety of local trees and plants to keep curious villagers out. His house is located 1.5 kilometers from the center of Thomale, a small fishing village of less than 600 households, located in the southern Sri Lankan district of Matara. It was early October 2012 when I found myself sitting in Bertrand's garden. I was 10 months into my doctoral fieldwork, which was being conducted between Thomale and the more tourist-oriented village of Po, 3 kilometers apart. Tensions had been high between Bertrand and the other villagers ever since he had built his house and moved in permanently a year earlier. His house had blocked off a popular drinking spot and he had refused to let locals pass. Bertrand and his wife had described the villagers to me as "backward fishermen who will try to cheat you every chance they get." I had been living in the same village for almost nine months by that time. I had not had similar experiences to Bertrand's. I had asked other villagers what they thought about Bertrand and his wife. Podi, a part-time fisherman, was puzzled by them. Podi was standing with his foot against a wall while I spoke to him, and two friends of his sat cross-legged below him leaning against the same wall. Podi explained that he found it odd that they had come to live in Thomale and not Po, where all the other foreigners lived. His friends nodded in agreement. He continued: "They came to live in our village and we thought they wanted to know us, maybe they liked our village. But then they built a big house with walls all around and many trees and they don't invite anyone. They come to our village but they keep the village out, then they always tell us 'don't do this' and 'don't go there'. The wife says she doesn't like fishermen so why did they build a house in *this* village?"

Bertrand had visited Sri Lanka in early 2008 with the intention of locating a piece of coastal land for development. He had visited the island twice since the tsunami and identified what he explained to be an opportunity to build his dream home, something he would never have been able to afford back in France. His garden is a sea of flowers and various fruit trees, and birdbaths had been placed at strategic intervals to attract exotic birds. As I walked through his garden for the first time that day in October 2012, he pointed around him and said, "Look at this. Look how beautiful; all of these plants are from this island. In the mornings and evenings it is full of birds; it's unbelievable. You see their [the villagers'] gardens and homes? They have all this beauty and they don't know how to use it."

As I sat sipping beer on Bertrand's back porch, Marta stormed back out with a new energy. I heard her shouting and cursing a few moments later, and I got up to peer round the side of the house. She was at the gate wagging her finger at a thin Sri Lankan man and another stocky local standing behind him. I heard her shout, "Ah you don't know? You think you can scare me with your police friend? I will call the embassy. We are not Sri Lankans; you will learn that with us you cannot pull these tricks. I will call the embassy now!" At the mention of embassy, both men appeared panicked and began waving their hands about and apologizing. Bertrand had joined the group and there was some muffled talk between them, followed by an audible "OK, Madam, I'm sorry Madam, OK." I walked up to the gate as the group disappeared down the path. A group of local men began frantically shoveling gravel from a mound on the path into the adjoining gardens. After catching sight of the operation I quickly scuttled back to the table, overcome by an inexplicable feeling of awkwardness and embarrassment.

Bertrand's efforts at creating a little corner for himself, his own epitome of a tropical paradise, have all been to an extent centered on control. The land was cleared and developed, and every detail in his property meticulously designed and coordinated. The act of enclosing the property is also an attempt at giving it a bounded and impenetrable quality. Christoph Hennig (2002) asserts that the tourist's conception of paradise is not only one composed of natural beauty but also includes particularities of otherness displayed by the native. Contrarily, expatriates in southern Sri Lanka are intent on recreating a controlled niche teeming with particularities of its own but that shuts out the native. The tensions with Bertrand's neighbors and other villagers seem to stem from his inability to control them or their actions. They stand in stark opposition to the world he is trying to create within his walls. He depicts the villagers as violent, uneducated, and uncivilized, whereas his home is a microcosm of the beauty reflected in the landscape that he deems the locals are unable to appreciate and that mirrors colonial accounts of the splendor of the landscape juxtaposed against the savagery of the native (Kravanja 2012).

Jagath, Bertrand's neighbor and a day laborer, explained the incident with Bertrand and his wife to me. Residents in the area had been complaining to the relevant authorities for a while that they needed to get the road paved. Finally, approval was given, but due to lack of funds an agreement was reached in which the materials and machinery for paving the road would be donated, but residents would have to perform most of the initial labor. Since the roller would be turning up the next morning, residents decided to prepare the road the afternoon before (Sunday). Podi, translating for Jagath and another neighbor, said, "See this is also their road now, but they do not help. Our friend, who was helping us and is a policeman, went up to talk to Madam when she started shouting. He told her, 'Madam, I am with the police …' then she started screaming, so we said, OK we will clear the road."

Jagath explained that they had tried to be friendly with them, but Bertrand and Marta were always angry and called them liars. Podi said, "It's possible other people lie to them, but we did nothing to them. They think that they can do what they want here. When they left with the car, we put the gravel back in the road and we left it there for three days. When they came back in the evening they were very angry, they couldn't find anyone to shout at, but we could see them. This is our village." It was only weeks later that I found out from Podi that Jagath and the other residents had not really put the gravel back in the road, out of fear of the repercussions, but had asked Podi to help them save face when relating the story to me.

Jagath and Bertrand's other neighbors were part of a strong social network—they were capable of mustering support from other villagers, they had friends in the police—and the village had a reputation for violence and toughness. Yet, when it came to confronting the foreigners in their village, they hesitated out of fear and fabricated a narrative of the event, perhaps a narrative of the way they had hoped to handle the situation. When I asked Podi what repercussions they feared, he explained that foreigners had a lot of influence; they could appeal to powers that were inaccessible to them such as their embassies. Podi explained, "After the tsunami there were many NGOs and foreigners in Matara District. They took many of the decisions and big people in the towns listened to them." He also suggested that many foreigners didn't like the fishermen. Why else would they exclude Thomale from receiving aid and give to other places like Po? Some villagers, Podi explained, associated foreigners with NGOs and resented them as a result. Some may have even been unfriendly to Bertrand and Marta.

The narrative provided by Jagath and the other villagers could be seen as an attempt to convey that they were taking control of their space. It may be seen as an apt metaphor for the politics of space being enacted here. Bertrand and Marta altered the land to develop a microcosmic ideal of what a tropical paradise should look like, in response to which locals altered the land to create an obstruction to that ideal. In their narrative the path was cleared to allow them to leave but blocked to prevent the foreign couple from reaching their ideal (enclosure). Seen this way, their narrative reflects the couple's own perception that the only impediment to their vision of paradise is the local and his/her interactions with them. Further, Jagath emphasizes the fact that they can't be found or contacted but yet are there casting their gaze. What is seen is not necessarily known but may become familiar (Velho 2001), just as foreigners were regularly seen as part of the post-tsunami landscape but were far from contact, at least to villagers in Thomale. The animosity between the foreign couple and the villagers is also a reflection of locals' view of the political hierarchy in the aftermath of the tsunami. In adopting a submissive stance to Bertrand and Marta's challenge, the villagers accept the foreign couple's superior status and their own vulnerability.

In the next section I present a case study from Po that illustrates an inverted situation to that in Thomale. Some villagers in Po have managed to utilize foreigners and their investments for their own benefit by employing strategies adapted from post-tsunami interactions with foreigners in their areas and the heightened competitiveness between those involved in the distribution of aid.

Competitive Subversion

While a number of foreign individuals, couples, and even families live in the village of Po for most of the year, the majority have built holiday homes where they spend only a short period of time every year. When these properties are vacant, they are entrusted to Lasantha's care. Lasantha is a guesthouse owner in Po who has managed to establish numerous close connections with foreigners over the years, including brokering the purchase of coastal land under his name. In return they allow him to rent rooms out to tourists when his guesthouse is full or when a large group of tourists is looking to rent a private property. On many occasions he, his brother, and their friends also use these properties to get away from their wives and have a drink.

Foreigners who have bought property and spend only short periods of time in the area every year are an important capital generating source to Lasantha and his family as a result of their property. Their house provides additional income and is also a place where covert activities take place and socialization of a different nature happens. The very fact that it is a foreign-owned property guarantees a certain amount of privacy, allowing activities that would not normally be accepted in the village space to occur undisturbed and to a degree unquestioned within its walls. It is both a part of the village and at the same time closed off to it. Thus, in this way, while some foreigners create homes representative of their ideal tropical setting, villagers use these same properties to enact their ideals, of covertness and concealment, from family and village.

In October 2012 Sunil, the local guesthouse owner introduced at the beginning of the chapter, invited me for a drink. He was visibly excited and informed me that in two weeks Gareth would be visiting for a month. Gareth, an English businessman, had known Sunil and his family since just before the tsunami and in 2010 with the aid of Sunil's younger brother Asanka, had bought a plot

of coastal land to build a boutique hotel. Asanka hired the masons and laborers, and his wife, a civil engineer, drafted the plans for the building. His father,
Hamzi, supervised the works. Hamzi told me, "You have to be careful; these
masons are thieves. You must always watch. When you're not looking they
steal materials for their own home." Asanka agreed to reserve the entire hotel
for Gareth when he visited, and for the rest of the year he would rent it out to
tourists and keep the profits himself.

The hotel was completed in early 2011 and decorated with enlarged photos
from Gareth's numerous travel destinations. It had a spacious lawn that spread
down to the sea and a private beach, with a small stretch of garden at one end
concealed by two walls and a gazebo. It is an ideal site for socialization. Being
an upmarket tourist establishment (at least for this area), it discourages other
villagers and wives from coming in, and the stretch of concealed garden at the
end allows for almost complete privacy. Most nights, men would collect at that
end of the garden and drink. Asanka utilized the hotel as a socialization point
to further his links with local businessmen and politicians.

When Gareth returned in late October 2012, he had moved into his hotel—
which had then ceased to cater to tourists, except when Sunil's brother Lasantha's place was full. Gareth ordered numerous cases of beer upon arrival and
invited Sunil, his local family members, and friends for drinks. At that time
Wilhelm, a retired Dutch man who had known the family for 25 years, was
visiting for two weeks. He had visited twice a year, every year since first coming to the village. I had met him numerous times, and each time he had been
introduced to me as 'uncle Wil'. Sunil had said, "He is like my uncle, like my
father's brother—he always stays at my house." However, on this occasion I
bumped into him having a meal at Lasantha's home and was surprised to see
him there. He told me he had gone straight to Sunil's but did not find anyone,
so he stayed at their mother's house that also catered as a guest house. When
Sunil passed by to visit his parents, Wilhelm welcomed and embraced him and
asked if he had a room available, to which Sunil said, "No—the place is full." It
came as a shock, as before I had any knowledge of this conversation, I blurted
out that I was the only person staying at Sunil's.

Wilhelm looked flustered and said, "It's that Gareth again; he is here so
they don't have any time for anyone else—Sunil is always going where there
is money. I love him like a brother, but he thinks only about his wallet. Three
days I have been trying to meet him and calling for a drink, but he says he is
always busy. I know where he is, drinking with Gareth, but they never join us
when he is here." Since Gareth had arrived five days earlier, Sunil was rarely
ever at home and spent every evening drinking with Gareth. Gareth had given
him money to restore his guesthouse. As more time passed a clear rift began to
develop between Gareth and the group of expatriates and regular visitors staying
in the village. Villagers praised him, and foreigners denounced him as arrogant.

One week after Gareth's arrival, he was invited to Sunil's for dinner and I
was asked to join. Gareth was accompanied by four British friends who were
visiting for a week. I introduced myself and sat down opposite. A number of
villagers had joined, and Gareth made a point of greeting each by name, asking

after their families and introducing them loudly to his friends, who sat in awe of his familiarity with villagers. Throughout the evening he dominated the discussion with accounts of his travels and exploits, inviting others at intervals to share their stories. Following dinner, he asked Sunil about the local situation and if there were any problems, adopting the pose of a godfather hearing his clients' requests. Sunil narrated a feud between his wife and Lasantha's wife. Sunil claimed that his wife had been attacked by his brother's sister-in-law. He and his brother Lasantha had been out drinking and on returning home, Lasantha's sister-in-law had attacked Sunil, whose wife jumped to his defense. After hearing their version of the story Gareth said, "This is not right on her part; she should apologize. I am surprised they allowed this to happen; I will talk to them tomorrow." Gareth was quick to give an opinion and a solution—and it seemed that he saw himself very much as a mediator, a situation I found to be common among some expatriates settled in Po.

Lasantha told me that the whole family was very fond of Gareth, especially since he had returned just after the tsunami to aid in their recovery. However, his wife expressed irritation with his interference in their domestic affairs, especially the situation concerning her sister. She was more irritated at Sunil, who she was sure had done this purposely. To have scolded or fought with her family would have caused trouble for him and his brother, but not for Gareth. Effectively, Sunil had used Gareth as a pawn in his quest for vindication. When I asked Sunil about the situation between him and Wilhelm, he said, "I like him a lot and we have been friends for a long time, but Gareth is like family. I want to invite him to my house, but it's not nice if I have guests, then it's like a business not a home." When I asked Lasantha about the situation he said, "This is not true. Wilhelm is always there for Sunil and it's not right for him to treat him like this. Now that he knows he won't stay with Sunil anymore. Sunil is my brother, but he always thinks of money. Gareth is here for business; he's a nice man, but he's here for business."

Lasantha states that his family protects Gareth's investments in property while he is away, and although the kin idiom is utilized, it is merely a mutually beneficial economic relationship. He invests in land and property that they then utilize to reap a profit, employ other villagers in construction, and position themselves as providers of employment, while his property is protected through their sponsorship (the property is registered in their family name).

Unlike Thomale, Po benefited from continual projects and NGO presence in the aftermath of the tsunami. Villagers were acquainted with foreigners, and even though property had been destroyed, structures were in place for the revitalization of the tourist industry tied in with village life. Villagers' constant interactions with foreigners allowed them to identify the common trends, attitudes, perceptions, and orientations in foreign interactions with villagers and their locality. Although lacking in comparable economic capital, villagers were able to devise methods to retain control over their space. In the case of Gareth, his dependence on the local protection of his investment, as well as Sunil and his brothers' dependence on the extra capital generated by his property and gifts, allowed both parties an equal stake in the relationship. The brothers catered to

Gareth's ego, allowing him to dispense advice when it suited their purpose. The utilitarian value of the relationship is confirmed by Lasantha's assertion that even though he is a nice man he is just here for business, suggesting that even Gareth is knowledgeable of the superficiality of the relationship.

Negotiating Identity at a Distance

Exoticization and counter-exoticization in the contexts I discuss in this chapter can be understood as processes whereby imagination and experience collide to give shape to representations of the Self and the Other, and the Self through the Other. Although the experience of encountering the Other implies a series of transactions and social interactions between groups and individuals, the examples of mutual exoticization I present here suggest that these encounters are more self-oriented. Preestablished imaginaries of the Other are transacted through the mutual process of exoticization and counter-exoticization. In other words, the experience of the Other is constantly counteracted upon to redefine the Self in juxtaposition to the Other as inferior. This power play, I have shown, implies concealment of the Self and maintaining social distance from the Other.

In recent years, an increasing number of studies (Fechter 2005, 2007; Knowles 2000; Korpela 2013; Leonard 2010) have dealt with the subject of Euro/American expatriates living in Asia and Africa. Anne-Meike Fechter (2005, 2007) illustrates how Euro/American expatriates in Jakarta are made conscious of their 'whiteness' on a daily basis through the constant pursuant gaze of Indonesians and the deployment of specific terms by locals to distinguish them as white Others. She notes that "gazes exchanged between foreigners and 'locals' can certainly be conceived of as a visual dialogue which can become very lopsided" (2005: 91). Fechter's argument may very well be seen as a statement that exoticization is never unidirectional—in other words, that both groups in her study, expatriates and Indonesians, negotiate identities of Self and Other at a distance. For the expatriate subjected to the scrutinizing gaze of the local, the experience is the cause of embarrassment and awkwardness rooted in the realization that they are being singled out as a category of white Other, and their desire to distance themselves from this identity being attributed to them. Fechter (2005) details how expatriates go to great lengths to create boundaries between themselves and locals, framing the local as childlike, uneducated, and racist in a bid to recraft themselves in contrast to the Indonesian Other and thus reclaim power or moral superiority. The Othering gaze is indicative of a social distance between outsider and local where the Self is mobilized in juxtaposition to an imagined Other.

In this chapter I have shown that the mutual exoticization of groups in coastal Sri Lanka was shaped by different experiences of the tsunami aftermath. The tsunami destroyed swathes of southern coastline, and villages were quickly inundated by a steady flow of foreign aid workers, tourists and curious travelers. Po's scenic beaches and benign environment conformed to the Western ideal of a tropical paradise, while Thomale did not. In Thomale, foreign organizations denied villagers aid and rendered them invisible through absence of attention. Villagers spoke of foreigners as having access to powers that were beyond their reach. The foreign couple who moved into their village erected walls around their property and adorned them with local trees, placing themselves beyond villagers' reach and in the process shutting off access to a popular drinking spot. For Bertrand's neighbors, this act paralleled their experience of foreigners in the tsunami aftermath—they were powerful and beyond contact, allowing themselves to be scrutinized only from a distance. Jagath's narrative emphasizes the latter—villagers gaze at the couple from the shadows, unseen. Exoticization, in the contexts I describe in this chapter, implies a negotiation of identities of Self and Other across a vast gulf of social distance. Through their narrative of the conflict, villagers in Thomale attempt to redefine themselves by depicting the foreign couple as powerless and under their control. Conversely, Bertrand's attempt at creating his epitome of a tropical paradise home involved transforming land in a locality that, in the Western imagination, does not conform to the ideal exotic tropical setting. Bertrand's efforts are in fact geared at shutting out any reminders of this imperfection, in this case his local neighbors. In Po, the investment that poured in following the tsunami allowed for the development of luxury foreign homes along its coast and a community of wealthy expatriates and foreign visitors who gave shape to the ideal of an exotic tropical setting. In Thomale, Bertrand was alone and surrounded by villagers who resented their exclusion by foreign investors and visitors.

The aftermath of the tsunami in Sri Lanka consolidated the image of the vulnerable, poor, and uncivilized coastal Sri Lankan, as a result of the widespread media images showing helpless villagers among the destruction of the tsunami. Po's exotic image as an ideal tropical setting allowed villagers to draw on this imaginary to forge relations with expatriates and sell them their piece of paradise. Villagers in Po also view foreigners as wealthy and powerful. However, unlike in Thomale, their extended experience of dealing with foreigners made them more attuned to foreign expectations of the Other. Rather than adopt a narrative of power and control, they portray themselves as submissive and docile, inviting foreigners to invest in properties that villagers will then benefit from for most of the year and through which they may enact their own ideals. As a result, foreigners are viewed as easily manipulated and youths are scolded when they do not sufficiently conceal this widespread perception. Villagers thus shape themselves as powerless while foreigners such as Gareth take on a role of superiority, crafting an image of himself as the benevolent village patron in front of his friends, all the while unaware that he is being used as a pawn to further individual interests. Foreign visitors resent Gareth as he draws local attention away from them, and Wilhelm portrays him as arrogant and Sunil as greedy, in the process redefining himself as their opposite and moral superior. The examples I have presented here illustrate that although exoticization is a process of Othering, it is also an act of self-definition through the framing of the Other in constantly changing local contexts. These examples further illustrate that exoticization is never unidirectional and this interrelational process sheds light on negotiation of local and foreign identities.

Maurice Said is an Honorary Research Fellow in the Department of Anthropology at Durham University. He has spent over a decade conducting fieldwork and research in southern Sri Lanka, focusing on post-tsunami reconstruction, kinship, patronage, and factionalism. During this time he has also conducted research on suicides and, in particular, the effects of tourism on factionalism and village-level politics in post-tsunami coastal communities in southern Sri Lanka. He is currently involved in a number of projects related to crisis management.

Notes

1. Names of people and places (with the exception of Matara) have been changed at the request of those involved.
2. A term of respect, usually affixed to a person's name to denote that they are highly regarded.

References

Bruner, Edward M. 1986. "Ethnography as Narrative." Pp. 139–155 in *The Anthropology of Experience*, ed. Victor W. Turner and Edward M Bruner. Urbana: University of Illinois Press.

Bruner, Edward M. 2005. *Culture on Tour: Ethnographies of Travel*. Chicago: University of Chicago Press.

Crick, Malcolm. 1991. "Tourists, Locals and Anthropologists: Quizzical Reflections on 'Otherness' in Tourist Encounters and in Tourism Research." *Australian Cultural History* 10: 6–18.

De Silva, D. A. M., and Masahiro Yamao. 2007. "Effects of the Tsunami on Fisheries and Coastal Livelihood: A Case Study of Tsunami-Ravaged Southern Sri Lanka." *Disasters* 31, no. 4: 386–404.

Fechter, Anne-Meike. 2005. "The 'Other' Stares Back: Experiencing Whiteness in Jakarta." *Ethnography* 6, no. 1: 87–103.

Fechter, Anne-Meike. 2007. *Transnational Lives: Expatriates in Indonesia*. Aldershot: Ashgate.

Frerks, Georg, and Bart Klem. 2005. *Tsunami Response in Sri Lanka, Report on a Field Visit from 6–20 February 2005*. Wageningen: Wageningen University Press.

Gamburd, Michele R. 2008. *Breaking the Ashes: The Culture of Illicit Liquor in Sri Lanka*. Bloomington: Indiana University Press

Gamburd, Michele R. 2014. *The Golden Wave: Culture and Politics after Sri Lanka's Tsunami Disaster*. Bloomington: Indiana University Press

Gunewardena, Nandini. 2008. "Peddling Paradise, Rebuilding Serendib: The 100-Meter Refugees versus the Tourism Industry in Post-tsunami Sri Lanka." Pp. 69–92 in *Capitalizing on Catastrophe: Neoliberal Strategies in Disaster Reconstruction*, ed. Nandini Gunewardena and Mark Schuller. Lanham, MD: Altamira Press.

Hennig, Christoph. 2002. "Tourism: Enacting Modern Myths." Trans. Alison Brown. Pp. 169–187 in *The Tourist as a Metaphor of the Social World*, ed. Graham M. S. Dann. Wallingford: CABI Publishing.

Kapferer, Bruce. 2011. "How Anthropologists Think: Figurations of the Exotic." Huxley Memorial Lecture. *Journal of the Royal Anthropological Institute* (n.s.) 19, no. 4: 813–836.

Klein, Naomi. 2005. "The Rise of Disaster Capitalism." *The Nation*, 14 April. http://www.thenation.com/article/rise-disaster-capitalism.

Knowles, Caroline. 2000. *Bedlam on the Streets*. London: Routledge.

Korpela, Mari. 2013. "'Westerners' in Varanasi, India: A Permanent yet Temporary Community." Pp. 37–58 in *Cocoon Communities: Togetherness in the 21st Century*, ed. Mari Korpela and Fred Dervin. Newcastle upon Tyne: Cambridge Scholars Publishing.

Kravanja, Boštjan. 2012. "On Conceptions of Paradise and the Tourist Spaces of Southern Sri Lanka." *Asian Ethnology* 71, no. 2: 179–205.

Kuhn, Randall. 2010. "Conflict, Coastal Vulnerability, and Resiliency in Tsunami-Affected Communities in Sri Lanka." Pp. 40–63 in *Tsunami Recovery in Sri Lanka: Ethnic and Regional Dimensions*, ed. Dennis McGilvray and Michele R. Gamburd. London: Routledge.

Leckie, Scott. 2005. "The Great Land Theft." Pp. 15–16 in *Forced Migration Review*. Special issue: "Tsunami: Learning from the Humanitarian Response."

Leonard, Pauline. 2010. *Expatriate Identities in Postcolonial Organizations: Working Whiteness*. Burlington, VT: Ashgate.

MacClancy, Jeremy. 2010. "Paradise Postponed: The Predicaments of Tourism." Pp. 418–429 in *Exotic No More: Anthropology on the Front Lines*, ed. Jeremy MacClancy. Chicago: University of Chicago Press.

Parliament of Sri Lanka. 2004. "Finance (Amendment) Act, No. 8 of 2004." *Gazette of the Democratic Socialist Republic of Sri Lanka*. http://www.ird.gov.lk/en/publications/Acts_Other%20Levies%20%20Taxes/FActNo.8[E]2004.pdf.

Ruhuna University. 2005. "Census on the Tsunami Victims in Matara District." http://www.ruh.ac.lk/tsunami/matara_stat.html (accessed 20 March 2012).

Ruwanpura, Kanchana N. 2009. "Putting Houses in Place: Rebuilding Communities in Post-tsunami Sri Lanka." *Disasters* 33, no. 3: 436–456.

Salazar, Noel B. 2012. "Tourism Imaginaries: A Conceptual Approach." *Annals of Tourism Research* 39, no. 2: 863–882.

Stirrat, Roderick L. 2006. "Competitive Humanitarianism: Relief and the Tsunami in Sri Lanka." *Anthropology Today* 22, no. 5: 11–16.

Stirrat, Roderick L., and Heiko Henkel. 1997. "The Development Gift: The Problem of Reciprocity in the NGO World." *Annals of the American Academy of Political and Social Science* 554: 66–80. Special issue: "The Role of NGOs: Charity and Empowerment."

Theodossopoulos, Dimitrios. 2014. "Scorn or Idealization? Tourism Imaginaries, Exoticization and Ambivalence in Emberá Indigenous Tourism." Pp. 57–79 in *Tourism Imaginaries: Anthropological Approaches*, ed. Noel B. Salazar and Nelson H. H. Graburn. New York: Berghahn Books.

Vaes, Birgit, and Martijn Goddeeris. 2012. *Sri Lankan Tsunami 2004: Lessons Learned*. Flanders: Belgian Red Cross.

Velho, Gilberto. 2001. "Observing the Familiar." *India International Centre Quarterly* 28, no. 2: 47–57.

Chapter 5

BAHIA OF ALL SAINTS, ENCHANTMENTS, AND DREAMS
Female Tourists, Capoeira Practitioners, and the Exotic

Theodora Lefkaditou

Bahia, Land of Happiness

The sound of the *berimbau* was clearly heard at Salvador's international airport, Deputado Luís Eduardo Magalhães. A small welcoming committee—women dressed in the Bahianas' typical white voluminous layered dresses, and young male capoeira practitioners playing capoeira's most cherished one-string instrument—handed small, colorful pieces of ribbon to the newcomers. Every year, thousands of people arrive at the city of Salvador in Bahia, the Bay of All Saints, with their luggage full of dreams, desires, and aspirations. Foreign and national tourists fill Pelourinho's steep streets in the center of Salvador. They visit social inclusion projects in underprivileged neighborhoods and spend time in historic sites, coastal resorts, and picturesque beaches and waterfalls. The imaginaries that fuel this movement of tourists involve a set of idealized understandings of the people of Bahia and their practices—conflicting yet complementary perceptions of the exotic.

Situated in the northeast of Brazil, the state of Bahia is portrayed as the 'Land of Happiness' after a popular song written by Dorival Caymmi. This idyllic

Notes for this chapter begin on page 112.

representation dates back to the 1930s, when intellectuals, artists, and scholars encouraged the romantic appraisal of what was perceived as Afrobrazilian cultural manifestations. In turn, this created particular imaginaries and expectations concerning Bahia, its people, and their practices. As Noel Salazar points out, "the vernacular imaginings people rely on, from the most spectacular fantasies to the most mundane reveries, are usually not expressed in theoretical terms but in images and discourses" (2012: 864).

Tourism websites build on the idea of a 'happy land' inhabited by 'vibrant' and 'cheerful' people. In their narratives, the natural, human, and cultural landscape are interwoven. Prospective tourists are given the promise to experience a 'contagious' and 'true' happiness embodied by the socially and economically disadvantaged Bahians. As a matter of fact, while walking about Salvador, local people encourage visitors to be blissful and to smile. As they characteristically say, "Smile, you are in Bahia!" Accordingly, tourist brochures and travel magazines depict black women, known as Bahianas, and half-naked capoeira practitioners with a friendly and inviting smile on their faces. Even if they "don't have money in their pocket, nor food on their table," the local Bahians say, they are nonetheless eager to share their 'sincere smile' with their guests. Poverty, joy, and cultural and racial mixture set the context for a potent identity economy that appeals to the senses. Black Bahians in particular are associated with stereotypical and often sensualized imaginaries that involve their dispositions, body, and mind.

These reified and paternalistic representations that celebrate social inequalities (see Freire-Medeiros 2013) speak volumes of Bahia's ambiguous place in Brazilian history, politics, and economy (see Romo 2010). The city of Salvador was officially founded in 1549 by the Portuguese Crown, and its history is intrinsically related to colonialism. By 1558, it played a leading role in the New World as one of the cities with the biggest imports of people from Africa, who were turned into slaves and later on distributed to work in the plantations (Nobre 2003). Cultural manifestations related with black people were suppressed, persecuted, and subjected to processes of hygienization. When Rio de Janeiro became Brazil's new administrational and political center in 1763, a configuration of power took place and Bahia became peripheral to the country's economy and political life. Eventually, though, and as public policies changed, Afrobrazilian expressions acquired new meanings and were transformed into romantic markers of an emerging and all encompassing Brazilian identity.

In the middle twentieth century, these romantic markers of identity were appropriated by the tourist market. Bahia and its capital, the 'Black Rome' (Calvo-González and Duccini 2010), gradually acquired exotic referents that foregrounded economic backwardness and an exoticized Afrobrazilian culture. Such contradictory imaginaries came to play a central role not only in the processes of national identity formation but, more importantly, in Brazil's developing tourist industry. The commodification of cultural difference—now in global display through tourism—involved the aesthetics and promise of black sexuality and has led to the production of an objectified exoticism.

With this in mind, I shift my attention to a specific Afrobrazilian cultural manifestation: capoeira.[1] I draw from the ethnographic material collected during 13 months of field research in Bahia and discuss the negotiation of the exotic in the interactions between male Bahian capoeira teachers and foreign female tourists. Capoeira is a game and a practice where players perform and communicate messages through bodily movements. Hence, it constitutes a field where sensuality, gender, and playfulness shape each other and quite often articulate with each other to form relations of power. My ethnographic account focuses on a collectivity to which I shall refer as 'Angoleiros da Bahia' and their experiences. Its young members—ranging from 20 to 35 years old— come from an island near the city of Salvador and are fishermen and surfers. Several teachers have left the island and live in Salvador's Historic Center, while others teach capoeira outside of Brazil, following transnational paths, or dream of leaving Bahia.[2] As such, their current transnational experiences challenge the idea of the fixed and immobile native who, after having lost his African homeland, grew roots in a Brazilian soil.

In the ethnography that follows I address how Bahian capoeira practitioners position themselves toward tourists, challenging, affirming, or subverting the exotic images that others have constructed for them. Following Noel Salazar and Nelson Graburn, I discuss imaginaries as 'implicit schemas of interpretation' that can be both 'seductive' and 'restrictive' (2014a: 1). Indeed, while imaginaries are structured around dichotomies, such as "here-there, male-female, inside-outside, local-global" (Salazar 2010: 864), they implicate the creative participation of different agents and interest groups—locals, tourists, and mediators—and are subject to change. Moreover, as Bruce Kapferer and Dimitrios Theodossopoulos argue in the introduction to this volume, exoticized subjects react to and modify externally imposed images and notions of the exotic in order to make them fit to new purposes.

In the Bahian context, exoticization and self-exoticization emerge as reciprocal processes: the capoeira practitioners negotiate the ways they choose to think about foreign visitors and re-articulate their self-representation, reemploying but also departing from previous exoticized referents. This negotiation and re-articulation of previous exotic stereotypes involves subtle practices of resistance, which become evident in the relationship of the local capoeira practitioners with foreigners, particularly in relationships that entail an erotic element.

In their interaction with foreign female tourists, capoeira practitioners attempt to gain recognition by building on the mystified and ambivalent figure of the *malandro*. Depending on the context and the speaker, the *malandro* is associated with both negative and positive qualities. He is either the free-spirited person who cleverly subverts life's difficulties and challenges the authorities, or the one who is considered intelligent but in a manner associated with cunning and deceitfulness. He may be perceived as idle and vagabond, or as hard working, outgoing, and creative. I conclude my ethnographic exploration by focusing on the anxieties and frustrations generated beyond the tourist encounter, when expectations and desires are not met or when recognition and self-assertion are threatened.

The 'People from Out There'

At least once a year, the Angoleiros da Bahia who live in Europe return home. They visit their families and capoeira 'brothers', their master (Mestre Prateado) who lives in Salvador's Historic Center, their place of origin, and its traditions to their foreign apprentices. It is a time to strengthen old ties, help the collectivity's members who still live in Bahia, and contribute to their community. Indeed, the arrival of big cruise ships, especially during January and February, signals the onset of the tourist season in Bahia. Tourism-related economies do not involve all agents in an equal way. Many capoeira *mestres* (masters) argue that just like the carnival, tourism is destined to benefit the 'elite'. The people who live in the Historic Center, however, and those coming from nearby neighborhoods or the island, try to make a living in every possible way. They struggle to find their place and improve their economic situation as artisans, painters, or cooks. Even street pickpockets anticipate the tourists' arrival. In turn, capoeira teachers and artisans take the ferryboat in order to sell their artifacts to tourists, foreign apprentices, and local shops in the city.

Due to capoeira's global expansion, capoeira players demonstrate flexibility and have learned to communicate rather easily with foreigners. For example, Siri and Neguinho are the youngest capoeira teachers from the Angoleiros da Bahia. At the time of research they were unemployed, so they used to occasionally provide information to tourists on how to find an exchange office or accommodation, especially when a friend of theirs rented a room or their own *mestre* had a vacancy in his hostel. By showing solidarity to their friends and *mestre*, they expected them to reciprocate the favor. Furthermore, it was a way to mediate between Bahians and tourists making use of their living abroad experiences and their familiarity with foreign capoeira apprentices.

For people in Bahia, the gringos and gringas who arrive from different places, bringing along imaginaries and desires for curios and souvenirs, are 'the people from out there'. This expression eloquently describes the idea of the existence of a world outside known boundaries. Their presence generates the process of self-reflection, as everyday activities, economies, politics, and imaginations are somehow related to these 'people from out there'. Pelourinho's residents have a vague idea about who these people are. According to them, most are "white and full of money." More importantly, though, Bahians claim they know what tourists expect and desire, and consequently they must choose whether they will conform to these desires. Mestre Prateado, for example, was puzzled with the changes that came along with foreigners. Being a renowned artisan of percussion instruments, he often complained that they had started painting colorful *berimbaus* "just like tourists want them," instead of the plain ones that maintain the wood's and pumpkin's natural colors. Changes in aesthetic criteria and the appropriation of people and culture were, according to him, intrinsically related to tourism and commodification. This subtle, yet very common expression of hostility toward tourists often disappointed visitors. To their surprise, Bahians did not easily share with their guests their 'sincere smile'.

The male capoeiras of what is known as 'capoeira for the tourist' in the Historic Center's main square played skillfully in exchange for money, while tourists rushed to take photos. Now and then, they stopped and sat by the church. While Angoleiros da Bahia often criticized them for performing capoeira 'for the tourist to see', they also claimed that contrary to the image of the laid back Bahian, those capoeiras were among the most hard-working people. During their pauses, Pelourinho's capoeira performers claimed to know what foreign women wanted by exhibiting a hypersexual black masculinity. Small incidents fueling gossips that circulated in the neighborhood were part of everyday life. Many stories that stirred the imagination of the Historic Center's residents had to do with capoeira practitioners, their quarrels and achievements, and most commonly, their relationships and sexual affairs with tourists. As it will become clear in the following sections, Bahians expressed ambivalence toward these practices, which oscillated between admiration, envy, and contempt.

Gringas, *Caçadores de Gringas*, and Cosmopolitans

William was a *menino de rua*, a child who spent most of his time walking about the streets in the Historic Center. He smoked crack and asked for food or money from tourists. He was, without doubt, the most polemic child in the Historic Center. Every time he saw a local—especially a man, and, in most cases, capoeira players—talking to a foreign woman, he said, "Hey, you, gringa hunter (*caçador de gringa*)," and then he started cursing. The phrase *caçador de gringa* echoed all over the place. William was so bothered by those interactions that once he went outside Mestre Prateado's atelier and threw a cockroach to his wife, originally a foreigner but living in Bahia for more than 20 years, while calling him a gringa hunter. The incident amused the *mestre*'s apprentices, and he playfully responded, justifying himself, "Well, yes, I was. I was a *caçador de gringas*. But I was a *caçador de gringas* while I was there, in Europe. Not, here."

Caçador de gringa is the young man who constantly pursues female tourists, especially foreign ones, engaging into sexual affairs with them. Street vendors, artisans, musicians, dancers, and capoeira players are among those who mostly interact with tourists and thus engage in these activities. Cabelo, a young Pelourinho resident, emphasized the relationships between the 'capoeira for the tourists' practitioners, whom he used to call 'exhibitionists', and female tourists. He said: "They go out to theaters, bars, restaurants and the women pay everything for them. They say they are Capoeiristas, but some of them are not even Capoeiristas. They are just male prostitutes. Once, one of these guys you see here, he met a girl, a tourist. When she left, she bought a ticket and she invited him to go and stay with her. But he was married and he brought his wife along. He said she was his sister and she stayed in the next room. Can you believe it?"

The Greek equivalent to the Bahian 'hunter' (*caçador*) is the 'spear' (*kamaki*). They designate specific comportments, especially in places frequented by tourists. 'Spears' do not focus exclusively on foreign tourists, but neither do 'hunters'. Like the 'beach boys' in Barbados (see Gmelch 2003), they are mostly men about 20 to 40 years old coming from the less privileged social classes, and compared to the women with whom they relate, they are all economically deprived. In Salvador, capoeira practitioners have a prominent place among local men because of their unmediated contact and easier communication with tourists. In addition, many women approach capoeira practitioners not only due to their physical appearance and the imaginaries generated by tourist agents in Bahia. They also relate to them because they play capoeira and foreign women aspire to improve their skills by taking classes from local men.

According to Mestre Prateado's wife, Dona Luisa, it had become rather common to see Bahian capoeiras going out with or getting married to foreigners. Today, even older capoeira practitioners and teachers—or men belonging to other social classes, although to a lesser degree—relate to foreigners. Reflecting on her personal experiences and the transformations that had taken place, she argued, "When my husband went to the island, the people there were not used to see someone with dreadlocks. They were intimidated. And he was married to a foreign woman. It seemed strange, unusual. Now, things have changed. More men wear dreadlocks and you see that even some you would not have imagined or expected also want to have foreign girlfriends."

As I mentioned earlier, the capoeira players' practices should be considered in relation to the historic figure of the *malandro*, of the man who spends most of his time at the street and engages in relationships with different women. In today's context, foreign women possibly add more value to capoeira practitioners. As such, going out with them is a way to be acknowledged by others as gendered subjects and as persons (*caras*).

Nonetheless, their activities provoked mixed reactions. Shop and hotel owners in the Historic Center maintained racist attitudes toward young men they considered *caçadores de gringas* and attributed to the *malandro* the negative stereotypes of the vagabond. Being black, unemployed, and underprivileged; playing capoeira at the street or at the beach; and hanging out with foreigners—men or women—place people at the margins. These attitudes augment Bahian capoeiras' anxiety and affect their self perceptions when they move away from their relatively comfort zones into more hostile spaces. Therefore, the teachers of the Angoleiros da Bahia tended to differentiate and distanced themselves from 'these guys in Pelourinho'. They insisted that 'these guys' were not even capoeira. They played 'capoeira for the tourist'. However, in Bahian society, proximity in space, ethnicity, social class, and the Angoleiros da Bahia's dubious involvement with tourists put them in an equally delicate position. They were perceived as too manipulative and calculative. As such, their interests and motivations were questioned.

"Here, the Exotic Is You"

All year round, Bahian capoeiras had the opportunity to meet foreign women and specially, capoeira practitioners. They played capoeira together; they trained or visited the island, making use of their foreign language proficiency and emphasizing their traveling experiences. They discussed a plethora of reasons for opting to go out with foreign women. As such, they preferred encounters that were transitory and non-repetitive, as it usually happens in tourist contexts Sometimes, foreigners returned and there was always the possibility to invite a teacher to their country. Living abroad was much desired. Those who remained home both admired and envied their friends' ability to learn new languages and to get to know different places. Their knowledge and interactions stressed the global significance of their practices and their own value as men.

Similar to the beach boys and the spears, capoeira teachers and practitioners seemed to appeal more to foreign tourists. Indeed, for Bahian women coming from the less privileged social classes, capoeira was still associated with stereotypes of laziness, as well as with the poverty and marginalization they aspired to eventually subvert. This avoidance was particularly reinforced by evangelical churches that preached against Afrobrazilian identity markers, including capoeira. Nonetheless, Bahian women quite often saw capoeira teachers in a more positive way and perceived as cosmopolitans. As a matter of fact, capoeira teachers should be distinguished by other Bahian men in the way they portray and display themselves. Their traveling experiences and transnational trajectories shape the way they think about themselves and their aesthetics.

In turn, men, as Bahian women complained, preferred foreign women to Bahians. Comparing them to the foreigners, they denigrated local women by saying that they were 'ignorants' who did not know how to dress and talk and that they never exercised. Bahians often suggested they were interested in meeting foreigners because it elevated their self-esteem, as well as 'out of curiosity'. As capoeira teachers used to admit, it was 'something different'. They justified their choices, claiming that being intrigued by someone, or something 'different', was nothing more than a 'common human attitude', and by appealing to a common humanity, they counteracted an exoticized difference.

Attempting to initiate a conversation with one of the young teachers, I made a comment on Bahia's landscape and exotic appeal. Rather surprised, he replied, "Do you really think Bahia is exotic? What is it in Bahia that makes it exotic? You are from Greece. Greece is exotic. All this history and mythology— these things are exotic, not Bahia. Here, the exotic is you." Clearly, the teacher's intention was to demonstrate his ability to engage with foreigners in a mutually comprehensible way of thinking and imagining. Even though I had never considered Greece an 'exotic place', I was invited to acknowledge that exoticization was not merely a 'Western' cultural trait. As Kapferer argues, "everything and anything is potentially in an exotic relation. Nothing is intrinsically exotic except through the relations into which it is drawn" (2013: 815). In Brazil, Greek islands and mythology were greatly exoticized, while many women dreamed of spending their honeymoon in Greece. In Barcelona, however, where I first started research among teachers from the same collectivity, I was not considered 'exotic', probably due to geographical proximity. Moreover, Angoleiros da Bahia defined themselves as 'natives from the island', and their island was perceived and presented as the most important identity marker. Since I also came from an island, they considered me 'native as well'. Thus, status may change and perceptions of the exotic, translated as difference, shift along with geographic mobility in a process of continuous estrangement and connectivity.

Imaginaries and expectations work both ways. Theodossopoulos notes that "[e]xoticisation ... can be a reciprocal process that produces parallel imaginaries" (2014: 58). For most foreign practitioners—both male and female—going to Salvador is a dream come true, a 'rite of passage' (Griffith 2011), a pilgrimage, and a 'living fantasy' (Downey 2005). It is an opportunity to familiarize with their teachers' place of origin, as well as with capoeira's origins and roots—a chance to get to know old capoeira *mestres* who no longer travel outside of Bahia, visit schools and academies, and train their skills. Regarding the female apprentices, their imaginaries are shaped by their teachers' discourses back home, by stories, by romanticized and eroticized images. The presence of Bahian teachers in Europe and the images that circulate on the Internet create certain expectations. Traveling to Bahia is already perceived as an encounter with 'biscuit-like' and 'chocolate-like' men. Therefore, their trips are conditioned by specific biased perceptions concerning sexuality and masculinity in Bahia in general and in capoeira specifically. Upon their arrival, their assumptions are tested by firsthand experiences in the field.

The foreign apprentices of the Angoleiros da Bahia spent their time visiting Salvador and the island. Most of them stayed at the collectivity's hostel on the island or in Mestre Prateado's hostel in Pelourinho. They engaged in a host of activities. They participated in capoeira *rodas* (capoeira circle or ring), trained, surfed, and accompanied members of the group in their daily tasks. In this spirit, when a female apprentice from England returned home, she posted a series of photos depicting their experiences on Facebook. The album's title was "An encounter with your true self." The photos materialized and crystallized specific imaginaries concerning 'simple', happy life and authenticity. They denoted an "unintentional primitivization" (Theodossopoulos 2014: 58), where the foreign social actor, by relating with islanders and their landscape, was connected with her true self. Separated and estranged from the Bahian context, the images circulated on the Internet, where they were displayed and idealized once again as 'exotic'. As Susan Stewart points out, "the exotic object represents distance appropriated" (1993: 147).

Back in Bahia, however, on several occasions, foreign women were frustrated by the violence they encountered while playing capoeira with their collectivity's members and their 'rudeness'. Away from their country of origin, they had to deal with the implications of gender, ethnicity, and social class in a new context. In other words, their notions of the exotic, as well as the ones Bahian men had, eventually 'met reality' (Salazar 2010).

For Siri, most people arrived and left Bahia having 'a fantasy in their minds'. Similarly, Peixe, another young teacher, commented rather puzzled on the biased assumptions regarding black Bahians' 'hypersexuality' and performance. According to Siri, these fantasies resulted from the construction and accumulation of a specific and idealized kind of knowledge that rarely responded to reality and to familiarity attained through experience. Thus, the collectivity's teachers encouraged both male and female apprentices to 'feel Brazil in their skin' by participating in everyday activities. Their critique was usually accompanied by a gesture they made touching their own skin and was suggestive of the hardships and experiences attached to being black, Bahian, or even a foreigner in Bahia—of boundaries, disconnections and misunderstandings. Their argument was based on how capoeira practitioners perceive and experience their practices and life itself. Life and knowledge are embodied experiences that can be captured with the passage of time, through imitation and attunement. Thus, the collectivity's comments that drew from capoeira's cultural and social specificities served as an invitation to capture social reality in its experiential sense leaving the path to communication open. Hence, understanding reality was perceived as a learning process that involved collaboration between Bahian teachers and foreign apprentices and eventually impacted both.

Anxieties

On various occasions, the young teachers attempted to validate their claim to status by talking about their success in relation to foreign women. Sometimes they even competed and placed bets. Gossiping and parodying foreigners was part of their performances. They presented a sexual and powerful self-image that others not only approved but also constantly reinforced. Nobody wanted to be considered a 'fool' (*otario*), and their sexuality was experienced and expressed through a series of emotions, practices, and ideas. Being a fool was a quality attributed to foreign male apprentices. At the same time, burlesquing foreign women and displaying rudeness, as George Gmelch (2003) also observed with the beach boys and Sofka Zinovieff (1991) with the spears, was a way to retaliate. As such, they hoped to challenge asymmetries and subvert their position in relation to women who came from socially and economically privileged social classes. Indeed, as Judith Butler claims, "recognition becomes a site of power" (2004: 2).

During their holidays, Peixe Espada and Cachaça used to bring to Bahia their wives, girlfriends, and apprentices. They aimed to make their traveling experiences meaningful and were transformed into unofficial historians and guides. They visited natural resorts, places, and people important to capoeira. While accompanying Peixe Espada and Cachaça, the teachers learned to see Bahia in a different way: from the 'foreigners' point of view'. They discovered the importance of specific places in rural Bahia that were more likely to attract foreigners' attention, and acknowledged the authority and power of old capoeira *mestres* who represented tradition. Yet, quite often, they ended up feeling frustration as, for example, when they realized they were the only black people frequenting particular places. They found themselves occupying a liminal space as they acquired the role of the mediator.

Mediation entails the acknowledgment of a particular role and presupposes some sort of conflict that needs to be resolved or avoided. An example of this was given when a street beggar approached us and asked from one of the teachers to give him money. When I observed that he never asked for money when they were not present, he replied, "He is not asking money from me. If he is asking, it is because you are here." Thus, mediation presupposes boundaries and reveals the potential danger when teachers can be perceived as strange and familiar to both locals and foreigners. Hence, in more complicated—and unpleasant—situations, some foreign female apprentices commented that they found themselves buying food or helping families and the friends of the capoeira teachers they knew. Confrontations and conflicts were not easily avoided, as the teachers returned and reconnected with their friends and family back home.

These incidents not only bring forth how mutuality and relatedness are experienced in Bahia. They also illustrate perceptions on gendered relationships and the place of women in capoeira. According to Mestre Prateado, many foreign female practitioners who visited Bahia "have no morality." As in Greece—especially during the 1970s, but also today (Zinovieff 1991)—and in Barbados, female tourists are stereotypically perceived as sexually loose (Gmelch 2003). Indeed, sexual relationships and sensuality are defined by internal politics and inequities. The assumption that foreigners go out with several capoeira practitioners from the same collectivity was quite commonly discussed with contempt. All these discourses entailed a moralizing element. As Suzette Heald proposes: "There is a link between moralities with ideas about the person. These ideas also articulate with perceptions of maleness and femaleness ... the standards of conduct expected of different members of a society differ, as do the evaluative modes that apply to their transgressions. But morality is never just a matter of double standards; it always involves multiple ones" (1999: 50–56).

Apparently, it was quite different being a woman from Bahia, a foreign capoeira practitioner and tourist, a student of the same group, the one to have an affair with or a wife. Similarly to what Marilyn Strathern underlined, there was a "categorical denigration of females and contextual evaluation of particular women" (1981: 166). One of the very few female *mestres* from Bahia noted that there was a gendered division that regulated interpersonal relationships. She said it was a sexual division of power and an affective one that involved duties. Women, who in almost all cases were also capoeira practitioners and former apprentices of their husbands, gained access to status—and in some cases, in making a livelihood—only through their relationships to men.

Women were, as Janaina, a female capoeira teacher from the Angoleiros da Bahia noted, the main reason for competition among men as they attempted to 'steal' them from others. Indeed, 'stealing' a woman or even an apprentice— male or female—demonstrated one's ability and skillfulness. The young teachers never stopped 'hunting'. Their desire was to keep being mobile by relating with different women in every place and country they went. They associated transnational mobility with personal freedom and challenged institutionalized discourses that wanted them rooted in Bahia and depended on the state. Sartre (in Judaken 2008), while reflecting on the human condition, sustains that people interiorize the labels and essences attributed to them, but the meaning they give may vary. In this case, capoeira practitioners joked by calling one another gringa hunters, and being a gringa hunter received positive connotations.

Once again, however, there are further implications and contradictions that are made explicit when Bahian capoeiras leave home. Contemplating on his experiences, Neguinho observed that once away from 'cultural Pelourinho', the symbolic markers of their identity—dreadlocks, clothes, and habits—led to their further marginalization. When Neguinho decided to get married to his French girlfriend and leave Bahia in order to get a job in France, he experienced frustration and anxiety. He discovered that his wife, who seemed to be a 'hippie', actually came from a very wealthy family he failed to please. The exoticized and, among capoeira circles in Bahia, positively valued self was transformed into something altogether negative. Indeed, many times, capoeira teachers who leave Bahia with a foreign woman 'fail to adapt' and return home. Their personal and collective expectations fail, and reality raises questions on the nature and viability of their imaginaries. In the new context, as Butler sustains, "the terms by which [they are] recognized" entail the possibility to "make their life unlivable" (2004: 4).

Making the decision not only to have sexual affairs with tourists but also to leave Bahia and get married to a foreign woman entails further risks. Among them is an assumed dependence from a white woman that leads to the men's disempowerment. Peter Wade discusses a political economy where the choices people make on whom "to marry or have sex with, what is beautiful and desirable ... shape and are shaped by hierarchies of race, gender and class" (2009: 156). Mestre Prateado was critical. He often warned younger Bahian men that foreign women wanted to "use them" and manipulated them in order to have an "adventure with a black man in Bahia."

During gatherings, capoeira *mestres*, particularly Mestre Prateado, pointed out that foreign people "if they could, they would take away everything," including both people and practices. By that, he touched on deeper issues of affective relationships, adding to the complexity of the encounters and relationships between foreign female tourists and young Bahian capoeira teachers. Similarly, another *mestre* used irony and criticized foreigners' attempts to 'domesticate' capoeira players by taking away their freedom and challenging their romanticized struggle against all sorts of authorities and obligations. Indeed, in official discourses, capoeira is described as a struggle in the past against slave owners and authorities. Today, capoeira *mestres* invest on these externally imposed imaginaries and use them against whomever or whatever seems to threaten their identity and independence. Hence, through creativity and self-reflection, a common identity is playfully constructed. Yet, the meanings and qualities attributed to this identity are open to negotiation as they may refer to what men, black people, capoeira practitioners, and Bahians have in common.

Conclusion

The tourism industry reproduces and builds upon specific essentialized tropes and images of black Bahians' identity and practices in order to attract tourists to the city of Salvador. Nonetheless, the residents of the Historic Center are aware of these imaginaries and act on them. The tourists' presence in Salvador encourages a process of self-reflection among the residents of the city, inviting different groups of local actors to position themselves towards the 'people from out there'. Yet, capoeira practitioners enter their relationship with foreigners from a position of greater cosmopolitan awareness. Due to their significant traveling experiences and their direct contact with significant numbers of foreign capoeira apprentices, they have developed the ability to communicate and interact across cultures with relative easiness. Their frequent contact with foreigners provides them with confidence to approach the exotic and their own exoticization by others, not as an inherent quality but as a matter of perspective.

Both foreigners and Bahians express curiosity toward one another—toward what they consider 'different' and appeals to them—and mutually discover Bahia's geography, capoeira's history, and personal and collective identities. The interaction with gringos and gringas positions the young members of the Angoleiros da Bahia in a risky place and reveals tensions, inequalities, and differentiations in the Bahian society. The Angoleiros da Bahia are perceived and presented as both cosmopolitans and exotic. They are criticized and treated with contempt, but at the same time they are also admired and envied for their language proficiency and cosmopolitan life style. They distance themselves from the 'other guys in Pelourinho', but, during gendered performances, they too project the image of the 'hunter'. Therefore, they alternate between performing and experiencing familiarity and estrangement toward foreign apprentices, other Bahians, and members of their capoeira collectivity.

While tourist mobilities toward Bahia have been central to the chapter, I have also acknowledged the importance of outward-looking mobilities and aspirations generated by the tourist encounter. Indeed, teachers migrate or return to Bahia as often as the tourists themselves. They bring back foreign friends and learn how to mediate foreign and local expectations. During these 'comings and goings', as they say, capoeira teachers learn about the values and viability of their own collectivities—their personal aspirations, fantasies, and individuality. Being or feeling exotic entails the idea of appropriating previous exotic referents, but also repositioning the Self in respects to such previous exotic referents—often in ways that engender a certain form of 'counter-exoticization'. The resulting negotiation of the capoeira imagery involves a continuous alternation between estrangement and connection, appropriation and separation. It is a constantly shifting imagery shaped by the geographic mobility and mobile aspirations of all the involved actors.

The proliferation of previous and emerging exotic images is also visible in the encounters between foreign female apprentices and Bahian capoeira teachers. It is the stereotypical and persistently exoticized nature of such relationships that challenges the possibility of creating relationships of equality between capoeira teachers and foreign women. As the meanings and values attributed to the exotic shift—primarily due to the cosmopolitan experience of the teachers themselves—the balance of power in the developing erotic relations is also transformed, creating new dependencies and relationships of submission. Mutual curiosity and appreciation may eventually lead to mutual frustration and disappointment when imaginaries are perceived as 'fantasies' that do not meet reality, or when capoeira practitioners challenge externally imposed exotic stereotypes.

The narratives and fluctuating perspectives of the Bahian capoeira teachers, as these revealed themselves in the ethnographic context examined in this chapter, suggest that the relationship between bottom-up and top-down modes of exoticization is complex and always changing. A focus on the mutuality and interrelationship of exoticization and self-exoticization can help us reconceptualize the exotic in less restrictive and static terms. The alternative, counter-exoticizing discourses of the capoeira teachers point to their complex relationship with history, their mobile experiences and aspirations, and their desire to actively reconstruct their identity—an example of "remaking the human" (Butler 2004: 4)—in an attempt to assert control over their lives and gain recognition. In this respect, counter-exoticization challenges previous hierarchical imaginaries and contributes in articulating a narrative about the Self, yet in terms more amenable to the exoticized subject.

Theodora Lefkaditou received her PhD in Social Anthropology in 2014. Her doctoral thesis is titled "The Social and Cultural Effects of Capoeira's Transnational Circulation in Salvador da Bahia and Barcelona." She has conducted research on transnational mobility, social transformations, and the concept of the person in Brazil, Spain, and Greece. Currently, she is exploring the use of social media in the context of the refugee crisis. She is the co-author, with Roger Canals, of "The Individualization of Kinship Ties in a Transnational Context: Bahian-Capoeira Collectivities and Afro-Venezuelan Religious Groups in Barcelona" (2016, in *Mobility and Family in Transnational Space*).

Notes

1. Capoeira's definitions are subject of disputes. The official tourist site of Bahia describes it as an all-encompassing practice: a martial art, mixture of dance and fight, philosophy of life, personal defense system originating from African slaves brought to Brazil, a local Afrobrazilian fight that conquered the world. Despite the best efforts of politicians, practitioners, researchers, and intellectuals to render it intelligible, capoeira still appears to be elusive yet precise in its relative imprecision. Until a few years ago, the main question was whether it came from Africa or Brazil. Some opted for a solution in the middle: it was invented by African slaves in Brazil and used as a way of resistance to colonial domination (Assunção Röhrig 2004: 5–6). As such, during the nineteenth century as well as in the beginnings of the twentieth century, capoeira was associated with marginalized people and street life. In the colonial era, those who practiced capoeira were severely punished. As a matter of fact, the Criminal Code of 1890 on vagrants and capoeiras, due to the Republic's civilizatory agenda, considered both idleness and practicing capoeira crimes (Albert Dias 2006; Assunção Röhrig 2004). Through ongoing

transformations from the 1930s on, capoeira moved away from a status of illegality and became symbol of Bahia and Brazil's intangible heritage and furthermore a valuable economic resource.

2. Angoleiros da Bahia, as all capoeira collectivities, has a master (*mestre*). *Mestre* is the ultimate title a capoeira practitioner may hope to attain. Their *mestre* teaches capoeira outside of the country and encourages his students to follow his example and leave Brazil. However, the research subjects have also been apprentices of another capoeira *mestre*, Mestre Prateado, who taught them how to make percussion instruments. Today, he owns a shop in the Old Center.

References

Albert Dias, Adriana. 2006. *Mandinga, manha e malicia: Uma história sobre os capoeiras na capital da Bahia, 1910–1925*. Salvador: Editora da Universidade Federal da Bahia.

Assunção Röhrig, Mathias. 2004. *Capoeira: The History of an Afro-Brazilian Martial Art*. New York: Routledge.

Butler, Judith. 2004. *Undoing Gender*. New York: Routledge.

Calvo-González, Elena, and Luciana Duccini. 2010. "On 'Black Culture' and 'Black Bodies': State Discourses, Tourism and Public Policies in Salvador da Bahia, Brazil." Pp. 134–152 in *Tourism, Power and Culture: Anthropological Insights*, ed. Donald V. L. Macleod and James G. Carrier. Bristol: Channel View Publications

Downey, Greg. 2005. *Learning Capoeira: Lessons in Cunning from an Afro-Brazilian Art*. Oxford: Oxford University Press.

Freire-Medeiros, Bianca. 2013. *Touring Poverty*. New York: Routledge.

Gmelch, George. 2003. *Behind the Smile: The Working Lives of Carribean Tourism*. Bloomington: Indiana University Press.

Griffith, Lauren M. 2011. "Capoeira Pilgrims: Negotiating Legitimacy in a Foreign Field." PhD diss., Indiana University.

Heald, Suzanne. 1999. *Manhood and Morality: Sex, Violence and Ritual in Gisu Society*. London: Routledge.

Judaken, Jonathan. 2008. "Sartre on Racism: From Existential Phenomenology to Globalization and 'the New Racism.'" Pp. 23–54 in *Race after Sartre: Antiracism, Africana Existentialism, Postcolonialism*, ed. Jonathan Judaken. Albany: State University of New York Press.

Kapferer, Bruce. 2013. "How Anthropologists Think: Configurations of the Exotic." *Journal of the Royal Anthropological Institute* 19, no. 4: 813–836.

Nobre, Eduardo A. C. 2003. "Intervenções urbanas em Salvador: Turismo e 'gentrificação' no proceso de renovação urbana do Pelourinho." Paper presented at "Encontro Nacional da Associação Nacional de Pesquisa e Pós-Graduação em Planejamento Urbano e Regional." ANPUR, Belo Horizonte, 26–30 May.

Romo, Anadelia A. 2010. *Brazil's Living Museum: Race, Reform, and Tradition in Bahia*. Chapel Hill: University of North Carolina Press.

Salazar, Noel B. 2010. *Envisioning Eden: Mobilizing Imaginaries in Tourism and Beyond*. New York: Berghahn Books.

Salazar, Noel B. 2012. "Tourism Imaginaries: A Conceptual Approach." *Annals of Tourism Research* 39, no. 2: 863–882.

Salazar, Noel B., and Nelson H. H. Graburn. 2014a. "Introduction: Toward an Anthropology of Tourism Imaginaries." Pp. 1–28 in Salazar and Graburn 2014b.

Salazar, Noel B., and Nelson H. H. Graburn, eds. 2014b. *Tourism Imaginaries: Anthropological Approaches*. New York: Berghahn Books.

Stewart, Susan. 1993. *On Longing: Narratives of the Miniature, the Gigantic, the Souvenir, the Collection*. Durham, NC: Duke University Press.

Strathern, Marilyn. 1988. *The Gender of the Gift: Problems with Women and Problems with Society in Melanesia*. Berkeley: University of California Press.

Theodossopoulos, Dimitrios. 2014. "Scorn or Idealization? Tourism Imaginaries, Exoticization and Ambivalence in Emberá Indigenous Tourism." Pp. 57–79 in Salazar and Graburn 2014b.

Wade, Peter. 2009. *Race and Sex in Latin America*. London: Pluto Press.

Zinovieff, Sofka. 1991. "Hunters and Hunted: *Kamaki* and the Ambiguities of Sexual Predation in a Greek Town." Pp. 203–220 in *Contested Identities: Gender and Kinship in Modern Greece*, ed. Peter Loizos and Evthymios Papataxiarchis. Princeton, NJ: Princeton University Press.

Chapter 6

FROM PRIMITIVE TO CULTURALLY DISTINCT
Patachitra and Self-Exoticization in West Bengal

Urmi Bhattacharyya

The concept of representation, whether this is engaged in describing an activity or identifying a particular group, has always been an integral part of the quest for anthropological knowledge. Following an era of exploration and discovery of new lands and societies, anthropology grew as a discipline that attempted to comprehend and understand the large category of the non-West. The 'objective' methods of observation followed by many anthropologists in the colonial times failed to provide an analytical commentary on the larger issues of power, politics, and imagination, which formed the context of the study of the 'Other'. This gave rise to the notion of the exotic, a significant category, which had serious ramifications on the growth of the discipline, as well as on the forces of colonialism.

This chapter represents an attempt to explore the construction of the 'exotic' in India, particularly in the colonial capital of Calcutta, West Bengal. It examines how power and imagination work together to introduce standards of uniformity by describing the Other. It also highlights how the category of the 'Other'—when this refers to particular human subjects—is subject to transformation through bottom-up processes of counter-exoticization and self-exoticization.

Notes for this chapter begin on page 134.

Such inversions of the colonial exoticizing process enable local actors to redefine their collective identity and experiment by negotiating new ideas about their self-representation.

In the Indian state of West Bengal, a hereditary community of artists, popularly known as the Patua, is engaged in the age-old tradition of painting on scrolls of cloth known as *patachitra* and narrating the symbolism of these scrolls in and around villages. *Pata* referring to the scrolls of cloth and *chitra* meaning art or rather illustration, the completed pictorial scrolls are referred to as the *patachitra*, as well as the distinct tradition of painting itself, which is known by the same name. Presently recognized as the Chitrakar, this community continues to associate itself with this caste-based occupation in spite of changes in their livelihood, occupation, and religious identity. Revolving around folklore, myths, epics, and popular legends, *patachitra* still plays a significant role in defining and reassuring the traditionally determined position of the Chitrakar within the larger society. The practice also plays an important role in the formation of a distinct cultural identity in the global market in the present day.

In the ethnography that follows I discuss the imperialist utilization of the discourse on the exotic in colonial India and its manipulation to signify a state of primitiveness. Following this I illustrate how the Chitrakar have simulated a counter process of self-exoticization through *patachitra* to assert the collective social identity of the colonized population in colonial Calcutta. Moving over to the present day, I subsequently discuss how the idea of the exotic is appropriated by the contemporary Chitrakar community in Bengal in their efforts to reassert their collective identity within a global context of consumerist art. Through this exploration, I attempt to shed some light on the need to understand the exotic as a dynamic category reconstructed continually through changing contexts of power, imagination, and experience.

Colonialism and the 'Exotic' Other

Historically speaking, it was with the colonial expansion of the West that the use of anthropology as a science assumed the task of disseminating ideas about parts of the world situated on the 'Other' side of the West (Cohn 1996). The notion of rationality was promoted as powerful discourse, able to shape and construct knowledge (Foucault 1980). Facts about other cultures were presented as evidence of the absence of those sociohistorical conditions that led to European Enlightenment and provided explanations about why allegedly non-Western cultures failed to achieve the same level of development (Kuper 1988). The construction of rational political knowledge led to the recognition of categories of difference and control that justified sovereign authority over the colonized (Scott 1985). This disinterestedness to reduce the distance between the observer and the colonial human subject, was then the very ground for the birth of the Other (Spivak 1988).

The abstract concept of the Other was, at most times, coterminous with the idea of the Orient in the context of colonialism. The presentation of the collective self of the Orient was supposed to be dependent on the European anthropologist for representation. Observations and perspectives of the anthropologist therefore helped in getting an idea of the Oriental civilizations (Lévi-Strauss 1966). These viewpoints and ideas also served as a source of representation and helped in the creation of further ideas and discourses through which difference could be gauged with the Western society. The political domination and economic exploitation of the colonies formed the base on which ideas of Western supremacy and superiority freely floated. Being a part of the colonial system, the 'objective' stance of the anthropologist was also to a great extent influenced by the prevailing stereotypical assumptions of the Orient in the colonial period (Lewis 1973).

Under these circumstances, the construction of the category of the Orient involved the invocation of the exotic. From an implied representation of the Orient, there was hence the construction of the Other as an object of enquiry and as a subject of control. With the notion of the Other, which was more a figment of the Western imagination than an actual depiction of an ethnographic reality, the non-Western world was portrayed in a relatively negative or inferior image, which justified the colonial rule (Lewis 1973). As Johannes Fabian suggests, this process of Othering was "never just found or encountered, but *made*" (1990: 755).

To defend the strangeness of the 'Cultural Other', there was hence the creation of the 'exotic'. The word 'exotic' is generally used to describe something that is not ordinary or usual, something foreign, or something from far away; the concept conveys a sense of distance (Kapferer and Theodossopoulos, introduction). In the larger context of anthropological knowledge, the exotic was used to signify "an image which asserts infinite possibilities for social transformation, cultural reconstruction, and geographic escape" (Foster 1982: 21). The exotic was also explained in a dialectical manner (Huggan 2001), as a symbolic system that defined the category of the Cultural Other, and as a taxonomic tool that facilitated categorization, and future prediction (Foster 1982).

The Primordial Exotic: The Case of Colonial India

For the early Western explorers, the Orient was the domain of the unknown and fantasy. During the colonial age, this view changed gradually into a reflection of power. The justification of European colonialism was supported by ideas of political, economic, and ideological supremacy. In India, under colonial rule, it was the notion of the native—conceived as the culturally different Other—that came to rationalize colonial power and authority. The idea of difference underpinned the colonial project of domination (P. Chatterjee 1993). For the colonizer, India demonstrated the picture of a culturally different and relatively premodern state (Cohn 1996).

The construction of the category of the Other and their control and domination were made possible not only through the use of political rationality (Scott 1985) but also through the authority of the law (Spivak 1988). The native population was made to believe that they were exotic, primitive, and thus in need of observation and subordination. Through a reconstruction of the past and a categorization of the practices of the native, the colonizer therefore justified its authority (Cohn 1996). It is for this reason that, over time, exoticism proved to be an effective tool of imperial power, engendering the "transformation of power-politics into spectacle" (Huggan 2001: 14)—a spectacle that hid from view the brutal side of reality. Notions of exoticism therefore existed in the colonial period as an "aesthetic substitution" (14): to conceal or disguise the unequal relation of power at play.

Gathering knowledge about the native population was one of the main objectives of the colonial empire. In this context, ethnographic narratives, the indological literature, and colonial surveys—which codified data about customs, people, and territory—served as vital sources to validate the moral and administrative authority of the British (Cohn 1996). The documentation of caste histories gradually gained significance for ascertaining Indian social identity and thereby maintaining imperial authority (Dirks 1992). Classification of the Indian population along ascribed categories of caste thus functioned to maintain and benefit the colonial gaze (Appadurai 1993). The object of subjugation (or gaze), it was assumed, was not supposed to look back, deny, defy, or protest against the colonial rulers. Exoticization was practically and materially ensconced in the bureaucratic and administrative system for the management of the colonial rule.

The crude reality of political domination and exploitation of resources for economic reasons were all concealed in a civilizing quest of the exotic Other. The very use of numbers and social classification was done under the assumption of the difference of the West from the Cultural Other (Appadurai 1993). While in the home country, the census project enabled the investigation of those at the social margins (e.g., the poor, the deviant, or the 'mad') in the colonies, "the *entire* population was seen as 'different' in problematic ways" (318). Exoticization thus not only had its implications on imperialism and colonial bureaucracy but also played an important role in shaping the very manner the colonizers viewed the Oriental Other. Along with census data, a number of ideological and colonial impositions enabled the mapping of the entire population; among these I should mention the role of Darwinist ideas and 'scientific racism' (Ludden 1993: 252), the enumeration of different castes from indigenous records and understandings of *jati*, the classification of tribes from different parts of the Indian subcontinent, and the criminalization of certain groups and communities (Cohn 1996; Dirks 1992).[1] Observation was, however, maneuvered through the discourses of racial, civilizational, and technological superiority of the West. This in turn influenced the processes and methods of data collection on the Indian population and also on classifying and explaining the data collected.

Counter-exoticization as Agency: Visual Representation through the *Patachitra* Tradition

The idea of a "paradigmatic fossilization" (Said 1985: 94) of the Orient dominated the discourses of power and control under situations of colonialism. But what this ambitious project of imperialism overlooked in due process was the other side of the story—the resistance made by the subject or the native population.

In Bengal, imperialism had brought along with it several other forces at work, ushering new opportunities and lifestyles and facilitating the cultivation of new, liberated ideologies. With the intensification of the colonial regime emerged a spirit of resistance among the Indian population, which was directed against imperial rule. This arousal of ethnic—and to a certain degree—social consciousness was inspired by an awareness of oppression and domination. It harped on the need to collectively engage in a spirit of nationalism, made possible through the recognition of a glorified non-colonized past and the loss of traditional cultural and social values due to the colonial rule.

There was, therefore, an intended rediscovering and reappropriation of tradition in Bengal,[2] especially in Calcutta, that was marked significantly as being on the rise during the late 1800s.[3] Popular cultural ideas, practices, and artifacts of the past, recreated and utilized for different purposes, played a very significant role in this context. The institutionalized practice of religion came to occupy a very significant position in the public sphere and the nationalist discourse in India at this point of time (Desai 1948). The revival of Hinduism and its use in the nationalist discourse increased its political significance (Pennington 2005). Rituals like goddess worship gained prominence in Bengal as a sociocultural activity for articulating regional identity (Ghosh 2003). Recreation of religious rituals, discourses, and practices aimed at strengthening social solidarity and common sentiments through an idealization[4] of the Indian society in terms of its religious past and cultural heritage.

It was within this historical context that a group of traditional painters, popularly called the Patua, migrated to Calcutta. This community of artists was hereditarily engaged with the representation of moral and religious themes in the rural areas of West Bengal. With their migration to the city, their painted images also contributed to the visual re-invocation of religious and traditional themes of the past in colonial Calcutta. Of all the folk forms of pictorial art still practiced in the rural villages of West Bengal, the most popular is the tradition of painting on scrolls of paper or cloth, known as the *pat*, painted by the folk artists known as the Chitrakar or the Patua.

The word *pat* originally signifies a piece of cloth. Functioning as early as the third century BCE, abundant references of this art form can be found in the Buddhist, Jain, and Sanskrit body of literature (Hauser 2002). In earlier times, when the use of paper was unknown or not widely in use, artists used scrolls of cloth to paint pictures on them. *Patachitra* (or *pattachitra*) therefore began being used to refer to the canvas on which paintings were drawn. Once painted, these artists traveled to nearby villages with their scrolls to engage in performative narration and improvised explication of the religious themes depicted on the scrolls. Although Patua refers to a caste in the Hindu social hierarchy, the community presently practices Islam. They trace their lineage to Hindu mythological texts written approximately around the thirteenth century. These texts mention the name of Chitrakar as one of the castes of the Hindu social structure (Bhattacharjee 1980).

The Patua community is found in many districts of West Bengal, including Medinipur, Purulia, and Birbhum. Historically, it was the construction of the

Kalighat temple in the city of colonial Calcutta that marked the migration of a substantial number of hereditary scrollpainters from rural regions of West Bengal. Dealing with the illustration and narration of paintings on scrolls of cloth,[5] these artists decided to move to the city for availing more economic opportunities. Once in the city, the traditional activity of the Patua—as this was previously related to painting and performing on scrolls—underwent modification. In response to the growth of the city and the temple as a popular source of tourist destination, the community took to selling painted pictures of the temple deity, Kali. From around the 1830s to the 1930s, these relatively inexpensive pictures illustrated on cheap quality paper were usually purchased by both pilgrims and tourists as souvenirs for worship or decoration (Ghosh 2003).

The Kalighat *patachitra*, as it came to be known, assumed a style of its own with the growing popularity of the temple and the availability of cheaply priced images that could be taken home by visitors. To increase their portability and their appeal, the traditional scrolls were restructured to single images or sheets. To produce for a mass market, they introduced paintings that could be used for worship or decoration. Along with the religious paintings, they painted contemporary events of sociohistorical, cultural, and political significance. The most popular theme included the image of the goddess Kali, depicted in the pattern of the Kalighat temple deity (fig. 6.1) or shown as the powerful goddess under whom the colonized powerless native would take refuge for protection and power (fig. 6.2).

Back in the villages, scrolls were painted mainly for accompanying the telling of tales through narratives. The Kalighat paintings being meant primarily for sale, however, invested attention on the beautification of the images and the development of a distinctive style. To popularize their images in the market, the Patua community also creatively engaged and experimented with new themes. Examples of these included the portraits of an educated Bengali social reformer, or themes that visually critiqued the repercussions of modernization on the changing values and increasing authority of women, or the influence of Westernization and industrialization more generally (fig. 6.3).

Being faced with a new task of painting images for the mass market, the community maintained a critically creative approach in their engagement with the visual in the reproduction of traditional themes. Rediscovering religious and cultural forms of representation through paintings, the artists engaged in a process of exoticizing the past. Directed toward the larger society, this rediscovering of the past emerged to counter the forces of exoticization by the colonizer, thereby facilitating attempts at self-exoticization of the native. By nurturing the imagery of the culturally distinct native in the mind of tourists, pilgrims, and other prospective buyers of the paintings, the Patua functioned as significant cultural agents. Through their paintings, they created a visual distinction between the colonizer and the native. The illustrations facilitated in the simulation of ideas concerning the cultural difference with the colonizer and its development as a separate cultural category of the Other. Through critique and satire of the colonized society of Bengal, the artists shed light on the need to look back at the traditional symbols and beliefs of the past to maintain collective cultural consciousness.

FIGURE 6.1 *Patachitra* depicting the deity Kali of the Kalighat temple

Source: Courtesy of the Indian Museum, Kolkata

Note: The goddess in this picture is mythically represented as the one of the prime symbols of the Shakti cult in Bengal. She is the manifestation of power, aimed at the destruction of all evil. In the image she is shown carrying the decapitated head of an evildoer in her hand. Her eyes are big and red with fury. Her hair is untied. Her tongue is out, mythically explained as a moment of realization when in the reckless spree of destruction; she possibly stepped on Lord Shiva. But as it is missing in this picture, her tongue, whose border is outlined in red, probably to indicate blood, could also be symbolic of her eagerness and yearning to kill.

In the meantime, the traditional meaning of this age-old caste-based occupation had been altered. In the city of Calcutta, these artists redefined themselves as painters, not performers. Their paintings mostly addressed the cultural and religious realms, and their critique was articulated through these domains.[6] In the face of the newly created industrial society and its concomitant culture, their accentuation of the religious icons, and their satirical approach to the depiction of the diminishing of traditional values and morality, worked toward romanticizing the cultural past of the native, thereby strengthening local social identities.[7] This counter-colonial approach, as reflected in the works of the Kalighat *patachitra*, encouraged the development of a tendency of self-exoticization of the colonized native in Bengal. The past practices and certain aspects of belief and collective thought were rediscovered through the medium of the visual in the *patachitra*. The Patua in this manner functioned as cultural agents

FIGURE 6.2 Kali as the Mother

Source: Courtesy of the Indian Museum, Kolkata

Note: In this *patachitra*, the same goddess Kali is shown in the image of the supreme Mother, or the divine protégé to whom devotees seek for protection. Her face gives a hint of smile, her tongue is not out, her power is depicted through her five hands, and her right foot is on the head of a human being, who is seen to revere her with folded hands.

who represented, through their artwork, the past as exotic and facilitated in the growth of a collective consciousness.

Idealization as Self-Exoticization: An Emerging Collective Social Identity in Calcutta

I have described so far the role of the Patua in awakening a sense of local social consciousness. It is here that the notion of the 'exotic' can be seen to shift from its preoccupation simply with the unusual, to signifying the ideal. The idealization of the Bengali community, and certain cultural practices, reinforced a sense

FIGURE 6.3 Reflections of the nonsacred world and its changing practices

Source: Courtesy of the Indian Museum, Kolkata

Note: This *patachitra* illustrates the image of a woman, possibly a courtesan who is seen to adorn herself for the night. This is an unfinished sketch of a Kalighat painting, and the drawing of the eyes has not been completed. She is shown wearing ornate earrings, a necklace, and bangles, with open hair. The images of courtesans were very popular during this period, probably to depict the growing popularity of the practice in Calcutta.

of collective identity. In this respect, self-idealization entailed a form of self-exoticization. In fact, the Patua, self-exoticized the entire social community in Calcutta, a process that further facilitated the revitalization of traditional practices.

By painting themes for the local tourists, the Patua community encouraged a reexamination of the past through a common lens—one that was provided by them. In Calcutta, then the colonial capital, the Patua came in contact with various social and political activities and movements that aimed toward nationalism. They also drew inspiration from the urban space, as opposed to older themes that were derived from life in the village. The education system, new work opportunities, and new socioeconomic classes provided the artists with a rich field of visual inspiration for their paintings. Their engagement with new urban themes could be understood as a form of amateur ethnographic reflection: a bottom-up reinterpretation of socioeconomic and cultural changes. Through the medium of the visual, the Patua played an important role in engaging with and promoting a critical discourse toward colonialism and the imposition of Western modernity. With their paintings, they voiced criticisms against the ill effects of modernization in the country and the adoption of new modes of cultural production including print media, cinema, and photography (Ghosh 2003).

Among the common themes of the Kalighat tradition, the most prominent was the painting of goddess Kali. In the city, as the practice grew around the Kalighat temple, the painting of this deity served as a popular source of souvenir. The Patua artists also depicted the goddess in the image of a mother, or the ultimate protector to whom the native had to surrender. With the intensification of feelings of nationalism, these artists also painted other Hindu religious deities. Through this recourse the idea of a distinct religious discourse idealizing a mythical past provided a sense of direction to the development of collective cultural identity among the colonized. Alongside political associations, the Kalighat *patachitra*, as an item of sale for worship or decoration, then visually contributed toward the escalation of the fervor of a collective anticolonial identity.

By popularizing the imagery of a mordant present while simultaneously projecting powerful religious symbols of the cultural past, these artists played a significant role in the way the native history was represented in colonial Calcutta. They nurtured the social imagination to reveal how the rediscovery of a decolonized past would encourage the development of cultural nationalism. This task was undertaken through the symbolic representation of religious icons. Coming from a tradition of hereditary painters associated with the representation of the religious, their practice was already common and their community was widely recognized in West Bengal. The traditional themes of their paintings primarily dealt with the prescription of moral myths. This pattern of representation required the mythical context to be projected as a historically ideal situation. In the Kalighat *patachitra*, it was then the religious symbols and figures that helped articulate the notion of the ideal and collective sense of the past, when the native culture was not infiltrated.[8] The mythical goddesses Kali and Durga acted as significant icons representing an admirable blend of femininity, as well as the agency of political action (Bhattacharya 2007).

The *patachitra* therefore served to redirect the collective consciousness to a common sentiment of cultural nationalism by invoking the power of religious identity. The past that was signified as ideal was that of a common religious past, brought to the forefront through the shared religious icons of worship and other symbols. Their illustration of popular gods and goddesses alongside their critique of the processes of Westernization and modernization brought to light the significance of the role of these painters, in articulating and strengthening ideas of religious identity (Ghosh 2003). The *patachitra* hence served as a critical source of representation facilitating the emergence and revival of the Bengali identity in colonial capital (Ghosh 2000).

In the early 1800s, social reform in Indian society by colonial administration aimed at addressing the shortcomings of the native social institutions and practices. With the intensification of the spirit of anticolonialism, however, the 'nationalist middle class' expressed their critique over this external source of social change (P. Chatterjee 1993). It was in this larger picture of the resistance to the project of colonial modernity that religious nationalism also developed. In this light, through the illustration of visuals on themes portraying the change in the dressing of men and women, and their attributes, the Kalighat *patachitra* reflected the critical attitude toward growing Westernization of the Bengali middle class. One of the popular themes portraying their social satire was about the changing values of society and their effect on the status and freedom of women. There were paintings of courtesans adorning and preparing themselves for their guests (fig. 6.3), and of the wife (the modern, educated, and Westernized Bengali female) exerting control over her husband in their relationship. Both indicated toward the increasing visibility of women in the public sphere, and instances of their exercise of power and authority. As this was understood to be the effect of colonial reform, which went against the traditional social order of patriarchy, these *patachitra* paintings reflected the prevailing discontentment through satire. The courtesan adorning herself with jewels was depicted ironically as the woman outside home, who would allure the men and distance them from their family life. Other paintings, like the wife controlling the husband, was satirically projected as being the result of the modern education of women, which was bound to lead to their increasing freedom and claims to equality.

By representing the contemporary cultural reality in satirical terms, and through a critical perspective, the Patua community portrayed the cultural past as ideal. Idealizing one's own past through the reimagining and rediscovering of shared historical and cultural practices can be better understood through the notion of self-exoticization. The common religious icons of Kali and Durga, and the secular themes of Kalighat *patachitra* were projected as powerful elements for invoking collective consciousness. The rediscovery of this art and its revitalization during colonial times—when the native culture was threatened by colonial modernization—can be seen as an attempt by the Patua community toward counter-exoticizing the cultural history of Bengal. The theme of Kali as the supreme goddess was linked to the idea of the nation as the motherland. The projection of religious deities alongside the ironical representation of courtesan women, or of the Westernized Bengali middle-class male, showed a clear picture of the tendency of in the *patachitra* to idealize the cultural past and look down upon the present. Hence, even though the secular themes were not painted for self-exoticization, their representation in a relatively negative light worked together with the religious images as themes engaged in counter-exoticization to reinforce the cultural values and practices of the past as ideal.

Conjuring critical ideas through the visual, the Patua artists in Kalighat asserted and maintained their own social position, while simultaneously contributing to the maintenance of collective cultural consciousness. Ascribed[9] to the caste of the Patua, who are hereditarily engaged in the illustration and performance of *patachitra*, it is their association to this traditional occupation that characterizes their social identity. Along with this, their affirmation of the caste title of Patua or Chitrakar strongly contributes to the collective sociocultural identity of their community. They function not only as artists but also as authentic spokespeople legitimated by the caste structure and the cultural system to depict the moral and the sacred in society. Their affiliation to the Patua caste and their simultaneous recognition as a community of *patachitra* artists thus affirmed their position in colonial Calcutta. In turn, it was through their painting of popular religious icons and certain satirical themes that they contributed to the development of a collective consciousness and a shared religious identity oriented toward nationhood in Bengal.

Apart from the Kalighat paintings, the Saheb-Pata and the Santhal-Bidroha Pata made important contributions to the context of the colonial situation and instances of revolt (R. Chatterjee 2000).[10] The absence of knowledge about preservation of these painted scrolls and sheets and the gradual rise of printed oleographs overtaking the aesthetic market gradually led to the decline of this significant school of art in Kalighat.

The Chitrakar, a Community of Scrollpainters in West Bengal

Traveling to the villages in Medinipur and Purulia districts of Bengal in search of the *patachitra* tradition, one witnesses a completely different picture today. The age-old practice of narrative scroll painting has adapted itself to the demands of the international market and the forces of globalization and has resurfaced in a new form. The Patua caste is further divided into subcastes such as the Mal Patua and the Bede Patua that are also associated with other tasks such as toy making, clay, and terracotta sculpting. The caste also comprises of the subcaste of Chitrakar Patua, related to the *patachitra* (Bhattacharjee 1980). This community is thus collectively known by the name of Chitrakar, which roughly means 'the one who paints'. The name is also used by the people of this community as their surname, possibly because it helps highlight the cultural identity of the artist more prominently, even to those who might not be well aware of the existence of this particular caste and its associated tradition.

In Bengal, it is in the village of Naya, in Medinipur district, that the community of Chitrakar is most actively associated with the illustration of the *patachitra*. As soon as one gets down from the local train at the nearest station to visit the village, taxis and buses seem to shout out the name of Naya, hoping to attract tourists. Over the years, owing to the participation of the artists in national and international exhibitions and art workshops, the village of Naya has gained widespread popularity. In most other districts of Bengal, artists from this community have actively engaged themselves in other forms of work to sustain their livelihood. The painting of *patachitra* is only a source of additional seasonal income. In Naya, however, almost all of the households in the Chitrakar community continue the practice of *patachitra* as their main source of income. Most members of the community currently practice Islam. The Patua caste in Bengal is historically documented to have always been accorded a very low social status in the Hindu caste hierarchy. This could be one of the prime reasons their historical records of religious conversion and reconversion between the communities of Islam and Hinduism can be seen as collective attempts to negotiate their social standing (Bhattacharjee 1980).

Being characterized by a rather nomadic life and given their historical fluctuations between the two religious communities in the past, the Chitrakar occupy a midway position in terms of their belief system, practices, and rituals. Their social life and cultural institutions like marriage and other collective practices display an interesting mix between Hindu and Muslim rituals. They continue to follow the surname of the Chitrakar, which is a Hindu subcaste. Sometimes they have Muslim names prefixed to their surnames, while some of them continue to have Hindu names, although they believe and follow Islam and despite the fact that they paint Hindu themes on their *patachitra* scrolls.

The history of religious oscillation experienced by the Chitrakar has led them to be looked down upon by both religious communities in the region. Although they are authorized to paint the Hindu themes concerning the sacred, their embracing of Islam has led them to be avoided by the Hindu community. For the larger Muslim community, the relation of the artists to the visualization and narration of Hindu themes has relegated them to a low sociocultural position. Not surprisingly, the Chitrakar now face a crisis of sociocultural identity, as evident in their relationship with the local and wider society. Given their relatively low ascribed social status, the Chitrakar do not have access to land for cultivation. Their pattern of residence in most villages in Bengal reveals separate cluster of houses mostly in a corner of the village or on its outskirts. Lack of education and employment opportunities place them in situations of abject poverty. It is then through their traditional occupation, the very condition that accounts for their crisis of identity and their rejection by other groups, that they attempt to renegotiate and reassert their social position.

The Self as Exotic: Negotiating Identity through Creativity

As I described in the previous section, the association of the Chitrakar with the *patachitra* places them in a challenging position within their own larger religious community. Remnant of a hereditary practice, the painting and the narration of religious scrolls fail to provide them a favorable position within the Hindu community. Their scrolls are regarded as sacred, and their performances are supposed to be auspicious. But its creators who double up as narrators of the practice are faced with a crisis of sociocultural identity. For the Chitrakar community, their illustration and the performance of the *patachitra* have less to do with their personal belief in the themes and are more of an occupation that traces and maintains their collective sociocultural identity. In the villages of Medinipur or Purulia districts, these artists still take their scrolls to perform in front of the local audience. When asked, one of the artists replied, "How can we leave this? This is our main work!" When further asked whether the practice is still popular in the villages and enough for sustenance, Prabir Chitrakar from Naya replied: "The scrolls are based on sacred themes and are revered by the villagers. The performance brings divine blessings, and so, when we go to perform, they don't usually refuse us. With the coming of television, the younger generation does not really want to hear us, and hence the number of performances has decreased over time. We do not get enough money and so we take part in exhibitions and art festivals where people come to buy our paintings."

Interaction with the artists revealed that their conception of work, which in this context has been translated from the Bengali term *kaaj*, does not necessarily or simply mean a mode of employment, facilitating income. Instead, it is the primary mode of action that gives shape and contributes to the identity of the individual as a part of a community in the larger society. It is through their association with the *patachitra*—its illustration and performance—that the Chitrakar community holds onto their traditional sociocultural identity as authentic artists representing the idea of the sacred and moral. Their themes of painting mostly relates to local myths and legends that highlight on the maintenance of social morals and the distinction of the sacred. Often the characters in the myths and stories assume sacred powers because of the purity of their moral virtues. In the painting and the narrative that describes it, the artists use their creativity to make modifications and highlighting on certain aspects while placing others in the background. The overall structure of the story, however, remains the same. Through the performances, the Chitrakar then visually depict and reaffirm what is seen as socially moral and religious in the collective consciousness of the wider Hindu community.

Although the Chitrakar belong to a different religious community, their age-old association with the *patachitra* tradition and their use of the title of Chitrakar renders their performance 'authentic' to the Hindu audience. Whether through its performance in nearby villages or its sale in the international and national markets, their involvement with this very tradition allows the Chitrakar to reassert their collective identity. By engaging in a process of self-exoticization as gatekeepers of a mythical imagined past, they claim the authenticity of their traditional practice in the contemporary village society. And by projecting themselves as mythical heirs of the *patachitra* tradition, the Chitrakar assert and redefine the idea of the sacred and the moral in the wider Bengali society. Thus, by emphasizing their distinctiveness, they also challenge their given—socially inferior—position and reaffirm their cultural identity in the village community.

Not all women in the Chitrakar community in Bengal engage in the painting of the *patachitra*. The male members of the family usually carry out its performance, while women stay back in their homes looking after the household and children. Since the community has a relatively limited population and is endogamous in nature, the artists are usually related and have knowledge about most of their kin, even those in other villages and districts. In Naya, most of the artists are very active in terms of their participation in festivals, fairs, and international events. Their homes display framed pictures of many of them receiving awards from the government. Most of the popular artists have visiting cards with their contact numbers and address given. They are aware not only of their demand in the market as art items but also their growing popularity in academic research. Visitors are asked whether they have come to learn about the tradition or purchase their paintings. Women from some families in Naya are also actively involved in the painting, and some accompany their husbands to workshops and events. When an elderly female *patachitra* artist, Rani Chitrakar, was asked about the present state of the traditional practice, her husband mentioned: "She has participated in more events than I have. Some art agencies showed interest in her work and offered her to present her work at an international exhibition. They prepared her passport and she went. I allowed her. She showed her paintings and performed her own narratives. I have grown old and my health does not permit me to travel to far off places. But she does. In the village or in nearby villages however, women never go around showing scrolls and narrating stories." The Chitrakar community in Bengal is aware of the growing recognition of their *patachitra* as art in the market. They understand that their distinctiveness in the international art market is contingent on their relation to *patachitra* tradition and the community of Chitrakar. They are also well aware that the global art market recognizes their age-old tradition, externally categorized as folk or exotic.

For the Chitrakar it is this external reputation of their practice—*patachitra* as something exotic—that inspires them to indulge in self-exoticization. To secure a culturally distinctive place in the international market, the community endeavors to produce art that is different and culturally exclusive. It is through its representation of the *patachitra*, and its production within a particular sociocultural context that the Chitrakar negotiate their own claim to globally recognized difference and distinction. By projecting themselves as a part of the community of Chitrakar, these artists therefore exoticize their occupation as 'antique', authentic, and distinctive. And furthermore, they underline, *patachitra*, is an exclusive and distinct tradition: emanating from a caste-based occupation of a community historically sanctioned to produce the specific art form.

No doubt, the styles and content of painting are based on an oral tradition that has been passed on through generations to the Chitrakar. They represent the community's historical embeddedness in a particular social position in the caste hierarchy. Altogether, this contributes toward the historically verified authority of the Chitrakar to produce the particular form of art that they call *patachitra*. Even when they experiment with new topics (fig. 6.4), their style of representation and narrative redefine the new global themes within the traditional space of the *patachitra* tradition. So Rani Chitrakar from Naya, on her trip to the United States, not only painted the scroll on the tsunami (fig. 6.5) but also performed her own narrative, so as to provide a view of the tradition as an audiovisual one. The idea of the new themes is shared, but its visual representation on the scroll is dependent on the creativity of the particular artists. These painters refer to the newspaper, the radio, or in some cases, the television, to re-present new information and visuals in a traditional format (Chatterji 2009).

Locating the construction of discourses and the trajectories of understanding them within specific sociocultural contexts of performance and representation becomes very relevant to the political implications of performance and representation. The creativity of the Chitrakar community and the *patachitra* themes developed by the artists can be understood as emanating from within the lifeworld and the hereditary engagement of the community with the practice. As Pnina Werbner states, "inventiveness arises from mastery of a culture

FIGURE 6.4 The nationalist movement in colonial India

Painting by Rani Chitrakar, photograph by Urmi Bhattacharyya

Note: This decorative *patachitra* illustrates the nationalist movement in colonial India and the participation of women in the freedom struggle. This is but a smaller version of the larger scroll, meant for sale.

or aesthetic genre more than from outside it" (chap. 2). In the *patachitra*, then, the boundary between the old and the new themes is blurred. As an oral tradition, the content of the themes in the *patachitra* have been open to the inflow of ideas, through the constant interaction of Chitrakar artists with other artists and other folk practices of painting when they travel for performances. In this respect, the *patachitra* does not merely represent an imitation of global themes or a continuation of old themes; it can be conceived as a practice whose content and performance is continuously modified as its creators, the Chitrakar, attempt to reassert their sociocultural identity.

In course of a conversation about the present condition of the *patachitra* and the changes and modifications in the content and practice of the tradition, Prabir Chitrakar, an artist from Naya, reflected upon the popularity of classic versus contemporary themes:

Traditional themes on *Ramayana* or the *ChandiMangal* will never lose their importance in *patachitra*, especially when it comes to performance. These are the older themes, religious myths; they will never fade away. They have been

FIGURE 6.5 Retelling tsunami through the categories of mythical time and space

Painting by Rani Chitrakar, photograph by Urmi Bhattacharyya

Note: This *patachitra* presents a visualization of the tsunami that took place in the Indian Ocean in 2004. Relating the form and representation as being similar to that of the sacred myths, this scroll portrays the catastrophe as a demon that took away several lives. The demon is therefore illustrated in a manner akin to the description of demons in myths. This part of the scroll also shows the intervention of the modern technology, as demonstrated by the white helicopter carrying food. The attire of the people in the scroll is depicted according to the traditional dressing pattern in rural Bengal. The addition of jewels on men is yet another style taken from the myths, where most of the characters, both men and women, are adorned with different jewels.

carried over generations. Contemporary themes will be popular for some time and then people will forget them. The villagers are not interested in them, and we mostly make them for the international audience. When we hear about an incident or an event from other painters, we decide to paint them on the scroll. We gather more information about it from newspapers and television and discuss it. Then we put in our own ideas to make it more attractive and create our own narratives based on the visual.

His father, Khadu Chitrakar, mentioned that he and his wife would be visiting Delhi for a workshop where they would teach schoolchildren the basic steps of painting the *patachitra*. He opened his diary of contacts and gave me the phone numbers of many art historians and museum curators in Delhi, with whom he has collaborated for exhibitions in recent times.

The artists of the Chitrakar community, such as Rani or Khadu, are well aware that the distinctiveness of their art consigns a connation of cultural exoticness to the *patachitra*. The ground on which they are tagged as exotic becomes the very lens through which the Chitrakar portray their own selves as exotic. Self-exoticization in this context involves the manipulation of the category of the 'folk' to represent one's culture or community as indigenous and therefore culturally distinct. It is locally understood, therefore, as a conscious attempt to present one's culture in an extraordinary manner, one that spells mysticism and thus attracts attention.

Conclusion

The idea of the exotic is entrenched in the discourse of power. And in many respects, the repository of knowledge about the exotic contributes in maintaining the structures of power. But within a wider world of inequality, particular communities, such as the Chitrakar artists of present-day West Bengal and the Kalighat Patua, define their own sphere of artistic imagination. They draw from established themes from the past or occasionally improvise by introducing new timely themes, yet always respecting the stylistic conventions that render their art form unique, extraordinary, and distinctive. It is through the presentation of their art form locally, and their distribution for sale in the global market, that the *patachitra* artists project themselves as culturally exotic, distinct, and aesthetically significant.

The popularity of the Kalighat paintings as souvenirs has led to a transition in this form of art: the paintings were gradually transformed from mythical representations of the sacred (consumed by the local community), to visual images of local-*cum*-exotic religious belief (consumed by the global market). With the decline of colonialism and the growth of neoliberal globalization, the role of the *patachitra* endured yet another transformation. With its recognition as souvenirs, its religious significance and political agency was gradually replaced with aesthetic uniqueness. *Patachitra* became popular as a product illustrating the aesthetic and cultural features of an exotic culture, which could be put on display at the homes of foreign tourists. From being an active agent of visual representation in promoting social organization and a sense of shared sociocultural identity, *patachitra* became a passive product of 'folk' art. With the dawn of print media, like the newspaper, and the birth of chromolithographs, the painted scrolls lost their special status as a unique source of visual imagery. Instead, they were admitted in museums as 'exotic' artifacts, representing a culturally distant space and time—an Indian folk 'allochrony', in Fabian's terms (1983). *Patachitra*, thus, became a part of the contemporary 'global' culture, an ethnocommodity (Comaroff and Comaroff 2009).

I have approached in this chapter the notion of the exotic as a discourse that is partly imagined and partly experienced, construed in dynamic terms. The *patachitra* tradition of West Bengal, as this developed in the colonial period and as it exists in the present day, can help us appreciate the shifting dimensions of the exotic as an imagined category. The exoticization of the native placed the Indian population on a temporal scale, within which they were then studied as unique—and different—social and ethnic categories (Fabian 1983). This very difference—conceived as exteriority, used originally to interiorize—is now employed in strategies of self-idealization. The Chitrakar community in Kalighat employed the visual imagery of a collective, 'national' self, embraced by an exoticized sacred past, to resist the colonial authority. In the contemporary postcolonial context, *patachitra*—the traditional occupation of the caste of Chitrakar—is marketed by reference to an archaic or 'folk' society. The exoticization of the international market has strongly affected this practice by reducing it to a form of pictorial art: a museum representation or a tourist souvenir. Aware of such trends in the global market, the Chitrakar community in the Medinipur and Purulia districts of West Bengal attempt to self-exoticize themselves as culturally distinct. While in the colonial period, self-exoticization aimed at inculcating ideas of resistance among the native population of Calcutta, in the present day, self-exoticization is directed toward protecting the social identity of Chitrakar community against the homogenizing and mass-producing tendencies of cultural globalization.

Seen from this point of view, self-exoticization, in its counter-exoticizing capacity, can be understood as a 'weapon of the weak' (Scott 1985). It is employed by peripheralized subjects to negotiate a form of indirect resistance. This may involve an awareness of marginalization, reinforced by the recognition of the collective self as culturally distinctive and unique. Embedded in the politics of difference, the category of the exotic maneuvers through structures and discourses of authority to maintain, as well as subvert, established structures of power. The transformation of historically rooted cultural practices, such as the *patachitra*, can therefore help appreciate the interrelationship between exoticization and self-exoticization, two processes that are intimately linked and often partake in a mutual negotiation. The Chitrakar of Bengal use their distinctive art form to disseminate knowledge and insights about the intricacies and inequalities of the wider society. And through their representations of a particular worldview of the sacred in *patachitra*, they invoke a sense of nostalgia about a mythically imagined and socially constructed memory of a collective past (cf. Theodossopoulos, chap. 1; Werbner, chap. 2), which legitimizes their position and occupation. In this dynamic representational context, the Chitrakar negotiate the knowledge they have acquired through practice to self-exoticize their community and reaffirming their cultural distinctiveness.

Urmi Bhattacharyya is a doctoral scholar at the Centre for the Study of Social Systems, School of Social Sciences, Jawaharlal Nehru University, New Delhi. Her ongoing research deals with the themes of collective identity and morality among hereditary artist communities in India, as represented through pictorial narrative traditions. Her previous work focused on the pedagogy of art and migration patterns of erstwhile nomadic communities in India. She is also currently teaching sociology at Sri Venkateswara College, University of Delhi.

Notes

1. For example, in the Criminal Tribes Act of 1871 that assumed crime to be hereditary determined through generations (Kumar 2004).
2. This idea of rediscovering of tradition as being different from what Eric Hobsbawm and Terence Ranger understood by the 'invention of tradition' (1983) has been pointed out by Dimitrios Theodossopoulos (2014) in his chapter on the Emberá indigenous tourism, wherein he states that invention would mean that the tradition was not an authentic one and was only invented under certain conditions.
3. As Partha Chatterjee (1993) writes, the spirit of nationalism was not prominent in the early 1800s until around the formation of the Indian National Congress in 1885. However, this idea of anticolonialism also manifested itself strongly through the recognition of the nation's distinct cultural practices and ideas to develop the cultural identity of the native.
4. This concept of idealization has been taken from Theodossopoulos's chapter on Emberá identity, where he explains how idealization also functions as a form of exoticization, alongside the tendencies of 'unintended primitivization' (2014: 58). What this chapter tries to argue is how this concept of idealization can then be used by the subject itself for purposes of self-exoticization.
5. These occupations were caste-based and therefore hereditary and exclusive in nature. Before the waves of industrialization made its inroads in the rural landscape of Indian society, the social structure and hierarchy in the villages did not allow for diversion from hereditary occupations, which were followed on intragenerational patron-client relationship.
6. In the villages, the Chitrakar or Patua community primarily associated itself with the illustration and narration of locally popular religious myths and episodes from epics to uncritically represent and continually reinstate the idea of the sacred among the Hindu community. Once in the city, their older themes were replaced by illustrations of popular religious figures or of the changing individual in the city. The purpose of the scroll had changed from episodic storytelling to serving as visual artifacts of worship or decoration. The Kalighat Patua community essentially endeavored to make their painting popular in the market for sale. Since it originated in the vicinity of the Kalighat temple in Calcutta, the painters sold the picture of the temple deity. Their purpose was not to narrate myths but to visually represent ideas, closely related to the growing religious nationalism and changing social culture in the city. Through their depiction of religious deities on the one hand and of the Westernized Bengali male elite and the modern powerful woman on the other, they engaged in criticism of the social situation in Calcutta.

7. The growing documentation on castes in India was used by the government for purposes of administration and surveillance, as well as for preventing the growth of a common spirit of nationalism. The understanding of caste was politicized and projected through ethnographic knowledge, and the existence of different legal provisions for different castes—their entry into occupations—enabled caste to reemerge in a central manner (Dirks 1992). The possibility of a common nationalist consciousness was then emotionally and nostalgically instilled in the minds of the native, through religious discourses that did not emphasize on the ascribed structure of hierarchy.

8. Through the depiction of the sacred, the Patua facilitated the development of common religious symbols to attract the collective conscience and nostalgia of the colonized. In the process, they also endeavored to attract the collective imagination of the colonized to a mythical yet morally ideal image of the past, thereby signifying the present as immoral.

9. Louis Dumont (1980) explains the caste structure of Indian society on the basis on ascribed status, one that was ordained to an individual by his or her birth into a particular caste. However, the understanding of caste could be misleading if generalized to portray the sense of a unified whole. Although this system of hierarchy justified itself through certain religious principles, it actual workings remained dependent on the pattern of network or relations in society. For the Patua or Chitrakar then, although their ascribed status assigned them relatively low socioreligious position in the society, it is through the practice of their hereditary occupation of the representation of the sacred that they challenged their given position and reaffirmed their collective sociocultural identity.

10. These painted scrolls mainly dealt with the themes of revolt and resistance. While the Saheb Pata illustrated instances relating to the domination and exploitation of the British colonizer, the Santhal-Bidrohi Pata highlighted the revolution of the Santhal tribe in response to colonial rule (R. Chatterjee 2000).

References

Appadurai, Arjun. 1993. "Number in the Colonial Imagination." Pp. 314–340 in Breckenridge and Veer 1993.

Bhattacharjee, Binoy. 1980. *Cultural Oscillations*. Calcutta: NayaProkash.

Bhattacharya, Tithi. 2007. "Tracking the Goddess: Religion, Community, and Identity in the Durga Puja Ceremonies of Nineteenth-Century Calcutta." *Journal of Asian Studies* 66, no. 4: 919–962.

Breckenridge, Carol A., and Peter van der Veer, eds. *Orientalism and the Postcolonial Predicament: Perspectives on South Asia*. Philadelphia: University of Pennsylvania Press.

Chatterjee, Partha. 1993. *The Nation and Its Fragments: Colonial and Postcolonial Histories*. Princeton, NJ: Princeton University Press.

Chatterjee, Ratnabali. 2000. "Representation of Gender in Folk Paintings of Bengal." *Social Scientist* 28, no. 3–4: 17–21.

Chatterji, Roma. 2009. "Global Events and Local Narratives: 9/11 and the Picture Storytellers of Bengal." *Indian Folklore Research Journal*, no. 9: 1–26.

Cohn, Bernard S. 1996. *Colonialism and Its Forms of Knowledge: The British in India*. Princeton, NJ: Princeton University Press.

Comaroff, John L., and Jean Comaroff. 2009. *Ethnicity, Inc.* Chicago: Chicago University Press.

Desai, Akshayakumar R. 1948. *Social Background of Indian Nationalism*. Bombay: Oxford University Press.

Dirks, Nicholas B. 1992. "Castes of Mind." *Representations* 37: 56–78. Special issue: "Imperial Fantasies and Postcolonial Histories."

Dumont, Louis. 1980. *Homo Hierarchicus: The Caste System and Its Implications*. Chicago: Chicago University Press.

Fabian, Johannes. 1983. *Time and the Other: How Anthropology Makes Its Object*. New York: Columbia University Press.

Fabian, Johannes. 1990. "Presence and Representation: The Other and Anthropological Writing." *Critical Inquiry* 16, no. 4: 753–772.

Foster, Stephen W. 1982. "The Exotic as a Symbolic System." *Dialectical Anthropology* 7, no. 1: 21–30.

Foucault, Michel. 1980. *Power/Knowledge: Selected Interviews and Other Writings 1972–1977*. Ed. Colin Gordon; trans. Colin Gordon, Leo Marshall, John Mepham, and Kate Sooper. New York: Pantheon Books.

Ghosh, Pika. 2000. "Kalighat Paintings from Nineteenth Century Calcutta in the Maxwell Sommerville Collection." *Expedition* 42, no. 3: 11–21.

Ghosh, Pika. 2003. "Unrolling a Narrative Scroll: Artistic Practice and Identity in Late-Nineteenth-Century Bengal." *Journal of Asian Studies* 62, no. 3: 835–871.

Hauser, Beatrix. 2002. "From Oral Tradition to 'Folk Art': Reevaluating Bengali Scroll Paintings." *Asian Folklore Studies* 61, no. 1: 105–122.

Hobsbawm, Eric, and Terence Ranger, eds. 1983. *The Invention of Tradition*. Cambridge: Cambridge University Press.

Huggan, Graham. 2001. *The Postcolonial Exotic: Marketing the Margins*. London: Routledge.

Kumar, Mukul. 2004. "Relationship of Caste and Crime in Colonial India: A Discourse Analysis." *Economic and Political Weekly* 39, no. 10: 1078–1087.

Kuper, Adam. 1988. *The Invention of Primitive Society: Transformations of an Illusion*. New York: Routledge.

Lévi-Strauss, Claude. 1966. "Anthropology: Its Achievements and Future." *Current Anthropology* 7, no. 2: 124–127.

Lewis, Diane. 1973. "Anthropology and Colonialism." *Current Anthropology* 14, no. 5: 581–602.

Ludden, David. 1993. "Orientalist Empiricism: Transformations of Colonial Knowledge." Pp. 250–278 in Breckenridge and Veer 1993.

Pennington, Brian K. 2005. *Was Hinduism Invented? Britons, Indians, and the Colonial Construction of Religion*. New York: Oxford University Press.

Said, Edward W. 1985. "Orientalism Reconsidered." *Cultural Critique* 1: 89–107.

Scott, David. 1995. "Colonial Governmentality." *Social Text* 43: 191–220.

Scott, James C. 1985. *Weapons of the Weak: Everyday Forms of Peasant Resistance*. New Haven, CT: Yale University Press.

Spivak, Gayatri C. 1988. "Can the Subaltern Speak?" Pp. 271–313 in *Marxism and the Interpretation of Culture*, ed. Cary Nelson and Lawrence Grossberg. London: Macmillan.

Theodossopoulos, Dimitrios. 2014. "Scorn or Idealization? Tourism Imaginaries, Exoticization and Ambivalence in Emberá Indigenous Tourism." Pp. 57–79 in *Tourism Imaginaries: Anthropological Approaches*, ed. Noel B. Salazar and Nelson H. H. Graburn. New York: Berghahn Books.

AFTERWORD
Lessons of the Exotic

Bruce Kapferer and Dimitrios Theodossopoulos

The issue of the exotic is central to anthropology and what the discipline is about. We make it clear that for us the exotic is that which is outside or does not fit prevailing assumptions, opinions, or theories guiding analyses in the humanities, social sciences, and sciences concerning differences or universalities in human sociocultural practice.

But what makes the exotic *exotic*, in the above sense, is thoroughly problematic for anthropologists who are (or should be) intensely aware that the recognition of the exotic can all too easily slip into exoticism. This is the paradox and the potential of an anthropology oriented, as it is, to the investigation of human sociocultural difference, a discipline that places a high value on difference and its comparative analysis for the general understanding of the unity that is human being. We have made it clear that we reject the over- or under-recognition of difference; that is, what we have broadly defined as exoticism, the distortion, falsification, obscuring, and prevention of the understanding of human practices. Exoticism impedes the constant critical effort of anthropology to build toward valid understandings of human action of larger import for humanity as a whole.

Our way out of the anthropological paradox—here apparent in the exotic/exoticism slippage—is effectively to de-link the notion of the exotic from any necessary connection with cultural difference and diversity or, at the very least, to intensely problematize such a connection. We have done this in the recognition that certain categories of anthropological classification and description that claim a generality or universality in application may themselves be open

References for this section begin on page 144.

to exoticism in the sense that they give universal applicability to what is a particular sociocultural historical construction of reality; an observation also made by Edmund Leach (1961) and significantly at a moment in the history of social anthropology when it was turning in a variety of new innovative directions. What we stress is that in our usage the concept of exotic refers to the extent to which particular forms and practices of human social action fall within or outside conventionally accepted terms of classification, description, and theoretical understanding. The concept of the exotic relates first and foremost to theoretical conceptualization and not to forms of life and practice in themselves.

We would like to turn the tables as it were. Sociocultural realities are not, in themselves, exotic. They only become exotic to the degree that social actors position and reposition themselves in exteriority to such realities. Assuming a view exterior to your own or other cultures can be a profoundly creative exercise, the very inspiration of cultural improvisation and imagination (see Bruner 1993; Hallam and Ingold 2007); but it can also slip into exoticism—for example, when concepts, theories, and descriptive terms falsify and imprison alterity by means of static labels and generalisations. In this sense, exoticism is closing the door to the pursuit of knowledge, a possibility that has been opened, at the first place, by the exotic itself (conceived here as exteriority).

The line of much of the questioning in this volume concerns the degree to which ways of describing and comprehending social action are exotic to the phenomenon under investigation and the limits this provides to existing generalizing theory. We can easily identify three general orientations that represent distinct approaches to the exotic:

- The first ignores the distortions set by exoticism and continues to record and analyse cultural difference, as if this emerges from parallel noncontiguous intellectual worlds (insulated from the researcher's own world).

- The second critically deconstructs exoticism—seen here as Orientalism, or unsubstantiated difference—treating the exotic as ethnocentric bias, a fragment of our imagination, a chimera.

- The third benefits from the deconstructive spirit of the second (with regard to exoticism), but attempts to approach the exotic (what comes from the outside) as a challenge for understanding, a possibility for reconfiguring knowledge beyond previously known and established boundaries (see Kapferer 2013).

The third approach is our favorite alternative, one that requires adopting a position of methodological openness.

For the sake of analysis let us name provisionally the three approaches we have just outlined. We have chosen to call the first 'intellectualist', the second 'deconstructive', and the third 'reconfiguring-knowledge' perspective to the study of the exotic. Such orientations are, obviously, accentuated and generalizing, employed with many reservations and for the purpose of illustration. To exemplify their advantages and limitations we will resort to a brief exercise of caricaturing. We will introduce an ideal type, a straw man, who identifies at first with the intellectualist approach to the exotic. We will call him, for the time being, the undifferentiated 'antiquarian ethnographer'.

The antiquarian ethnographer is an enthusiastic collector of exotica and classifier of difference. He has perfected through hard work and dedication his skill in narrating, translating, and reorganizing the cultural content of the exotic. In recording (and amassing) the fine details of cultural diversity, the antiquarian ethnographer intellectualizes exteriority. And by doing so, our straw man works hard to liberate the exotic from the reductionism of function, an admirable contribution. The exotic now becomes an object of thought. It is classified, theorized, interpreted by an analyst that dwells—often, unreflexively—on the inside of scientific knowledge, a Eurocentric location predicated upon the distinction between Self and Other. This sense of Eurocentric inside-ness—taken for granted by our 'antiquarian ethnographer' (and further projected on his readership)—is generative of analytical dualism(s).

Apart from dualism, however, there is a further danger lurking in the intellectualist approach to the exotic. Hand in hand with the intellectualization of sociocultural diversity comes its depoliticization (see also Fabian 1983; Trouillot 2003). Difference-*cum*-exteriority (ethnic, gendered, and classed) becomes domesticated (territorialized, temporalized) through the accumulation and translation of cultural content. Alterity is developed into an issue of classification, a mind game. Our 'antiquarian ethnographer' can be compared to a butterfly-knowledge-collector and his mind to a museum of Otherness.

So much appreciation of detail, coupled with admirable dedication in recording the content of difference can hide from our view the simple fact that the exotic has been a product of dispossession and inequality. Here, the rifts of the exotic—disjunctures (Appadurai 1996) and frictions (Tsing 2005)—are distorted by descriptive (or even interpretative) narratives that elucidate the happy (nonpolitical) face of exteriority—comparable to Ulf Hannerz's (2004) happy face of cosmopolitanism. Fredrik Barth (1969) would have argued that our 'antiquarian ethnographer' pays too much attention on the content of culture; he has forgotten the boundaries—tensions and points of contestation—that make exteriority politically meaningful. By producing a narrative on the content of difference, our straw man, as many intellectualist analysts of the exotic before him, has added a small building block on the wall of incommensurable Otherness.

We should not forget at this point that our 'antiquarian ethnographer' is a caricature and that caricatures—as most ideal types in the transient world of academia—change over time. So, let us suppose that the 'antiquarian ethnographer' has abandoned his intellectualist proclivity, and is now engaging with the exotic in a more critical manner. Let us imagine he has adopted instead a deconstructive view, enthused by a serious commitment to unravel the asymmetries in the production of knowledge about the exotic. His view of exteriority is now dynamic, aware of rifts and fractures and the structuring effect of history in defining the narrative and signification of the exotic. Assuming that such a transformation has indeed taken place within our straw man, we may very rename him the 'revisionist ethnographer'.

With respect to the study of the exotic, a central tenet of the deconstructive approach is a refusal to homogenize alterity. Our 'revised' straw man, the revisionist ethnographer, has embarked in a self-critique that encourages a reflexive consideration of the production of difference through academic engagement. Such a critical standpoint can potentially interrogate the very constitution of exoticism: the desire of academic analysts to see the people they study as 'Other'. An advantage of this approach is the possibility of escaping temporarily from the dualism of the Self-Other distinction. A second advantage is the potential of de-homogenizing culture, or evading static, self-contained depictions of 'other-practices'. Closer attention to subjectivity enables the 'revisionist ethnographer' to approach exteriority as emerging from the interrelationship of structure and agency; the exotic can become, for example, an imposition, but also a strategic engagement.

The deconstructive approach can help us acknowledge the exoticism of self-representation, which often takes the form of negating or opposing the Orientalist exotic. Local communities often attempt to evade discrimination, or use the exotic as a vehicle for gaining visibility or global allies (see chaps. 4–6; Strathern and Stewart 2010; Theodossopoulos 2010). The 'revisionist ethnographer' is likely to pay attention to local self-exoticizing narratives, recognize the proliferation of previous colonial referents in such narratives, but also identify how self-exoticization operates within emerging frameworks of defensive nationalism. More importantly, and despite criticizing such limitations, the 'revisionist ethnographer' is likely to appreciate the subversive potential of the counter-exotic, and the challenge it poses to stereotyping and prejudice.

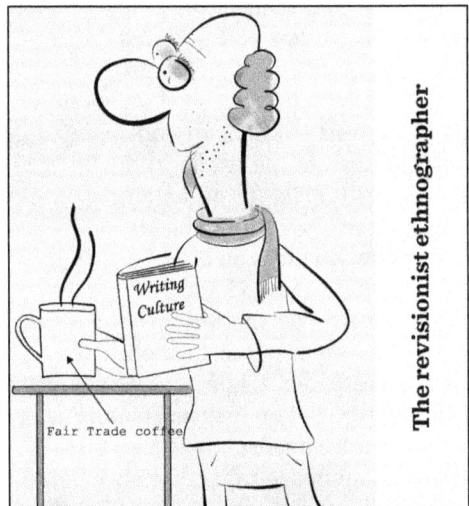

The undeniable advantages of the deconstructive approach may encourage the revisionist ethnographer to rest on his/her analytical laurels. And our caricature of such a generic deconstructive analyst resembles (way too closely) our colleague next door (farther down our academic corridor); our caricature is an abstract representation of a generation of deservedly successful scholars, who liberated anthropology from its otherworldly connotations. Yet, to the degree that a deconstructionist stance toward the exotic represents an accepted—and thus domesticated—perspective in academic theorizing, we feel prompted to push our analysis a little bit further. Instead of turning our back to the exotic in critical dismissal, we propose that there is scope to learn from it: for example, to allow our engagement with exteriority to lead us to new challenges that enhance our knowledge about *both* Self and Other.

Is there a way to combine a view of the de-homogenized exotic (as achieved by the 'deconstructive' approach) with the reinstatement of exteriority as an object of thought (as pioneered by our 'intellectualist' predecessors)? In an attempt to contemplate such a composite, not-dualist approach, we will introduce here a third ideal character, the 'reconfiguring-knowledge ethnographer', a trickster who detemporalizes and deterritorializes the exotic as both practice and value. Exteriority is a possibility inherent to all dimensions of human experience, a pivotal point of comparison to contemplate unity and diversity. In these terms, the exotic can be seen as an artificial and fluid boundary that generates tension and transformation, continuities and discontinuities. This provocative view allows us to approach the exotic as the boundary of exteriority that substantiates difference, opening the way to contemplate sameness, "the epistemological space within which it becomes possible to study Others—as human beings, or as human beings whose culture is of the same value as ours" (Argyrou 1999: S31).

The ideal type of the reconfiguring-knowledge ethnographer is freshly formed and not yet generalizable. It represents a desire, on our part and of a growing number of colleagues, to defy the dualistic quandary of relativism and universalism that lie at the very heart of our discussion about the exotic. The plurality of views and perspectives—the cultural content recorded and championed by anthropology—is closely depended upon exteriority, the possibility of the Other being exotic to the Self. And the plurality of views, the many forms of exteriority, are relevant and commensurable only to the degree that we recognize a common ground, a single world from which plurality emerges. "There is only one world but, yes, there

The reconfiguring-knowledge ethnographer

Against Exoticism

#wearethesameand,also,different/

are interpretative communities," argues João de Pina-Cabral, "if there were truly incommensurable then there would be no ethnography" (2014: 68).

In this fundamental respect, the exotic—seen *not* as Orientalism, but as the idea of exteriority—has structured, and continues to inspire the production of anthropological work. It operates as the conceptual block of alterity (the many anthropological worldviews recorded and to be recorded) but also as the point of return to sameness (a signpost that commensurability is possible). If we trace our footsteps backward—from the exotic back to the familiar—there is a good chance to establish a common language for describing the conditions of humanity. The plurality of exteriority, when traced back to its source, provides a testimony of the fundamental unity of human beings.

The twist in our approach to the exotic is largely born of the fact that anthropologists are no less constituted as social beings within particular historical trajectories than those whom they study, a fact that is integral to the very way difference is ethnographically objectified (or self-represented), which in turn influences the way social realities are conceptualized and engaged to general or universalizing theoretical concern. This is a common or garden understanding of anthropologists that is both positive and negative to the pursuit of anthropological knowledge, our prime focus. What we argue is that the self in the other, as it were, produces more than bias (see Douglas 1978) but is vital in the production of conceptualization and theory that is exotic to the phenomenon addressed and, in consequence, implicated in the production of exoticism. This is of two kinds, often entangled: that, on the one hand, widely discussed as Orientalism and, on the other hand, that which conceptually occludes or subsumes (in the interest of theory at the expense of evidence) what may be substantially distinct. Some universalizing perspectives present such a risk, as do those that are predisposed to irreducible difference.

It is with regard to the last point that we stress the importance of collapsing what still seems to be naggingly persistent in the discipline—the opposition between universalism and relativism. We underline our point that either are open to exoticism: the former by acts of denial (universalist assertions sometimes having ideologically performative potency) whereby bias is obviated; the latter, as we have presented (see introduction), by an overvaluation of difference, a feature of much avowed relativism that overlooks the possibility that it has exposed a potential feature of value and practice that is more general, if suppressed, in other realities.

In our rejection of exoticism as the mirror of production of the exotic (exotic as a concept and theory) we have stressed lines of anthropological practice that remove some of the grounds of exoticism and particularly that of the much critiqued Orientalist sort. Our orientation is one which moves well outside those in anthropology that sought to characterize the value systems of entire societies, cultures, or civilizations as if these constituted bounded homogeneous wholes rather than open and internally heterogeneous systems, continually differentiating in value and practice (relative to situated problematics). Undoubtedly, there are continuing traces of what we aim to overcome, and reject, in much anthropology and sociology. This is evident in what has been called the ontological turn in anthropology and underpins the criticism expressed by essays in this volume. It is also apparent in the work of Louis Dumont in whose work many would see a strong element of Max Weber's style of Orientalism as exemplified in Weber's comparative continuum of world religions.

We have argued that Dumont is actually anti-Orientalist. Moreover, his perspective is not that of inverted exoticism that re-insists the sort of dualism he would oppose (whereby the Other rather than the Self becomes the basis for descriptive conceptualization and theory). Rather, he attempts to unify what others divide seeing differences as historical variations upon principles that are unifying in human being (and underpin human being in general). Nonetheless, Dumont is open to the Orientalist charge (if often mistakenly construed) perhaps because he starts from the ethnography of India, the mother site of classical Orientalism paradoxically, perhaps, in an effort to overcome it.

Our concern is not to defend Dumont but to note a potential of his approach that is worth developing. This is to concentrate on practices (rather than on societies and systems as wholes), to focus on issues or problematics (both specific and general), and, finally, to approach particularities holistically—that is, to determine the logic of practice in relation to its ethnographically demonstrated relevant set (or the value logics of the set in reference to which specific practices gain their significance and limitation). We contend that this is a rigorous way of approaching comparative understanding for a subject that is through and through centered on the diversity of humankind while insisting that all human beings are one. We stress, especially, anthropology as issue and problem-centric rather than society-centric. That is, what society is must be relative to the problem examined.

Society is an abstraction and achieves its most particular concretization in specific events and practices and their situated (or contextualizing) processes. There is, in this approach to society, an aspect of the kind of holism that interests us; that is, society as open, never closed, or finite, continually in process. Any universalism or general statement about what its fundamental basis might be (or overarching normative or value arrangement is) must be contingent. This is so in the sense of society (and the social) as phenomena in history—as processes of continual differentiation or in the dynamic of reproduction (i.e., constant change, transmutation, transformation, or constant emergence). It is in such regard, combined with the powerful awareness of sociocultural difference or variation across the globe, that anthropology is alert to the potential of the exotic (of theory) to human created realities (as they continually and differentially unfold) and the exoticism (of understanding) that may be the consequence. Insofar as this volume opens and develops such a perspective, so may it be seen as one contribution to a methodological debate concerning anthropology and a vital role in the humanities, social sciences, and other human sciences.

Bruce Kapferer is Director of an ERC Advanced Grant on Egalitarianism at the University of Bergen. He was the Foundation Professor of Social Anthropology at the University of Adelaide and later James Cook University. He was the Professor and Chair of Anthropology at University College London, where he is now also Honorary Professor. He is the author of several monographs, including *Legends of People, Myths of State* (2011) and *2001 and Counting: Kubrick, Nietzsche, and Anthropology* (2014), and editor of many volumes, among which are *Beyond Rationalism* (2003) and *In the Event* (2015, with Lotte Meinert). He has conducted ethnographic research in Zambia, Sri Lanka, Australia, India, and South Africa.

Dimitrios Theodossopoulos is Professor of Social Anthropology at the University of Kent. He has conducted research in Panama and Greece, focusing on processes of resistance, exoticization, authenticity, tourism, and environmentalism and on the politics of cultural representation and protest. He is the author of *Exoticisation Undressed* (2016) and *Troubles with Turtles* (2003), and editor of *De-Pathologising Resistance* (2015), *Great Expectations* (2011), *United in Discontent* (2010), and *When Greeks Think about Turks* (2007).

References

Appadurai, Arjun. 1996. *Modernity at Large: Cultural Dimensions of Globalization*. Minneapolis: University of Minnesota Press.

Argyrou, Vassos. 1999. "Sameness and the Ethnological Will to Meaning." *Current Anthropology* 40, no. S1: S29–S41.

Barth, Fredrik. 1969. "Introduction." Pp. 9–38 in *Ethnic Groups and Boundaries: The Social Organization of Culture Difference*, ed. Fredrik Barth. London: Allen & Unwin.

Bruner, Edward M. 1993. "Epilogue: Creativity Persona and the Problem of Authenticity." Pp. 321–334 in *Creativity/Anthropology*, ed. Smadar Lavie, Kirin Narayan, and Renato Rosaldo. Ithaca, NY: Cornell University Press.

Douglas, Mary. 1978. "Cultural Bias." Occasional Paper No. 35. London: Royal Anthropological Institute.

Fabian, Johannes. 1983. *Time and the Other: How Anthropology Makes Its Object*. New York: Columbia University Press.

Hallam, Elizabeth, and Tim Ingold. 2007. "Creativity and Cultural Improvisation: An Introduction." Pp. 1–24 in *Creativity and Cultural Improvisation*, ed. Elizabeth Hallam and Tim Ingold. Oxford: Berg.

Hannerz, Ulf. 2004. "Cosmopolitanism." Pp. 69–85 in *A Companion to the Anthropology of Politics*, ed. David Nugent and Joan Vincent. Oxford: Blackwell.

Kapferer, Bruce. 2013. "How Anthropologists Think: Configurations of the Exotic." *Journal of the Royal Anthropological Institute* 19, no. 4: 813–836.

Leach, E. R. 1961. *Rethinking Anthropology*. London: Athlone Press.

Pina-Cabral, João de. 2014. "World: An Anthropological Examination (Part 1)." *HAU: Journal of Ethnographic Theory* 4, no. 1: 49–73.

Strathern, Andrew, and Pamela J. Stewart. 2010. "Shifting Centres, Tense Peripheries: Indigenous Cosmopolitanisms." Pp. 20–44 in Theodossopoulos and Kirtsoglou 2010.

Theodossopoulos, Dimitrios. 2010. "Introduction: United in Discontent." Pp. 1–19 in Theodossopoulos and Kirtsoglou 2010.

Theodossopoulos, Dimitrios, and Elisabeth Kirtsoglou, eds. 2010. *United in Discontent: Local Responses to Cosmopolitanism and Globalization.* New York: Berghahn Books.

Trouillot, Michel-Rolph. 2003. *Global Transformations: Anthropology and the Modern World.* Basingstoke: Palgrave Macmillan.

Tsing, Anna L. 2005. *Friction: An Ethnography of Global Connection.* Princeton, NJ: Princeton University Press.

INDEX

www.ingramcontent.com/pod-product-compliance
Lightning Source LLC
Chambersburg PA
CBHW060043030426
42334CB00019B/2473